BOYSTOWN

BOYSTOWN

Sex & Community in Chicago

JASON ORNE

Photographs by Dylan Stuckey

THE UNIVERSITY OF CHICAGO PRESS
Chicago & London

The University of Chicago Press, Chicago 60637
The University of Chicago Press, Ltd., London
© 2017 by The University of Chicago
All rights reserved. Published 2017.
Printed in the United States of America

26 25 24 23 22 21 20 19 18 17   1 2 3 4 5

ISBN-13: 978-0-226-41325-9 (cloth)
ISBN-13: 978-0-226-41339-6 (paper)
ISBN-13: 978-0-226-41342-6 (e-book)
DOI: 10.7208/chicago/9780226413426.001.0001

Library of Congress Cataloging-in-Publication Data

Names: Orne, Jason, author. | Stuckey, Dylan, photographer.
Title: Boystown : sex and community in Chicago / Jason Orne ; photographs
    by Dylan Stuckey.
Description: Chicago ; London : The University of Chicago Press, 2017. |
    Includes bibliographical references and index.
Identifiers: LCCN 2016028700 | ISBN 9780226413259 (cloth : alk. paper) |
    ISBN 9780226413396 (pbk. : alk. paper) | ISBN 9780226413426 (e-book)
Subjects: LCSH: Gay community—Illinois—Chicago. | Gay culture—Illinois—
    Chicago. | Gay men—Illinois—Chicago—Social life and customs. | Gay bars—
    Social aspects—Illinois—Chicago. | Sex—Social aspects. | Gay culture. |
    Lakeview (Chicago, Ill.)
Classification: LCC HQ76.3.U52 L4466 2017 | DDC 306.76/60977311—dc23 LC record
available at https://lccn.loc.gov/2016028700

♾ This paper meets the requirements of ANSI/NISO Z39.48–1992
(Permanence of Paper).

… this intimacy, I have some questions
for you. Did you mean it?
Democratic America joined by
delight in the beauty of boys.

especially working-class ones? I joke.
I know you meant adhesiveness,
that bond of flesh to equal flesh,
might be the bedrock of an order.

a compact founded on skin's durable,
knowable flame. I've felt what I think
you meant. I don't mean to romance this, Walt,
but much of what I've known of fellowship

I've apprehended in the basest church,
—where we're seldom dressed, and the affable
equality among worshipers is
sometimes like your democratic vista,

men held in common by our common skin.…

CONTENTS

1

Nightfall

The crush of people standing in the hallway just within view of the stage delineated the boundary between the front and back bars at Cocktail on Saturday nights. At five foot six, I'm a smaller man. I can squeeze through crowds more easily, so I stood in front pushing sideways, pulling Austin along with me by the hand. The three-foot-long tables lined up perpendicular to the western wall took up valuable real estate for spectators at this hour, leaving us on the edge of the ring of empty space surrounding the stripper's stage.

"Oh, it's Peoria," Austin, my then-boyfriend, now-husband, nudged me to look over to our left, where three middle-aged, straight, white women stood, talking excitedly to their white, gay, male coworker who had brought them down from the suburbs for a fun night out on the town—I'm an eavesdropper.

"Ooh, that's mean," I said. "I'm calling you out on that." I pulled out my phone to take a few notes on the scene.

To our right, a middle-aged Latino man in a long, yellow polo shirt, stylish black-framed glasses, and the gelled Caesar haircut I had in eighth grade laughed with his older friend, a gaunt white man. With debaucherous glee, the older man—his face's tight, distorted skin a badge of survival from a time before HIV was more easily hidden—pushed him toward the stage where BELIEVE was dancing.

I first met BELIEVE with Frank, a white queer man I had been following for fieldwork months earlier, in April.[1] BELIEVE is Frank's favorite go-go boy. White. Tall. Muscular. Straight. The word "believe" in black block letters is tattooed across his chest. As Frank and I leaned against the front bar, BELIEVE hung on Frank as he asked us for money.

"I do this to support my kids," he smiled confidently. Succumbing to the allure of the straight boy—gay for pay—Frank tucked a few dollars down the front of his underwear and received a manly squeeze on the arm with a smile in return.

The December night that Austin and I saw him, BELIEVE supported his kids a few different ways. He squatted on stage, his crotch at eye level as he leaned forward to whisper in the ear of the man in the yellow polo. Three dollar bills in one hand, a vodka soda in the other, the Latino man brushed the bills down BELIEVE's chest, across his abs, and into the front pouch of his underwear, pulled down to the base of his cock, straining legality. His fingers lingered long enough to feel BELIEVE's buzzed pubic hair. The Latino man's giggle turned into raucous disbelieving laughter as he spun around and headed back to his also-laughing friend.

Another go-go boy, this one unsurprisingly also tall, white, and muscular—but gay from the way he twerked his ass as he leaned forward against the back wall—took over the stage for BELIEVE to start to work the crowd.

BELIEVE headed straight for an even more lucrative audience than drunk, older gay men: a young white woman in leopard-skin pants. His demeanor changed completely when he started talking with these women. With the man in the yellow polo, he was cocky, brash. With women, he caressed first. His lips grazed her ear as he whispered softly.

Her taller friend in a white dress and heels egged her on. With this encouragement—permission?—BELIEVE started stroking her thighs as they gyrated. I could see him rubbing his dick against her from behind. It bulged slightly from within his too-tight briefs. They were laughing, obviously having a great time.

With a howl, another group of white women came through the front door. One wore a pink boa, seemingly ignoring the small sign outside against the brick wall: "No Bachelorette Parties."

Straight people come for the glamour, forgetting sometimes that real people are behind the enchantment as they look to have their own night out on the town. Austin and I took the arrival of this group as our cue to leave what had quickly become a straight strip club. We pressed again through the crowd to reach the front, bursting out into the cold night air onto the corner of Halsted and Roscoe.

"Where do you want to go?" I asked Austin. "Roscoe's?" I gestured across the street.

With a line of people standing outside, Roscoe's looked more packed than Cocktail. A bachelorette party emerged through the front door: four white women in heels, dresses too thin for winter, and party tiaras. The lead woman's tiara read "BRIDE."

"Jesus. Can we go someplace *gay*, Jason? I'm not paying a cover for this." Austin said.

■ ■ ■

Figure 1.1. Hydrate Nightclub, by day and night

From neighborhoods as big as Chelsea or the Castro to places only as big as clubs like the Shamrock in Madison, Wisconsin, or Sidewinders in Albuquerque, New Mexico, gay areas are becoming normal. Straight people flood in. Gay people flee out. Scholars call this transformation assimilation. Some argue that we—gay and straight alike—are becoming "postgay."[2]

In *There Goes the Gayborhood*, Amin Ghaziani argues that gay people can live anywhere now, no longer forced inside the gay ghetto.[3] When gay people go to live elsewhere, straight people move into those gay neighborhoods—or gayborhoods, as many of us are fond of calling it—for such amenities as good schools and rising property values. Moreover, gay people can sometimes stay home, living in small towns rather than fleeing to gay meccas. Although no longer essential, dedicated gayborhoods are still needed, Ghaziani contends, to provide gays with some measure of safety and as multicultural enclaves celebrating LGBT identity.[4]

The years I've been studying Boystown, Chicago's gayborhood, have given me a different perspective: gayborhoods don't celebrate differences; they create them. Through fostering a space outside the mainstream, gay places allow people to develop an alternative culture, a queer culture that celebrates sex. In gay clubs around America, one learns different values, a way to judge people by different rules. When night falls, we learn new lessons.

Yet these spaces change when sold to a new audience. When queer people arrive on the 36 bus, the Red Line "L" train at Belmont Avenue, or find a parking spot on Pine Grove Avenue, few will be as welcome as white straight women. Those who are sexual deviants, who are genderfucking and trans, who are too brown and black, or who are too poor, Boystown rejects these people now. They don't fit Boystown's new image as a gay Disneyland, a safe theme park, a petting zoo.

America is not becoming "postgay," a label that is laden with homophobia, as though gay identity is a stage to be transcended.[5] Gay America is "post-queer." By shedding the queer elements, Boystown trades sexuality for normalcy. It trades queer sexual connection for legal equality.

"Gay" and "queer"—words often used interchangeably, but referring to different aspects of the homosexual experience.

Gayle Rubin's "charmed circle" diagrams how sexual practices interrelate.[6] The circle's inside wedges are mainstream and hegemonic. These practices represent how good moral, normal people have sex. The outside practices oppose these wedges. Society stigmatizes these subversive sexualities. Sex in the outer limits is queer.

Only one wedge describes sexual orientation, the person's sex/gender with whom you are having sex. The other practices are other sexual aspects: the place, timing, group composition, and so forth. These other traits became the basis of stereotypes. Sexual deviant. Promiscuous. Slut. AIDS ridden.

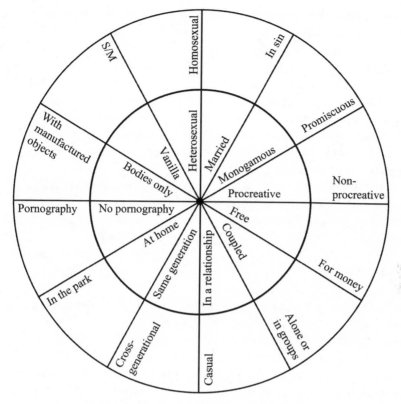

Figure 1.2. The charmed circle

Facing one section's stigma, gay communities also reject the other wedge's morality—or they did. If you question the morality of discrimination because of who you love, you might also question the morality of other sexual decisions. The inside wedges join together against the outside circle. One must follow all these practices to escape stigma.

The homosexuality/heterosexuality wedge is unique. Homosexuality became an identity. Being gay is an orientation. Today, society considers sexual orientation essential to one's being. A political movement transformed conventional sexual morality by creating gay identity.[7]

The U.S. Supreme Court recognized this change as well. *Bowers v. Hardwick* held sodomy laws constitutional because the law regulated *conduct*.[8] *Lawrence v. Texas* reversed *Bowers* because homosexuality is an immutable *identity*.[9] Homosexuals gained legal rights by proving essential identities. Gays and lesbians are oppressed *classes* of people. The state can regulate conduct. The court did not protect a right to have sex as we choose.

Therefore, in Ruben's circle, we also see how assimilation works. If a boundary disappears, then acceptance into the inner circle means new morals. Gay neighborhoods stay gay—affiliated with homosexuality—but they become less queer, stripped of the outside's alternative sexuality.

Gay identity versus queer sexuality. Old divisions, a familiar dynamic. Nearly twenty years ago, Michael Warner wrote about the disconnect between queer liberation and gay assimilationist movements.[10] Lisa Duggan warned us of "homonormativity," a white, gay male, upper-class, family-man normality.[11] Almost a decade ago, Jane Ward saw a new "respectable" queer.[12] Gay movements want a return to privilege's embrace; queer movements resist the inner circle's vice grip.

We stand now on a new edge. The gay movement won marriage, military inclusion, legitimacy, and legal rights. How has life in the gayborhood changed? Are gay men normal? Is queer sexuality banished, destined for extinction? Or can we still learn the lessons of the night?

■ ■ ■

Austin never wants to go to Roscoe's. The mix of dollhouse decorations, dark wood, and too-earnest baby gays isn't his scene. The bachelorette party and cover charge were a convenient excuse to pull us out of line.

The Lucky Horseshoe, however, has a darker scene.

White cocktail napkins billowed like tumbleweeds down Halsted in the warm winter air. The streets, though, were far from deserted. Once the cold starts to settle in around November, even the slightest rise in temperature brings people out onto the streets. With so little time outdoors, many will take any chance they can get. During the summer, the crowds can get even worse. With a huge mass of people, density and heat means fission. At times, violence erupts.

Boystown is an entertainment district: a neighborhood with residences but also a theme park for gay desire. Groups of people walk along the street at night. Some bar hop, going from ride to ride, getting lost in the Disneyland magic of the night. For others, that magic *is* the street.

We walked down Halsted Street, holding hands in the one place we can. A bit drunk, Austin and I were laughing at each other's jokes. He swept me up in his arms and planted his lips on mine.

"Woooo! Do it again!" a white woman screamed at us, poking her head out of a passing cab.

Crossing Belmont, we escaped into the Lucky Horseshoe, the windows tinted in faux shame.

The Lucky Horseshoe is nothing like a straight strip club, no matter the similarities between people dancing on the bar for tips and private dances

Figure 1.3. The Lucky Horseshoe Lounge

in the back. The boys working for tips in their jockstraps take their cue more from their drag queen sisters than from their similarly scantily clad stripper kin.

The front center stage, surrounded by the namesake horseshoe bar, had a cute dancer: his beefy football body squeezed into the usual too-small jockstrap, the jiggle of his meaty ass overhanging the squeezing straps.[13] However, I wasn't there to watch the dancers, and it was too busy to find a space at the bar. We pushed past the crowd to the middle bar where the dancers hung out between sets, and, like BELIEVE, they tried to talk men out of their dollars rather than dancing for them. Someone walking out of the bathroom—no more than two small swinging saloon doors concealing a toilet— almost ran into us, but we got situated at two stools down at the end of the long line bar, opposite the video poker machine that the dancers congregated around.

We like the Shoe, as Boystown regulars call it, because it is literally dirty enough that no bachelorette would venture in. But also dirty in the good way. Between the inhospitable—some might say sexist—bathroom arrangements, skeezy vibe, and the almost tragic dancers who seldom have the same level of muscularity or masculine Chippendales' attitude Cocktail's dancers have, the Shoe is not the party destination for straight women looking for a night out on the town.[14]

Instead, everyone else in Boystown seemed to have congregated here. The Shoe seems overrun with hot men, much busier than normal, making it hard to get a drink. As Boystown's gay clubs fill with straight women, these raunchy spaces are doing better, are more popular. Finally flagging a bartender, I ordered us two whiskeys on the rocks to sip while we watched the crowd.

As I did at Cocktail, I eavesdropped and observed. Clumped in groups, men stood and handed money to the men on stage. The stripper within eyeshot of our stools flexed his arms at the older white man stuffing money down his underwear. Turning around, he showed off his muscular black ass, only a thin line of fabric holding the thong in place.

The Shoe felt like a sexy haven in the gentrified wilderness. Queer in the midst of gay clubs playing nice for straight dollars. A cozy dark corner from Boystown's newfound light. The Shoe echoes an earlier time—perhaps a time living only in our nostalgia—for the nightlife of dark rooms, a people bound together by shame, and the sexual thrill that came from doing it anyway.

■ ■ ■

Sex is important.

Americans consider sex private, yet we talk about nothing else. Sexuality is an intimate experience that defines our public lives.

During the day, we get married. We form families. We raise kids. We choose careers. We work our bodies, fashion our clothes, and buy products to sway others' opinions. We make choices so others see us as good, attractive, normal people. The right kind of person.

During the night, when darkness shrouds the world, Boystown flickers to life. The "wrong" person emerges. The kind that has sex in public. The kind that has sex with people of the same sex. The kind that cruises and takes someone home from the bar. The kind that has sex with more than one person, while drunk and high, in a sleazy backroom. Society shames these people.

Society shames queers. Queers resisted by forming their own spaces.

As homosexuality becomes mainstream, even sexuality studies shy away from sex, from understanding queer people's unique, radical sexual cultures, despite the key place sex holds in gay life. Today, sociologists study the politics of choosing a gay or a queer label. This book is not about identities.

This book is about sex.

When people say in surprise, "My! How far gay people have come!" they are speaking about legal equality. We had already gone further than straight people in sexual innovation. Queer men built radical sexual culture out of the ruins of rejection. Queers developed an alternative culture to cope during the long drought, when we drank our lives away to numb the pain of our families' lost love. Now, love floods our lives again. But the rising tide of straight acceptance threatens to wash away the queer erotic sensibility.

Assimilation is the cultural impact of HIV.[15] Patrick Moore, in *Beyond Shame*, argues gay men led a queer sexual revolution, the "sexual experiment": sexual freedom allowing alternative relationship forms and families of choice within a milieu treating sex as a form of art "where the artist doesn't wait for the audience to show up." This libertine sexual fantasy with a darker side of drug addiction was in its adolescence when HIV came. Just as these gay men began to integrate sex culture into a life engaged with straight institutions and women, HIV inextricably linked sex with death. Just as an older generation could have explained queer sexuality to younger men, to help them avoid past mistakes, HIV killed them. An entire generation lost.

Gay men turned toward normality for fear of sexual freedom's consequences. The reaction—overcorrection—was to begin to advocate legitimacy. We embraced the charmed circle. We're just like everyone else. Sex belongs in the home. We only use condoms, and we use them forever. We only have sex in relationships. We're vanilla. We get married.[16]

One cannot appreciate that fear without understanding the cataclysmic proportions of the AIDS epidemic. I've never seen statistics on HIV's total toll on the queer male population in the eighties and nineties. Here's my conservative estimate: in 1995, when AIDS deaths peaked, 21 percent of American queer men had died.[17]

I try to imagine a fifth of my friends dead. Devastating, life changing.

That's a total, not divided into specific social networks, like the new communities queers created in their sexual experiment. Death clustered in those spaces where men were experimenting with a sexual freedom "beyond shame." When faced with such a loss, gay men retreated to the inside of the charmed circle. The sexual experiment of intimacy outside family, a revolution that built new families, died without followers. Who knows how much further the queer revolution could have gone? What new social forms could have developed?

Straight people could have gone further, too. In 1986, the *New York Times* published an article titled, "With AIDS about, Heterosexuals Are Rethinking Casual Sex." Advances in contraception and women's liberation made casual sex a possibility. The risk of contracting HIV cast everyone back into a time of sexual fear. The sexual revolution was not just a queer revolution, though perhaps queers kept its lessons alive.

In Boystown, we see the beginning of the tail end of that wave of sexual fear. The culture that Moore shows dying, in *Beyond Shame*, rises from the ashes again. Not like a phoenix but like a seedling after a devastating wildfire. Today, queer men retain those lessons of sexual freedom. Resurgent, sexual spaces live on. The sexual landscape is different now. Marriage is on the scene, but different relationship forms are folded within. We don't have to live in the gayborhood. We can meet men elsewhere in the city. Yet, there are benefits to these explicit sexual spaces that continue to exist, even under attack from gentrification and respectability.

You can find those queer lessons in the backrooms of gay bars, in online hookup websites, in leather families, and on drunken Sunday afternoons. As gay men retreat to the suburbs to raise kids, new residents take their place. Straight women, tired of sexual harassment, look to gay neighborhoods to find the same freedom—though not always with the best consequences—to grasp a life beyond shame, embracing the sexual body, to learn about the outside of the charmed circle from the night's denizens.

This book is about those lessons of the night.

By going into the darkness—whether in the backroom of a raunchy club or in the sunshine on a boat along the coast of Lake Michigan—I am able to present a theory, formulated through ethnographic social scientific methods, about the power of sex to connect people together across boundaries. I document a queer phenomenon: *sexy communities*.

Sexy communities form in hybrid collective sexual spaces: a social mixed-use public space containing flirting, hooking up, or fucking. Pleasure—sex, the erotic energy of a space—connects people together, forging naked intimacy in the crucible of the night.

These spaces are racially diverse, bridging boundaries separating us during the day. In this book, I discuss sexual racism, a perspective on racial boundaries within sex and romance as structural, cultural, and interactional, not as personal prejudice or preference alone. Sexy communities are less sexually racist. Conversely, assimilated spaces are more sexually racist. Assimilation not only brings gay men into the inside of the charmed circle, it also makes gay spaces structurally, culturally, and interactionally whiter. Becoming normal means becoming white. Becoming white is part of becoming normal.

Yet separation protects from the outside straight world; sexy communities rely on boundaries. Intersectionality, an academic movement, seeks to understand the ways in which structures of social oppression—race, class, gender, sexuality, and so on—interrelate. Some sexy communities reject women. Some are upper class and reject those who are too poor. When racial boundaries recede, other barriers, like gender and class, deepen. While sex can bridge boundaries, oppression is tangled. Loosen one string, others tighten. I call this problem the intersectional knot. Through the push-pull of Boystown, the fight between sexuality and normality, I will demonstrate there are no easy solutions to social inequalities. Whether in queer "antiracist" politics or on the dance floor, the intersectional knot makes oppression hard to loosen.

■ ■ ■

Individual streets, stores, and houses make a neighborhood. Zoom out. The streets combine, hundreds of neighborhoods dotting Chicago, together forming a metropolis with complex logic when interconnected, but are seemingly simple when viewed up close. Before we descend again to the streets of Boystown, I want to hover for a moment, zoomed out, to talk about the lessons for those other neighborhoods.

Sexy communities have been pushed out of Boystown's core to the margins as gay men assimilate into mainstream straight society. Once a standard feature of the gay bar—hatred pushing together people unable to go elsewhere—Boystown's sexy communities exist on the periphery in the shadiest spaces, the darkest bars in the deepest night. Or on the periphery of the physical world, as men augment their reality with the latest digital app. Or on the periphery of the city in leather bars or expensive boats floating on Lake Michigan.

Boystown pushes sexy communities to the edge because they are edgy, unrespectable. Society accepts gay men, but not queer sex. As gay neighborhoods integrate into the fabric of American society, gay culture frays. Gay men assimilate, and Boystown transforms. Boystown becomes richer, whiter, straighter. In a word, "normal."

These things happen, however, not to kill gay culture but because businesses attempt to save the gay neighborhood. Boystown's life depends on straight dollars, tourists buying a fun fashionable romp. As businesses sell Boystown to new people through a process of heritage commodification, Boystown's queer sensibility, the lessons of sexy communities, fade away as new customers go on safari into queer spaces, transforming them with their tourist gaze into normal areas. To stay gay, Boystown becomes less queer.

When spaces change, we change. The places we are involved with—normal or sexy, inside the circle or on the outer limits—teach us. We learn culture from our spaces, our ecological context, but we also learn something beyond culture.

In response to relentless scientific individualism—masquerading as economic rationalism—sociologists have been reviving the Chicago school, the focus on how our ecological context shapes our behavior. We are more than the interplay of genes, more than essential psychological identities. This book doesn't seek to disprove those influences.

The places where we live influence us; these are the "neighborhood effects" discussed by the Chicago school of sociology.[18] However, I argue that the neighborhoods we live in teach us more than just for which political party to vote or which food we like to eat. Our neighborhoods teach us our sexuality.

Our understanding of neighborhood effects is too bound to our residence. The political economy of neighborhoods shapes the social psychology of people living there. However, we traverse more spaces than where we live, especially today in our mobile global economy. We shop. We eat. We drink and fuck. We partake in the pleasures of life. Where we consume matters to our understanding of space. Time factors in as well. I call these lessons of the night because night is the time of day they predominantly occur. The temporal rhythms of consumption—when?—shape who we are.

Yet culture alone is insufficient to understand sexuality. We learn a sexual culture from our neighborhoods, but spaces also shape who we are viscerally. We consume, often for pleasure. We have to consider the body: our movements, our tastes, our physical desires.[19]

I use carnal sociology as a solution.[20] Carnal sociology argues that sociologists should use a "flesh-and-blood" understanding of social life, in which we are embodied, as opposed to traditional sociology, which sees us as actors in our minds attached to inert bodies that robotically follow our wishes. To understand social life, we have to pay attention to the physical body that feels, senses, moves, suffers, fails, and sometimes succeeds in changing our environment.

I push carnal sociology to consider the most overt connotation: the sexual pleasurable body that desires. We seek sensation, pleasure, and the erotic. This book aims to expand the term "carnal sociology" to this field of pleasure, sex, and eroticism. We learn from pleasure. We seek pleasure. Understanding social life requires understanding the carnal body as not only corporeal—physical, acting upon the world—but pleasure seeking and consuming.[21] I also hope to correct a tendency within queer theory to prefer stultifying jargon and the rational mind of identity over the messy sexual body that purportedly aims to be sexuality studies' focus.

With this flesh-and-blood focus on our bodies in action, on physical sensations, and on emotions, our consumption takes on new importance. We learn through pleasure. We consume to change who we are. The spaces that we move through, the people with whom we talk, the scenes in which we hang out are important. But so are the cocktails we drink, the food we eat, the people we fuck, and the places we dance.

Thus, through Boystown's sexual arena, we can see the connection between the people that we become, the cultures we have, and the decisions that we make for pleasure within an economy. By paying attention to the pleasurable erotic body, neighborhood effects become more than residential.

They also become more agentic; we are in control. Individualism seduces because we want to be masters of our destiny. We bristle at social structure because it seems to imply we are nothing but automatons acting out social commands given to us by structures made long ago. We may not be individuals constrained by nothing but our reason and resources, but we are not social robots.

When we pay attention to pleasure, we see that people intentionally seek out new experiences to shape who they want to become. Where we are and where we consume shapes who we are. We recognize that reality and seek out a better self. Straight women going to gay clubs, queer liberationists with antisex attitudes, baby gays going down into a backroom for the first time. These groups become more understandable when we focus on their pleasure.

In Boystown, I propose a carnal sociology that considers us as desiring creatures. By paying attention to those shamed that live on the outside of the charmed circle, by paying attention to pleasure, we can gain new perspectives on assimilation and oppression. We can learn to ask new questions about the connective power of sex.

■ ■ ■

What can the night teach us?

The night teaches us about the day.

Sociology's goal is to discover something about life, the human experience, and how our societies work. Ethnography teaches about the general from the specific. We meet a place, a people, and a culture. Through learning about this place, this people, this culture, we learn about our own. A trip into the nightlife of Boystown takes us into the daylight of our everyday lives.

In this book, I explain the radical lessons of queer sexuality, but these lessons aren't just for queer people. Using this lens of connective public sexuality, the lives of other people outside of the charmed circle, vying for respectability, become explicable. The intersectional knot helps explain oppression's continued bondage, our inability to easily untie ourselves. A carnal sociology of pleasure pushes social science to consider sexuality not as a sidelined niche but as a critical component of our decision making and social world.

In most ethnographies, you meet characters and know them deeply. In this book, I want you to know the character of a neighborhood. I want you to meet a kind of community. I want you to understand the nature, the sounds, the look, and the soul of a space. A place I fear disappearing into my memories but lives on in my field notes.

Gay poet Mark Doty wrote: "To think through things, that is [the artist's] work... artists require a tangible vocabulary, a worldly lexicon. A language of ideas is, in itself, a phantom language, lacking in the substance of worldly things, those containers of feeling and experience, memory and time. We are instructed by the objects that come to speak with us, those material presences."[22] To think through worldly things is also the ethnographer's work. My use of carnal sociology also implies a different perspective on ethnography.[23] If participants learn through the body, through consumption and pleasure, then so too must the ethnographer. Every ethnography uses the researcher as a scientific instrument to collect data. In this book, I write about myself in the action. I was not a spectator. I am a gay man. I have queer sex. I share my physicality, my emotions, and my place with you so that you can come to understand how I developed the ideas I present.

Rather than ephemeral theory, dislocated ideas, I demonstrate through concrete places: "a worldly lexicon." I compare experiences, mine and others. I ask unpleasant questions.[24] I lived in Boystown and other parts of Chicago to understand the material conditions of a culture. As a queer man, I have experienced radical sexual culture firsthand to share a truth about our sexual lives, perhaps an uncomfortable one.

For three years, I studied Boystown and the queer tendrils that extend across Chicago. I've collected the stories of many nights. Through fieldwork,

I attended a variety of social scenes and events to answer my research questions. I hung out with many people in every bar in Boystown, and many others across Chicago. One night I might shoot Jägermeister with JJ's working-class Latino friends at Circuit. The next, I would sip vodka sodas with "the plastics," a group of upper-class gay men, at Minibar before jetting off to drink PBR (or Pabst Blue Ribbon, for the unhip), with "bears" at Big Chicks or swirl martinis with a bachelorette party.[25]

I especially followed six groups of people, whose experiences varied by race and social class and who also attended very different parts of Boystown's nightclub scene: JJ's Latino and Black working-class group; Darrin and Jon, two friends of color, students, with whom I regularly attended *RuPaul's Drag Race* showings and karaoke; Sean's "poz" guys, a middle-class white group of HIV+ men; Marcus's leather family, an extended family of choice affiliated with the BDSM/kink communities; and Frank's white "queers," a leftist political group of friends and activists.

In scenes across this book, I will introduce you to their social spaces to compare and contrast their experiences, not as individuals but as people participating in a social process. Not all of these groups receive the same attention within this book, nor did I spend the same amount of time with each. Ethnographic work shows only pieces of a larger body of field notes. While I show you illustrative scenes, I developed these theories using qualitative analysis techniques, such as a process of "constant comparison" and "theoretical sampling."

One such analysis technique is triangulation. In addition to participant observation and enactive ethnography, I interviewed people about their experiences with Boystown and the topics I will discuss. These people rarely overlapped with the people I followed ethnographically. They were bar—tenders, journalists, business owners, former homeless youth, prostitutes, and organizational leaders. I also analyzed hundreds of media reports and people reflecting about Boystown on Facebook, Twitter, Tumblr, and other online spaces.

I blend these sources together using multilogical qualitative methods, a methodological strategy that balances the ethnographer's experiences, participants' voices, and other researchers' knowledge. For you to understand my analysis, I must explain my choices in phasing between these perspectives. I discuss those challenges throughout this book as the need arises to understand the evidence I present, but I encourage you to read the supplement, "Producing Ethnography." Read it early. To learn from an ethnography, you must trust the ethnographer. Rather than expect trust by author-ity, I hope to earn it by presenting you with the context of my decisions.

The names that appear throughout this book are not the ones that their mothers or fathers gave them. Some chose their own pseudonyms. That's the method that I prefer, so there is no likelihood that I will accidentally give them a name that others will be able to connect back to them. Coming up with their own pseudonyms was difficult for many people. Trans and genderqueer participants often found the process tedious. "I already chose a name once," some would tell me.

Many of the people that I met out in the streets, I did not talk to long enough to warrant a selection of a pseudonym because I never got their name to begin with. Others told me just to pick one for them. In that case, I used a name generator, trying to pick names with similar levels of obscurity and, when I could, ethnic origin.

Boystown isn't a pseudonym, but it could be. "Boystowns" exist all over America, little havens for queer people, but mostly gay men, in major cities and small towns. Whether the Boystown is as small as the local gay bar or as big as a neighborhood, gayborhoods and queer spaces shape the life of LGBTQ people. I'm writing about a particular Boystown, a specific Boystown that lies between Belmont Avenue and Irving Park Road east of the train system's Red Line, but that doesn't mean that what happens is unique.

That's a lot about names, but I care about transparency. Ethnographies contain many secrets. Not everything I did is reported in these pages because such a full account would be impossible—and boring. Moreover, I've changed details I considered analytically irrelevant at times, not only to protect the innocent and guilty alike but also to blur their edges. These are real people I discuss, in public spaces, but this book isn't about their individual lives. It is about the social context in which they live. I keep some details secret for analytical as well as ethical reasons. One must deal with these secrets by being transparent about choices behind the scenes.

The choices I made resulted in a book that is particular, written from my experience in these spaces; triangulated with the perspectives of people I followed, other people I interviewed, and essays I read; and put into a conversation with other scholars. I could not write about everything in Boystown. I followed lines of inquiry that emerged.

Two omissions will stand out. The queer sexual revolution and the devastation of HIV are *male* radical sexual communities. I write about gay, bi, and queer men.[26] While I discuss spaces outside of Chicago, this book isn't about all of LGBTQ Chicago. I haven't researched queer women's communities, for instance.[27] However, women are present. Women—queer and straight—are a part of Boystown's story. I talked with many women to understand gender's influence.

Separate LGBTQ communities of color also exist in Chicago. Boystown is one neighborhood of a metropolis. I could have followed different lines of inquiry extending out of Boystown—for instance, one focused more on the interplay between the Black gay communities of the south side and those of Boystown. Again, acknowledgment of this focus doesn't mean I research white gay men only. I focused my activities outside of Boystown on the explicit sexual spaces I saw leaving the neighborhood, researching the race relations in these two kinds of spaces.

Two groups—once together, now separating—gay spaces assimilating to straight culture and queer sexy communities, the day and the night. This ethnography sheds light on those that have been kept in darkness. To bring their possibilities to light, we have to go into the darkness under the sheets.

2

On Safari

"To the birthday girl!" I toasted, hitting the glass against the bar before slinging back a shot of Jameson at Hydrate's Manhole night. Each of the five straight white women in front of me took their shots as well. One grimaced, managing to shoot about half. As the warmth hit my stomach, I thought, this place is not quite as Sam described.

■　■　■

Two months earlier on a warm April afternoon, Sam and I sat outside a café in Chicago's Roger Park neighborhood, sipping iced coffees. Sam was walking me through the kinds of clubs in Boystown. As a Black man involved in the nightlife industry, he knew the scenes each club represented. As my third interviewee, I expected we would talk about racism because of my initial research questions. Instead, he said a lot about the clubs' sexual energy, each space's sexiness. With a crude map of Halsted Street sitting between us that I had hastily scrawled in runny blue pen on yellow legal paper, I wrote each club's name on the map as we discussed it.

"Wang's," I wrote down as Sam spoke, "is trying to recapture that old energy. That old feeling of having gay space where you could really just go and be comfortable gaying-out." A space filled with sexual energy. A place you could go to pick someone up, flirt, or get laid.

Wang's attracted national attention for banning women after 11 P.M. Ten years ago, straight women wouldn't be in the club that late anyway.[1] Today, Boystown has seen an influx of straight white women tourists. Wang's attempted to re-create the old scene by preventing women from coming inside. Some people called the policy discrimination. Others thought it was the only way to preserve sexual space. Gay clubs look different with women on safari, prompting Sam to say, "Why can't [gay men] just have this raunchy gay space? Let them have it."

"What other bars would you say are like that in Boystown?" I asked.

"None to that extent." He paused to consider, "There are some parties you'll see at Hydrate that go that way. I've never heard any accusations of women not being allowed in, or that sort of thing, but they certainly tend to go more raunchy. Before it was Hydrate, it was a bar called Manhole."

When I laughed, he said, "You have that knowing smile. So yeah,"

"No, but you tell me." I insisted. I needed it on tape.

"Manhole was that gay space. The backroom of it, which wasn't like a backroom in the traditional sense. There are still one or two bars that have a classic backroom in Chicago, but not in Boystown. But their backroom, you had to take your shirt off or be in leather. There was still this raunch element to it."

Sam is underselling it. Manhole closed, becoming the tamer Hydrate, long before I came to the neighborhood, but older guys still tell a few explicit stories about Manhole's backroom. For instance, down in the basement, people could get wet in a few bathtubs and showers. When it wasn't water from the showers, people played watersports with recycled beer.

Today, Hydrate is known more for gym rats and circuit boys than people pissing on each other in the basement. Today's revelers are sweaty from using crystal meth and dancing until 5 A.M., not having sex all night in a stuffy basement.

"But once a month, like every six weeks or so, this group of guys puts on Manhole parties that harken back to those days of that sort of thing. The last one was called Phys Ed about jocks and sportswear. The next one is Tom of Finland themed," Sam told me.[2]

Sounded like fun. A wild party full of sexual energy. A great place to see queer spaces' alternative sexual cultures. It would be different from most nights I spent out in Boystown dodging bachelorette parties.

■ ■ ■

It wasn't. I've seen other Manhole nights since then that were as Sam described. However, my first night was different. The five women there to celebrate a birthday stood before me wearing dresses, skirts, and heels. Not quite the attire Tom of Finland depicted in his drawings.

I had been in the front bar waiting with Jon, an early-thirties Latino gay man, for his friend Darrin, a twenty-five-year-old Black gay man. We were discussing the International Mister Leather conference's Leather Market— so expensive!—when five white women entered. When they rounded the corner into the club, we were the first people they saw.

Almost immediately, we fell into old patterns. Gay men and straight women have an easy script. The characters are stereotypes but fun to play

Figure 2.1. Men and women outside Hydrate Nightclub

nevertheless. They'll say we look like fun. I'll compliment their shoes. They'll bemoan that all the hot guys are gay. Within ten minutes, we were taking birthday shots, merrily chatting about popular culture. As dated as this reference sounds now, Madonna's tour would be in Chicago in just a few months: What did everyone think of her new CD?

Like I always did, I told them I was writing a book about Boystown. I asked them about their visit. Why come to Manhole night?

"What?" the birthday girl told me, "We were walking down the street and this place looked like fun. This is my first time here."

One of her friends scowled. She had recently moved to the neighborhood. She told me later she didn't want her friends to embarrass her on their first night out in Boystown.[3]

Jon and I wanted to go to the back to dance, and the ladies decided to come with us. The trouble began when they tried to get through the curtains to the dance floor, the "backroom." Jon and I took off our shirts, paying the visual toll to the bouncer, showing some skin to keep the space erotically charged. The bouncer—a bear, his leather harness stretched over his rotund hairy frame—moved to block the hallway after we passed when the women tried to follow us back.

"No shirts." They didn't look pleased.

Although the club was too loud to hear what she was saying from a distance, I watched the young woman who lived in Boystown persuade her friends. Each pulled her dress's top down and the bouncer waved them through.

"Woooo! This is wild!" the birthday girl laughed as she skipped onto the main dance floor clad only in her bra from the waist up.

No shirts? Close enough.

■ ■ ■

Women were at Manhole the next time, too. Two shirtless lesbians made out with each other in the corner. One pushed the other against the wall, pulling her onto one of her legs, trusting her hips in time to the music. One hand cupped a bare breast, a thumb running over her erect nipple. They blended into the scene.

Men packed the room, most dancers grinding. Leather and other fetish gear everywhere. Austin and I drank whiskey gingers against the right-hand-side bar while talking with a friend who was wearing a full suit of rubber gear. His boyfriend stood behind him, dressed similarly except for the dog collar and leash.

Later, I saw a tall Iowa boy, chunky and muscular, get his dick sucked in the dance floor's back corner near the DJ booth. A leather harness wrapped around his chest before extending down over his stomach to attach to a leather cock ring. I tried to avoid looking, lest I make them feel self-conscious.

When the boy from Iowa was less preoccupied, he told me he drove hours to be at Manhole night. "Nothing like this where I live," he yelled to me over the music before smacking my ass. Not your everyday research.

■ ■ ■

No one was on their knees that first night. As we marched back, the birthday girls produced an aura of purity, or an aura of sexual shame depending on your perspective. While the place was similarly full as the visit just described, the men around us kept their distance, making me feel like we were dancing in a bubble. Sure, people were still dancing sexually, but with none of the groping I would see on that next visit.

Yet.

After twenty minutes of dancing, the birthday party decided to move to another bar. We hugged, and I pressed my business card into their hands while we made our good-byes. When they left, I felt a notable shift in the crowd's mood. Suddenly Darrin started making out with a young white guy wearing tight jeans, whose thick chest hair curled around the straps of a leather harness.

Time warps when you dance, the electronic tones and remixed divas washing over you as you gyrate to the tunes. The bubble surrounding me when I was with the birthday girls had burst, dudes crashing in, pushing skin against me. I couldn't tell whether thirty minutes or two hours had passed, but Darrin and the guy he was making out with had long finished their session. Darrin moved to dance about three inches away from me on the dance floor. He pulled up behind me, grinding into my back. When I danced away, pulling out of his unwanted embrace—resulting in a need to hash out later in text messages that I didn't like him in that way—I ran straight into the arms of the leather-bound man with whom he had been trading spit earlier.

"You want a beer?" he asked. I did.

Several beers later, we were holding hands, running through the pouring rain to Charlie's, another late-night bar on Boystown's northern edge, my Mohawk drooping down the side of my face. He pulled me against a nearby building and kissed me.

Another successful night out in Boystown.

■　■　■

People go out on the town for many reasons. A primary one is sex, or at least the possibility of it. Zach Stafford, in a piece for Chicago's alternative newspaper *RedEye*, put it this way: "When we all go out—gay or straight—a lot of us are looking to meet someone. Whether it's for a one-night stand, a potential first date or just some innocent flirtation as we hang out with friends, we usually are looking for some fun with someone we find attractive."[4] His title asks: "Is It Time to Bust Out of Boystown?" Following Betteridge's law of headlines, Stafford answers no.[5] Gay men want, perhaps need, to go to Boystown, he says, because their chance of finding another gay guy there is higher than elsewhere in the city. Best estimates put the number of out gay, bisexual, and queer men in America at 2–3 percent of the population. Finding other gay men in a nongay bar is statistically unlikely, let alone finding someone who meets their unique desires.[6]

Yet Boystown's nightlife is losing some sexual charge that made finding a hookup easy. Although the bars have no shortage of queer men, these spaces' sexual culture is changing because more people are coming to gay bars on safari. More straight women are out for Boystown's novelty, disrupting the sexual vibe. A night out at Manhole is now a theme night, rather than a regular occurrence.[7] Getting to the backrooms of Rogers Park's leather bars takes a forty-five-minute bus ride north on the 36. In general, Boystown is much more about social drinking than picking someone up.

At the Rogers Park coffee shop, I asked Sam what he thought was the biggest change to Boystown since he moved to Chicago over a decade ago.

"Boystown still represents nightlife and fun with friends," Sam told me, "But there is an aspect to it. It's the gawking aspect. You know, you have a lot of people come in, especially straight women who fetishize gay men and the gay lifestyle a little bit and they can be a bit overzealous in their appreciation for it."

"There are a lot of guys who want to go to a gay bar to be free," Sam continued, "To like take off your shirt and be raunchy. To just have at it without this whole table full of straight girls saying, 'Oh gay men are so safe and pretty and I love you.' Bitch, get off of me! I'm trying to suck this guy's dick."

I must have looked a bit shocked—I've never been known for my poker face, though it's a good skill for interviewers to practice—so he quickly added, "I'm sorry, just being completely open here."

After some reassurance that the interviews were confidential, he continued. "The general acceptance of gay and lesbians has led to . . ." He trailed off.

"Sometimes Boystown is a bit of a zoo. I don't even go to the Pride Parade anymore. I can't fucking handle it." He threw his hands in the air dramatically, exasperated with the world, making me laugh out loud.

"Because it's mostly just straight people." His voice squealed into a caricature of straight women, "Oh they are so cute! Gay men are so buff! All of them!" Raising his eyebrow, he indicated his own plus-size body.

"It's just become like this petting zoo where they come and look and gawk at the gays and it's not as much just the gay neighborhood as it is where people go to see the gay people. A lot of people don't like that. I don't like that. I can't stand it when a woman will come up to me at a bar like 'You're gay, you're my best friends!' like that kind of attitude."

His voice started to break with laughter, as he said: "Like I don't know about you, but just because you've seen gays on TV doesn't mean I'm going to be your best friend."

"Do you have a story or example of a time that happened? Where you felt like you were being observed that way?" I asked.

"There's not one story, because it always happens. You know, I'll be in a bar. I'll be hanging out with friends and a straight girl will barge into our conversation throw her arms around me, tell me how much she loves gay people and then, you know, just make it—All. About. Her."

Boystown sells straight women a gay lifestyle of fun fashionable drinks in stylish surroundings. Boystown offers a place for straight women to escape straight clubs' ever-present possibility of violence. But Boystown also sells the gay men and their sexual space. Boystown promises straight women a petting zoo where they can see the gays. Boystown is a novelty promising a wild night out. Boystown is a chance to go on safari.

■ ■ ■

Someone is on safari when they consider the consumption of a space as a new authentic experience to be more important than appreciating the space's purpose. The birthday girls cared more about having a wild time than they cared about knowing what Hydrate's Manhole night was. They didn't intentionally want their birthday party to disrupt Manhole's sexual field. Indeed, they wanted it to be sexy, to a point.[8]

They had the privilege, however, of being entitled to go wherever they wished. For them, it was a chance to do something weird. For gay men, Manhole is a place to hang out, flirt, maybe even suck someone's dick in the corner of the dance floor. If these women knew how some of the gay men felt about their presence, they would likely be horrified. However unintentional, the space changes as everyone tries to ensure they have a good time.

The sociologist Erving Goffman described social interaction using the metaphor of the theater. People mutually define what kind of scene is taking place, using scripts to help figure out what to do. We all have a role to play on the stage. Scripts help us muddle through everyday life. While every situation is a little bit different, general rules help. When definitions conflict—different ideas about what is happening—scripts help those in power to assert their definition.[9] To offer others something to do is to tell them what is happening. While someone may have thought one thing was taking place, they'll follow along and do another altogether if that's what the script seems to call for.[10]

In the gay bar, when different uses for the space conflict, the heterosexual definition of the situation is often adopted. "Normal" sexuality and rules of propriety—you would never see someone having sex in the corner of your neighborhood pub—win out over queer alternative sexuality. The outside of Rubin's charmed circle wanes and the inner circle wins out.

The adoption doesn't happen automatically, but the script straight women assume in these situations is seductive. When the birthday girls came to Manhole, they didn't force me to compliment their clothes, but that is another line of script between straight women and gay men. Their expectations for a gay night on the town make playing a role in their drama easier for me than to resist them, be rude, and preserve a raunchy queer definition.

Later, I will discuss the businesses' role in selling gay culture, known as heritage commodification. For now, I want to focus on the sexual consequences of their expectations. Straight women on safari in these situations have what sociologist John Urry calls a "tourist gaze."[11]

Someone with a tourist gaze has expectations about what an "authentic" experience should be and others act accordingly. For instance, a white American visiting an American Indian reservation might expect certain handmade goods to be for sale, traditional ceremonies to be performed, or to witness other "Indian" things seen in popular culture that form their definition of authentic Indianness. The people living on the reservation, in need of the economic resources the tourists provide, have incentives to act in the manner the tourists expect. The white American doesn't intend to exploit or stereotype, but their tourist gaze shapes the shared script everyone will act on regardless.

The tourist gaze of those on safari in Boystown's gay clubs transforms gay men from full-fledged cast members, to continue Goffman's dramaturgical analogy, to supporting characters. Gay men become another accessory straight women can buy on a night out. Like the script I performed with the birthday girls, the gay bar becomes a space to engage in the mutual banter of the gay best friend.

These expectations hover over any nightlife interaction between straight women and gay men. When Austin and I went on a date to the Chicago Beer Festival, a pair of straight women clocked us as two gay men. Since we were wearing leather jackets—October in Chicago—a midtwenties white woman with long, black hair felt the need to walk over and tell us we were her "favorite biker gays." Laughing, she rubbed her hands along my sleeve. I felt as though she had never met a gay person before in her life. I felt objectified. We were an accessory to make her night more fun.

And, I had fun. Like the birthday girls at Manhole, I laughed along, enjoying our shared script despite my discomfort. Austin kept more silent than usual. After we left the venue, he told me he was uninterested in friendship with someone who didn't treat him like a real person. Some gay men play along; others resist; most do both. Based on my conversations with other straight women during fieldwork, if they knew Austin had felt this way, these two women would have felt uncomfortable. Regardless of their intentions, their tourist orientation to our interaction created these consequences.

The script Sam wants to engage in—"Bitch, get off me! I'm trying to suck this guy's dick!"—gets overwritten when a woman comes up behind him, appropriating his friend group for her fun night, without realizing these men have a different use for the space. While her own sexual field—the places she goes to look for a hookup—are across the tracks in Wrigleyville, Sam's sexual field is right here. If Sam acted in Wrigleyville like he was in his sexual field, he would be attacked.

Because, while those on safari want an authentic experience, they don't know what "authentic" looks like. Someone on safari doesn't understand the scripts for queer sexual space, the rules for the situation that come with queer cultural knowledge. To gain these requires genuine engagement over time.[12]

Barbara Crowley, in the aptly titled "Why I Sometimes Feel Uncomfortable around Straight People," writes:

> I can't ignore the fact that I often find myself feeling uncomfortable around my heterosexual friends.... No, it usually isn't their actions at all. These feelings often manifest during certain conversations that remind me that, while I'm getting the rather comfortable feeling of belonging, they will never understand major parts of me and my experience being queer.
>
> This is not to say I expect them to or that any of us perfectly understands anyone else. Rather, I have recently noticed major gaps in their understanding, not only of the queer and genderqueer communities, but of me as a queer person. A few questions and comments, in particular, serve as unpleasant reminders that as hard as we try, there will always be barriers between us when it comes to my sexuality and love-life.[13]

For Crowley, her straight friends' questions—"What's queer?"—or comments—"That's gay"—remind her of her difference. Similarly, out in the gay bars, those on safari often lack queer cultural knowledge, misunderstandings that make the queer people around grit their teeth, reminders of society's stigma.

Without knowing how to act in the space, those on safari end up disrupting the flirtations of the gay men around them. Even well-meaning straight people can obstruct the sexual situations of their friends when they don't know the rules of the game. Samir, an Indian American man in his late twenties, told me about his experience at Dollop, a Buena Park coffee shop just outside Boystown.

"So they'll go up to some guy and say, 'Oh my god, my friend thinks you're really cute,'" he said leaning over the table. "And that's because they don't know the sort of—not etiquette but codes of sexual conduct. They really interrupt it by being really forward, being really obvious versus flirting or cruising. Which is sometimes very endearing and sometimes very, like, vulgar."

He searched for words. "Or disorienting. Or annoying. I've been told more often by women than by men that I'm cute in a club. So there's something affirming about them being there. But there's also like, how do—."

He paused again, struggling to articulate the subtle nonverbal differences between cruising and the traditional straight way of picking up someone by initiating conversation.

"These codes are different. That women are operating—queer and straight women—are operating with gay men, there's a way in which they provide a validation that doesn't always come by being a person of color in the club. So there's that as well. But them actually coming out and saying these things is very different from cruising," he said.

As Samir points out, the script gay men and straight women act out together can be validating. Who doesn't like to be told they are attractive? But this flirtation circles back, shutting down other flirtation in the space. It crowds it out.

One night at Jackhammer, a Rogers Park leather bar, when I was working the coat check, I could tell this midtwenties white guy was trying to flirt with me. People often flirt with bar employees. Standing in my underwear checking coats has a way of drawing that out, along with unwanted aggressive attention. He wanted to go downstairs to the Hole, where the dress code dictates fetish gear or underwear. As he took off his clothes, he bent over to pull down his pants, gazing a bit too long at my crotch, before turning his head up to smile at me.[14]

His friend, a tall white woman in a black lace corset pushing her massive breasts together, leaned forward, interrupting our interaction. "You just are so fit. Do you work out a lot?"[15]

Turning my gaze toward her to answer her question, I ignored her friend's nonverbal flirting. Moments later, he finished packing his clothes into a brown paper bag. I wrote his bag number in sharpie on his left shoulder as I continued talking to his friend. He slipped a couple of dollars into the waistband of my underwear, before marching to the bar.

Things aren't supposed to go this way. Cruising—the sustained eye contact, sexual jokes, and other clues that you are into someone—requires that friends get out of the way.[16] Someone continually inserting themselves into a flirtatious interaction is said to be "cockblocking."[17] Overly concerned with seeing new things—having a tourist gaze—those on safari often watch too intently or involve themselves too much in the ongoing flirtation that can lead to sex.

Those on safari can also overwhelm a space making the gay identity of the space hazy. Several bars in Boystown have such a high proportion of straight people that some men don't bother to hit on anyone because of the high chances of hitting on a straight guy. While some gay men find straight men alluring, few want to spend a night attempting to hook up with someone when going home with him is only a remote possibility.[18]

Berlin, for instance, sits next to the Belmont stop of the Red Line "L" train, just over the line to Wrigleyville. Most count Berlin as part of Boystown anyway. Berlin plays alternative music, with traveling DJs and theme nights. Berlin's late-night liquor license allows/forces them to stay open until 5 A.M. on weekends and 4 A.M. on weeknights. Many nights of fieldwork ended in a line waiting to enter, as the people I followed were eager to dance, inhibitions lowered after a long night of drinking.[19]

On an early June night, I was waiting in line to catch up with Carlos, a Latino genderqueer gay man in his midtwenties, for our Tuesday dollar-PBR ritual. Luckily, I had my headphones out or I would not have heard the conversation of several straight men behind me.

"You think there's going to be a bunch of fags here tonight?" The dude behind me at least had the consciousness to ask this quietly of the friend beside him.

Not wanting to give myself away as one of those fags, I waited a few beats before turning around to confirm who the speaker was. Yes, three young white men in T-shirts, jeans, and baseball caps. While Carlos and other gay men may have thought this club was in Boystown, these men clearly thought otherwise. For the rest of the night—and honestly, every time at Berlin since—I heard those men softly saying "fag" when I saw gay men dancing together. They imported their stigma into what had been a queer space.

At the most extreme, if enough straight people are in attendance, even if they are the most queer friendly and have no interest in going on safari, their mere presence can transform a gay bar. The space begins to look like the straight sexual fields, with *their* sexual rituals, more than a queer space. A Thursday night out at Scarlet intentionally evokes the homoerotic yet heterosexual masculinity of a frat house. Everyone stands around drinking 40s and small personal pitchers of Long Island iced tea or playing beer pong.[20] Scarlet is one of the best places in Boystown to dance. The lack of dance spaces in the straight-identified parts of Chicago drives straight women into the dance clubs of Boystown, and straight men follow. With mostly straight groups on the dance floor, some of the straight men working the crowd to separate a woman from her friends, you might forget you are in Boystown. Even straight couples that are only in Scarlet to get drunk on cheap Long Islands and to dance give the club the feeling of a straight bar.

Who wants to go to a straight bar?

■　■　■

Not many queer men.

When a conflict between queer sexual culture and people on safari develops, gay men respond to the loss of sexual space in different ways. Some gay men have retreated from spaces known to have many straight women or escape from those spaces when groups of women overwhelm the bar, fleeing, instead, to bars known for their raunchy atmospheres.

On another night, Austin and I were walking down Halsted to Sidetrack to meet a few friends when we ran into one of Austin's buddies from law school. After the hugs and introductions, we asked him where he had just been.

"Scarlet. Ugh." He groaned. "I had to get out of there. There were four different bachelorette parties there."

He imitated the bachelorette party's well-known call: "Wooooooooo!" He sighed. "I just couldn't take it."

Austin and I looked at each other nervously, hoping Sidetrack wouldn't be filled to the brim with those about to be married. "Where are you going now, then?" Austin asked.

"I'm going to catch a bus up to Jackhammer."

Many gay men are doing the same, traveling from all over the city to the two raunchy clubs in Rogers Park, Jackhammer and Touché.

While Boystown's backrooms closed, these bars still have spaces for people to hook up. The people who don't go into those areas still benefit from the sexual energy of bars with hookup spaces, as I discuss later.

The entrance to Jackhammer's backroom space called the Hole is via some narrow stairs, hidden to the left of the main bar. On a night like the Recon Party during the International Mister Leather (IML) conference held in Chicago every year, the stairs seem far from hidden.[21] The first time I went down into The Hole, I was following Alan, an Asian American gay man in his early thirties, and several other Asian American men visiting him from out of town for IML over Memorial Day weekend, 2012. After paying our twenty-dollar cover at the door, we bypassed the main bars to get downstairs to the action.

The long cab ride up to Rogers Park from Boystown was as long as the line into the Hole.

"TO THE LEFT," Marcus, a midfifties Black gay man and the Hole's bouncer, dressed in a full rubber suit and knee-high boots, would scream when people clumped up trying to talk to friends as they waited. Everyone scrambled to get against the wall; no one dared disobey Marcus's orders.

Once patrons reached the bottom of the stairs, Marcus enforced the dress code. Like Manhole nights, a visual toll must be paid to enter the sexually charged atmosphere. The Hole is more hard-core than Manhole or Wang's in this respect. On Recon night, dress code required fetish gear—leather, rubber, or sports gear—or to strip down to underwear. At the time, I didn't have a leather harness yet, so I stripped down to my jockstrap and carried my clothes over to the clothing check, depositing everything—except for some cash I stuck in my shoe—into a brown paper bag.[22]

At the time, the Hole was a barely finished basement at best. An open bathroom at one end—since closed off with doors as required by the city inspector—and a small bar in the center dot an otherwise empty expanse. The space must be sparse to hold the crowd. After I put my clothes away, our group grabbed drinks while surveying the crowd pressing around us. To the left in the corner, a man strapped to a Saint Andrew's cross was being spanked with a crop as he moaned for the crowd. To the right, crowds disappeared farther into the next room or around the corner to a small dark hallway to have sex.[23]

After one drink, Alan's friend Kevin tugged my arm, raising his eyebrows suggestively toward the side room brimming with men. I followed him back into the dim haze. All around me, people were cruising. Some stood in small groups drinking with seminude friends they had just met. Two tall muscular men with beers in their hands stood near the entrance talking casually, while two men on their knees behind them rimmed their asses. Farther near the back, tucked into the darkness, men were fucking, the bottoms bracing themselves against the wall. When Air's "Sexy Boy" started playing over the speakers, I looked up, expecting glitter to fall from the ceiling. I was in an episode of *Queer as Folk*.

These days though, on an average night, even these sexual spaces of queer male escapism see people on safari. Straight women are coming down into the Hole. Marcus confessed to me that he has to monitor the room more closely. Too many women have wandered back into the corner hallway reserved for sex. If a straight woman gets back there, her presence causes the gay men having sex to scatter back into the bar area, uninterested in being the show for her tourist's gaze.

Marcus doesn't care if women want to drink downstairs in the bar with their friends. After all, if a tourist gaze transforms the space into a petting zoo, as the zookeepers, Marcus and other employees benefit financially from the increased traffic. As with the seductive scripts, their material interests collude to ensure everyone, even those on safari, has a good time.

Marcus expects everyone to follow the rules, at least minimally, excluding those on safari. I watched Marcus eject a straight white woman because she refused to follow the no-hallway rule. I was standing at the bar talking to one of the bartenders, now wearing my leather harness, which meant I could keep my pants on. She wandered down the stairs with a friend, seemingly unsure of where they were going. Her gay male friend certainly knew, since he immediately took his shirt off. Marcus explained the dress code to her. She needed to take her shirt off if she wanted to come downstairs. Based on her giggling and the slight roll to the way she held her drink, she'd already had a few.

Clothed in her bra and jeans, she stood against the wall for several minutes soaking in the half-clothed sights around the two of them. She must have noticed men wandering into the back hallway to cruise, so she walked over and stuck her head in, again giggling at what was happening inside. Marcus came over and explained the area was for sex. If she wasn't going to be having sex, she shouldn't go back.

Five minutes later, she was at it again, poking her head around the corner. Marcus, ever patient with customers even if he could be stern, told her to stay out. When she wouldn't take no for an answer and tried to push past him back into the hallway, he told her she had to leave. Indignant, she grabbed her gay male friend's arm and took him back upstairs.

■ ■ ■

If even the Hole has people on safari, where are gay men to go? Online mobile hookup applications allow gay men to layer over spaces with the possibility of sex. If the area around them doesn't have the kind of sexual culture they wish to engage in, then they can pull up Grindr, Scruff, or one of several other mobile applications.

Walk into a Boystown bar and the unmistakable "bloop!" of the Grindr message notification can be heard if you listen closely enough. Like most of the mobile applications, Grindr uses the GPS location of the user's cell phone to display the profiles of others close to them. In a place with a high concentration of active users like Boystown, the closest will often be within the margin of error, meaning they could be standing close by. One of my apartments in Boystown had at least four users in the small building.

Since you can take Grindr with you, it is the perfect device to engage in "augmented reality," the layering of digital information over physical locations.[24] Augmented reality began as a technological design term, referring to applications that literally used a phone's camera to display a video feed overlaid with information. For instance, within the Yelp iOS application, the Monocle feature allows the user to use the phone as a lens on the world. Restaurant names and ratings are displayed over their approximate location. Standing in front of Boystown's Rollapalooza, you might wonder: "Is that place any good?" Point the monocle and the rating will appear.

When someone engages something like Grindr, though, in augmented reality, they add information to their surroundings socially. The app allows people to see the other gay men around them, send them naughty pictures, flirt, or just chat like they would in a gay bar. If a bar is filled with people on safari, then Grindr allows gay men to have a secret back channel. While straight men might be in the bar Berlin, you know the men on Grindr are gay. If you can't cruise because someone on safari is watching, the privacy of the application creates another layer of community.

A night out at Minibar, the Boystown cocktail bar associated with the plastics, upper-class mostly white gay men, is a perfect example. Like many nights I sat alone in Boystown bars, I saw the other men in the bar looking on their smartphones throughout the night. From my vantage point, I saw a white man in his early forties chat with people on Grindr while drinking at the bar. After significant time talking via Grindr, another man approached him. From their body language, it seemed they were meeting in person for the first time, by all indications through Grindr. Other participants I've talked with have mentioned similar scenarios.

Even these online spaces see women on safari. At a housewarming party, several groups of subjects I'd been observing came together, although as usual, the space between ethnographic participants and friends had blurred.[25] Samir was with several of his Indian American friends. A few people from the poz guys showed up. Of course, most of the plastics didn't come, but at least one graced us with his presence. Interspersed throughout were a few college friends who had moved to Chicago, as well as Austin's friends.

As the party started, a few members of each group had arrived. Introducing them to each other, one of Austin's friends, whom I'd just met, asked me my profession. Telling him about this book, he exclaimed, "Like girls on Grindr!" Murmurs of agreement came from around the room. Nearly everyone had seen one before. A few even had a female friend on Grindr, some secretly by pretending to be men. Dramatized by the website Buzzfeed, women on Grindr engage in many of the same on safari tactics I've described here, such as looking for gay best friends, gay men to shop with, or just someone to be their gay accessory for a night out on the town.

When the Buzzfeed article's photos were posted to Facebook, one gay male Chicago resident commented: "Straight women have become very disrespectful towards gay men, insomuch as to be invalidating of their personal boundaries, and invasive of their public spaces. (read: women invading gay bars to the point that it no longer can be considered a safe space) Considering this is taking place on Grindr this is a great example of that."

The Hole. Grindr. No place is safe from people coming in on safari, tourists in queer spaces hoping to have a good night at the expense of the sexual culture.

■   ■   ■

Preventing people from coming out on safari is impossible. Many gay men blame straight women, as though they were the only people capable of going on safari. The controversy over Wang's Men's Room night demonstrated those defending these sexual spaces often did so by banning all women—

straight and queer alike. Lesser versions of the same policy exist in several gay bars around Boystown like the No Bachelorette Parties sign on Cocktail's front door. Yet this sign did not prevent groups of straight women from coming in—unaccompanied by queer people—to have a wild night stuffing dollar bills down the go-go boys' underwear. As I would have predicted, the straight women I've talked to have never encountered anyone telling them they aren't allowed in the clubs.

In my conversation with Celeste, a white straight woman in her late twenties, she was explaining the reasons she loved Boystown, a topic I will return to later, but I wanted to see if she perceived any negative feedback from gay men about straight women's presence in the bars.

"Have you ever had any negative interactions?" I asked.

"No, I don't think so. None that stand out. I've never had anyone say anything negative to us. No," she said.

"OK," I replied, but paused, unsure how that could be true. "I just ask because I've interviewed a lot of different kinds of people and I think, Cocktail, that bar that used to be on the corner over there, used to have a No Bachelorette Parties sign."

"What?"

"Yeah, so I was wondering if you ever encountered anyone saying they didn't want bachelorette parties?"

These were leading questions, but I couldn't understand at the time why her presence in a gay space had never been questioned.

"No, I never have encountered that," she said.

"OK, it's good for me to know! I see the sign, but I'm, like, does that actually happen?" I attempted to recover.

"I've been out on a lot of bachelorette parties and I've never encountered that. I can see that there might be some resistance in terms of girls going in and thinking that they are going to run the show, kind of, and stepping on some toes that way," she said.

"How would they step?"

"Like wooing, being loud."

"Woooo!" I mimicked.

She laughed, nodding. "Like, maybe you're there for night with your friend or boyfriend or whatever and then you have to deal with annoying people? Because we can be annoying. I can see why there might be some pushback but I've never encountered it, but even if someone said something snarky I think I would just brush it off, but I've never had bad service."

"You've had all good experiences?"

"I've always had a good experience," she insisted.

Not all straight women have good experiences. I've talked to many who,

Figure 2.2. A bachelorette party outside the Kit Kat Lounge and Supper Club

while out on the town in Boystown, have reported negative aspects, like slow service from bartenders. However, the overwhelming experience is positive. Their tourist gaze transforms the space such that everyone ensures they have a good time.

When bars like Wang's declare themselves off-limits to women, many people in both the straight and queer communities were quick to declare the rule discriminatory. Of course, no business is allowed to prevent a legally protected class from accessing their business. Later, I will explore the reasons why straight women come to Boystown and the sexism greeting them when they arrive. For now, I want to emphasize the sense of entitlement that people on safari have to the spaces they want to observe.

For instance, the popular online feminist blog *Jezebel* posted an article titled "Get Out of My Gay Bar, Straight Girl." Chloë Curran's argument, written in typical Internet clickbait hyperbolic style, was that straight women needed to stay out of queer women's spaces.[26]

"I'm not here to argue for a ban on straight people in gay clubs; that's discrimination, and clearly wrong." She writes, "However I will ask you to a) rethink the entitlement you feel to occupy every space and b) respect that no matter how much you 'love the gays,' sometimes gay people need to be amongst their peers and therefore apart from you."

Despite her disclaimer about not wanting to ban straight people, the piece ignited a firestorm on social media, both inside and outside of Boys-town. Many people declared, like in the Wang's flap, it was a kind of "reverse discrimination."

The problem is that both sides of this issue are focusing on the identi-ties of the people occupying the space rather than on their actions. Straight women in gay bars are not the problem. The problem is people coming in with a tourist gaze, appropriating others' space on safari. The problem is that dominant people feel entitled to all spaces, not recognizing times when minorities need spaces away from dominant culture. The problem is that people on safari put their own desires for a good time above the sexual cul-ture they are disrupting. The problem is that people on safari are unaware of a sexual culture in queer spaces to begin with.

People not on safari, even if they are straight women, are respected in these settings. For example, up at the Jackhammer in the Hole, staff mem-bers recognize the difference between straight people on safari and those participating in the energy of the space, respecting and not gawking. They host a variety of parties aimed at straight people who are also in need of alternative sexual space, like nudist groups.

As Marcus told me, "My favorite time is when a straight girl is pegging her boyfriend in the back."[27]

Even conventional penis-in-vagina intercourse is acceptable in the Hole. At another Recon Party, in the back recesses of the side room, in the dark-ness past the slings, I saw a white man fucking a white woman, her blond hair occasionally obscuring her face as it swirled around her. No one around them batted an eye. They were of the space, participating in the same kinds of activities as those around them.[28]

Furthermore, straight women aren't the only people capable of being on safari. Those with the "right" identities to fit the space can also be on sa-fari. Oftentimes, people new to the gay scene are still ignorant of the queer scripts for these spaces. Sometimes, down in the Hole, Marcus must kick out gay men who refuse to follow the dress code or who are gawking.

One bartender told me that straight women on safari were not the prob-lem. Rather, their gay male friends should know better. In the early morn-ing dawn, after I had worked a shift on coat check, he told me, as he wiped down liquor bottles, "I really blame their boy toys that bring them here. They are just here to look at the freaks just as much. They want to join in, but use their girls for safety."

He sighed. "If they knew better, they wouldn't bring howling straight girls in the first place."

Samir, when I interviewed him, agreed with the idea that gay men can also be spectators. "I've been a tourist in Boystown myself," he said, explaining that he went to places like Roscoe's and Sidetrack when he first came to Chicago because others more experienced told him to do so. "Now, I kind of stay away from these places where everyone's sort of wide-eyed."

Every gay man has been on safari. Perhaps one day it will be different, but few gay men grow up in queer cultures. Everyone comes from a straight family, coming to a place like Boystown in adulthood. Everyone has to learn the script.

The first time I was in a gay club at age eighteen—the Bonham Exchange in San Antonio—I brought my friend Dana along. We sat at a table in the corner of the dance floor. While she stared at the table, bored out of her mind, I gawked at everything happening around me. Men dancing. Men kissing each other. Everything seemed so different, grand, and gay. One might even say that, in writing this book, I'm taking some readers on safari as well, clueing the uninitiated into the rules of a subculture different from their own.

Should we expect everyone to know the rules of these environments before they arrive there? I don't think so. But we should expect people to be respectful. As the saying goes, if you sit down at poker table and you don't recognize the mark, you're the mark. If you aren't sure who is on safari in a space, you're it.

"You know whose privilege I find a lot more oppressive than straight white women?" a Chicago gay graduate student posted as a response to a comment I made on Facebook about the *Jezebel* article:

> Upper middle class gay men who will only interact with their other upper middle class friends who they met at the gym or their Audi dealership. Gay couples who think the fact that they are going to drive home to their two adopted kids and three shelter cats entitles them to a space where they get to dictate who belongs and who doesn't. Gay men who act like it is normal to treat HIV+ men as less than human. Gay men who think body type dictates sociability.
>
> Those people and their privilege are oppressive to me, but I am not arguing that they should stay out of (or be kept out of) places I want to claim as my own. Even straight white women who are celebrating a bachelorette party—often cited as the worst offenders in intruding into gay spaces—with their gawking and finger pointing, are less offensive or oppressive than many gays. They are there at least celebrating the safe space where breaking societal norms of gender and sexuality is embraced, rather than building additional walls to keep others out.

Indeed, they are. Thinking back to the birthday girl embarrassed by her friends' blatant sense of novelty, as someone living in the neighborhood, she didn't come to a Boystown gay club because of proximity alone. The fun of Boystown hinges on its sexual difference and sexiness. To be successful, heritage commodification must be "authentic."

Yet a tourist gaze transforms. These bars must now adopt an acceptable sexiness. No longer allowing for radical queer difference, Boystown's gay bars assimilate, reinforcing other aspects of assimilation taking place in the neighborhood.

All the forces my Facebook friend mentioned are oppressive, but they are connected. Just like the women on safari, other forms of discrimination occur in gay bars. Not coincidentally, the places most protected from those on safari are those most preserved from these other forms of discrimination. The places most filled with bachelorette parties are the most sexually racist. Rather than being a competition between oppressions—HIV stigma or women in gay clubs?—they are connected. Queer sexuality, the outside of the charmed circle, erodes these other forms of discrimination.

3

—

Naked Intimacy

Music inspires memory. Anytime Tesla Boy's "Spirit of the Night" begins playing—the chimes ringing up the scale like the startup to a futuristic computer, the electronic beats flashing in fast tempo—I'm transported. I'm alone on the 151 bus, riding down Devon Avenue. My shirt is a little too tight, revealing the straps of my leather harness underneath, obvious under the bus's harsh fluorescents. Tesla Boy blasts through my white iPhone headphones.

At the corner of Clark and Devon, the night is unusually cool for June; the cold metal of the harness's buckles chill my skin. Across the street, I can barely see the men standing outside, the glow of their cigarette tips like fireflies.

Jackhammer brings warmth against the cool night, administered as a tight hug from Ricky, the doorman, who doesn't bother to check my ID. I pull my headphones off, Tesla Boy's savory electronics replaced by Katy Perry's saccharine tunes thumping from the speakers. I pass the bar to my left, with Omar, a bartender, pouring one of many rounds of Jäger he will have that night.

Thunk. Thunk. Thunk.

The metal stairs at Jackhammer clink under my black boots as I descend step by step into the Hole. I pull my shirt over my head, tucking it into the back of my pants. I look every inch the image of the leatherman: Mohawk with tight, short sides, black leather harness, black boots, dark blue jeans. I've become him. Alice in Chains crashes occasionally out the door at the bottom. I'm entering a different space. I can feel it.

■　■　■

Smell transports; the body remembers. I could be on the street when I smell a strong whiff of the testosterone-laden body odor of someone walking home from the gym passing too close. The lights go out. I feel claustrophobic. Too

Figure 3.1. The stairwell down into the Hole

many people press against me on all sides. It is the middle of Chicago winter, but the room is unventilated and a hundred degrees. The air is sweaty, pungent with musk.

And suddenly, I'm at Men's Room. The bar isn't Wang's now, a place to sit nicely sipping fourteen-dollar martinis. It has transformed. Now the spirit is here, inhabiting this space.

The Black front man at Men's Room, clipboard in hand, pretends to check the list at the door—a fiction that gives him leeway to deny entrance to whomever he wants—and gives the speech: "Top or bottom off. Take out your phone and you'll be asked to leave."

So, like nearly everyone, I choose top—in no relation to *that* sexual meaning of top and bottom—and go shirtless. I'm in character now.

I take refuge from the horde by a pillar near the back wall. I lose sight of Leo and Caleb, the couple that I came with, immediately on entering. When I can't find them, I get a nine-dollar whiskey soda—this busy, they can charge whatever they want—and settled in to watch and to chat with others in the easy intimacy.

The white man squished into my right side, his back to the wall, has a sleeve of aquatic tattoos, Japanese koi swimming up his left arm. Leaning into each other's ear, we make quick conversation of the usual tattoo talk: Who is your artist? Where? Plans for your next one?

I never learn his name, but I learn many more intimate details over our next forty-five minutes of conversation. An avid cyclist, he has thick thighs, corded muscle stretching his blue jeans. He's preparing for the HIV/AIDS ride, biking ten, twenty, fifty miles a day. I learn his sister doesn't know he's positive because they've had a strained relationship, but he's thinking of telling her before the ride.

Conversation ranges from intimate to silly, our voices pitched in lower tones to be heard over the din. He's telling me a funny story about his dog, when his smile curls devilishly to reveal a few weirdly crooked teeth, cuter for the imperfection. His cycling cap slightly covers his eyes with its short brim as he looks down to watch the muscle boy on his knees in front of him unzip his jeans, one hand on the wall to steady himself against the people standing behind him. The juxtaposition of a cute story told during a raunchy blow job strikes me as funny, and I try to stifle laughter lest I become no better than those on safari. He gives me a conspiratorial wink, and I see those few crooked teeth again.

The Latino muscle boy, who probably has seventy-five pounds on me, turns slightly, shifting his considerable body weight, and starts rubbing my cock through my pants, while his main focus remains on the cyclist. His friend, a tall, skinny, white guy with a full beard, turns around, looks down, laughs in feigned surprise, and says something to him that I can't hear. He leans down to my level, yelling into my ear: "HEY, WHAT DO YOU DO?"

I say I'm writing a book. "ABOUT BOYSTOWN. I'M A SOCIOLOGIST."

We chat for the barest moment before, my head turned to talk to him, I spot Leo. Just as easily as the conversation started, it ends, as I set out through the crowd.

My head clears of this forceful memory. I'm back on the street. The man from the gym farther away. Even here in the middle of the day, I feel the spirit of the night. I feel connected, bound through naked intimacy.

■ ■ ■

The music, the smells, the sensual details carry the transformative power of these spaces. They connect me back to sexy community.

Sexy community, a queer phenomenon, lives in these spaces rejecting the respectability of the inside of Gayle Rubin's charmed circle. In these spaces, people bind together through a process of naked intimacy. The spirit of the night inhabits these erotic ritual spaces, bringing us out of ourselves. One doesn't need to be having sex because the space itself and the objects one wears symbolize erotic power. Naked intimacy is a carnal interaction ritual. The out-of-body experience puts one back in the body, a reminder of a shared humanity, "uncrowning" us.[1] Bound together, people in these spaces experience kinship, family-outside-of-family, community.

Assimilation pushes sexy community to the edge: of the city, of the night, of the physical world. Boystown ejects sexy community, no longer pushed into a single neighborhood by straight stigma. However, losing sexy community has consequences. Sexy communities built through the erotic ritual of naked intimacy bridge racial divides. The loss of sexy community in Boystown is a penalty it has imposed on itself to appease straight society.

Not lost. These spaces continue on the margins of the night in sleazy hookup bars. Digital applications re-create it on the margins of the physical world. You can find sexy community on the margins of the city in bars outside of Boystown, and in leather bars, BDSM spaces, and HIV+ social circles. Furthermore, people move through many of these as well as Boystown's assimilated spaces. As they do, they carry the spirit of the night with them in their daytime lives. Sexy community, a lesson of the night, the radical gift of queers.

■ ■ ■

As I approached the bottom of the stairs, I noticed no line. A slower night, but I was also early. The Hole had only opened an hour before at 10 P.M. and wouldn't get busy until 2 A.M., when the hoards from Boystown's bars would start arriving as those spaces closed.

Marcus, dressed in his blue rubber suit, sat on a stool at the bottom. I met his gaze, both of us smiling.

"Marcus!" I said, throwing my arms around him.

"Hey! Come on in," he said.

Unlike others, I didn't have to take off my pants and stand around only in my underwear. Although everyone, including me, still had to take off their shirts, I wore my harness and I have large tattoos, marks that brand me as a bearer of the erotic ritual. That is, I was already adhering to dress code.

After grabbing a drink at the bar, Marcus and I shared a conversation about work, sexual stories, and funny drunken moments, often bringing others into the conversation, as they moved to and fro from the back hallway, where men fumbled with each other in the dark. Owen, a Black man in his midthirties, wandered in and out of the back hall, losing track of our conversations. Derek, a six foot five white giant towered over me in his underwear, proudly showing anyone who would look his new Prince Albert piercing keeping him out of the action.

Other times, those of us surrounding Marcus at the door would help him enforce the moral order, "forcing" someone to strip.

Why was taking our clothes off so important? Nakedness helps create the nature of the space, stripping people of their everyday identities.

Out of our clothes, out of ourselves.

■ ■ ■

Samir, the Southeast Asian man in his late twenties, described it this way when I interviewed him: "When you're stripped of clothes, you're not reading people's social class in their clothes. There's more mixing, but there are less social cues. So there's a way in which that diversity question is muddled there."

Of course, there's more to social class than the clothes that people wear. Plenty of clues to class exist in our appearance, our grooming, our smell, in the very way that we hold our bodies. There's also the way that we interact with others, our deportment, our word choices and education—the many social parts of what social theorist Pierre Bourdieu calls "habitus," a concept that I will return to in later chapters of this book.[2]

What Samir seems to be saying isn't that it is impossible to tell someone's social class, but that people seem to become more than that. As they strip their clothes off, they come out of their hierarchical, social selves and into their individual bodies. They become more collective by becoming less so.

Georg Simmel, sociologist of the early twentieth century, noted this aspect of clothing in his writings on individuality, modernity, and urbanization. For Simmel, clothing, and fashion more broadly, represented presentations of not just class but also individuality, our sense of self as separate from others around us: "Fashion is the imitation of a given example and satisfies the demand for social adaption; it leads the individual upon the road which all travel, it furnishes a general condition, which resolves the conduct of every individual into a mere example. At the same time it satisfies in no less degree the need for differentiation, the tendency towards dissimilarity, the desire for change and contrast."[3]

Some people today see fashion as a way of integrating ourselves with others as a result of purchasing similarly styled clothing available from big-box stores that is mass produced in factories and sold around the world. However, the style of clothes we select for the day does say something about ourselves. Perhaps this is even truer today, given the vast choices we have, compared to the limited consumer selections of the past. Removing our clothes has the effect of removing a marker of that individuality.

However, it's not that upon entering the Hole I feel like I'm playing a character, per Erving Goffman's dramaturgical analysis. The theater metaphor argues that the person is like an actor but also implies full awareness they are playing a role, even when saying lines with full conviction.[4]

Rather, the space, our naked bodies, and the objects within are associated with the erotic encounter to the extent they induce those collective emotions.[5] More religious than theatrical, the spirit of the night sweeps you up. Those within the space feel outside of themselves, more-than, different from their everyday life, which waits for them back up Jackhammer's metal stairs. Upstairs, they are judges or custodians. Down in the Hole, they are dirty pigs.

Literally, the Hole has a great mix of these people, many of whom do not know the power/status/class of others. Executives, judges, and doctors mix with waiters, custodians, and construction workers. I know only because I asked.

A few years later, I was talking upstairs with a few out-of-towners at Jackhammer for International Mr. Leather about what they liked about these spaces, these moments in which they felt outside of themselves. One of them, Francis, a nongovernmental organization consultant, used that actual phrase, "out of myself."

His friend Will, an accountant with a major firm, disagreed. "I don't feel outside of myself. I am who I am. I feel that I am more myself."

This experience frees him because he contains himself every day, because sexuality is not allowed in ordinary society, the society of the inner charmed circle. Will compared these moments to his experience at Burning Man, another experience outside of the bounds of everyday society. He feels his more authentic self, something he can take back with him to his workaday world.

In fact, the BDSM community has a term for his feeling, the out-of-body experience where one feels more authentic, more oneself: "headspace." A submissive who is in "headspace" or "subspace" is outside of the social mores they are required to follow in daily interactions. They are more themselves by taking on a role.

Down in the Hole, when people experience naked intimacy, they get a new headspace. They get infused with the spirit of the night. They experience what Émile Durkheim calls collective effervescence.[6]

Collective effervescence is Durkheim's explanation for the out-of-body, heightened, more-than-themselves feeling people often have during religious and political events when brought together with many other people experiencing similar emotions.

As Durkheim explains, "This stimulated and invigorating effect of society is particularly apparent... in the midst of an assembly that becomes worked up, we become capable of feelings and conduct of which we are incapable when left to our individual resources. When it is dissolved and we are again on our own, we fall back to our ordinary level and can then take full measure of how far above ourselves we were."

Durkheim developed the concept to explain the moments of religious frenzy that he saw within anthropological accounts of the Australian Aborigines. In a classic example of scientific racism, Durkheim saw within their society a more primitive state that he could use to peer into earlier human civilization, which he then compared to "more advanced" White European society. He sought to explain religious thought and its function, power, and origin.

Among the Aborigines, he saw a sharp distinction between mundane moments of everyday dullness and heightened moments of religious ritual. Daily life involved the manual labor of staying alive, time during which the Aborigines were reportedly spread out across wide areas. The population density vastly increased, however, during religious moments, in which people came together for festivals and rituals. At such times, the physical proximity and the changing material conditions brought people out of themselves.

"People are so far outside the ordinary conditions of life, and so conscious of the fact, that they feel a certain need to set themselves above and beyond ordinary morality," wrote Durkheim.

With typical scientific racism, Durkheim interpreted the actions of the Aborigines during these rituals as animalistic and uncontrolled: "A sort of electricity is generated from their closeness and quickly launches them to an extraordinary height of exaltation.... Passions so heated and so free from all control cannot help but spill over from every side until there are nothing but wild movements, shouts, downright howls, and deafening noises of all kinds that further intensify the state they are expressing.... The passions unleashed are so torrential that nothing can hold them."

Note the focus in Durkheim's analysis on the carnal, the sensual physical details of their experience. Their movements and the physicality of these moments induced their collective emotions.

This force binds the group together once they leave the space. As he writes, "Shouting the same cry, saying the same words," brings the group together in agreement, solidifying their shared awareness of their morality and social cohesion.

Of course, Durkheim thought of the Aborigine as primitive, representing an earlier stage of humanity through which Europeans had passed. Durkheim also used the concept of collective effervescence and the distinction between these sacred and profane times, spaces, and objects to explain how groups bind themselves together in European society as well, though he viewed the moments there as less bifurcated. In his time, he argued, the difference between the two emotional states might not be as sharp, and so wouldn't require the kind of ecstatic rituals that release the primal, but the two states still exist.

Today, sociologists refer to this connection between collective effervescence, group connection, and collective emotions as an "interaction ritual." We use interaction rituals whenever we synchronize our bodies with others; doing an activity together also synchronizes our emotions.

For instance, singing the national anthem at an American baseball game, for instance, binds people together, outside of themselves. For a moment, they are not Monica or Jim, but Americans. They carry that connection with each other even after the last verse. Similarly, the music at a concert—perhaps you are watching Kanye West at a large stadium—sweeps you up. You are outside of yourself, singing along. One voice through many mouths.[7]

The ritual frame and heightened emotions of collective effervescence help to explain the experience of naked intimacy in erotic spaces like the Hole. Durkheim recognized that sex was a condensed version of these moments of oscillating sacred and profane, bringing people together: "Through this communion, the two persons united become one."[8] This is a common moral understanding of the sense of connection that sex brings, such that other rituals often repeat these words during moments celebrating the inner charmed circle, such as weddings. Because inner circle morality declares sex private, we assume that group sex and collective public sexuality are not similarly religious, emotional, and intimate in this manner. However, just as sex between two people connects them, collective sexuality similarly brings people out of themselves and into oneness.

■ ■ ■

It's not just that people are having sex in the space. The space becomes transformed, imbued with the erotic potentiality of the sexual rituals that have taken place there. Durkheim uses the concept of a totem to describe this kind of transference. Totems are objects used in rituals that begin to collect the emotions associated with these moments of collective effervescence. He uses the analogy of funerals.[9] Westerners wear black to funerals, so when seeing people wearing black, the clothes reminds us of a funeral and we think sad thoughts. In this respect, totems are the collective equivalent of Stanley Schachter and Jerome Singer's two-factor theory of emotions: we use social cues to identify the emotional states our body is feeling.[10] This process allows for reverse causality. We may interpret ourselves as sad because we are crying, or happy because we are smiling, unless a social cue exists to otherwise explain our actions, like crying at a wedding. Similarly, a totem comes to represent, and therefore evoke, the feelings aroused—in this case literally—through collective effervescence.

The most obvious totem for sexy community is the gear that people sometimes wear to the space. Fetish gear, like rubber suits, harnesses, or boots,

Figure 3.2. A Saint Andrews cross inside the Hole

represents sex, intimate connections, and pleasure of the space. Wearing gear brings one closer to experiencing the erotic ritual again and each fuck in the backroom of the Hole only strengthens the association. Some kinds of gear, like tattoos and piercings, might become permanent fashion accessories, allowing one to carry the feeling outside of the space. When a Daddy gives his boy a chain and padlock to wear around his neck outside of BDSM scenes, the lock simultaneously acts as a source of identity to others and a constant reminder of erotic potentiality.

The spaces, often the entire bars, become totems, too. The spirit of the night settles into those spaces, such that having a backroom, fetish space, or place where people experience sexy community tinges the entire area. It profanes those spaces but makes them sacred as well. Therefore, even places that no longer have the explicit sexual spaces still share in some of the spirit. It fades over time, though, without continual ritual reproduction, but it does exist, even if only faintly.

Lastly, the body can become a totem. "Sacredness is highly contagious," Durkheim writes, "and it spreads from the totemic being to everything that directly or remotely has to do with it."[11] Our bodies, connected as they are to sex, remind us of these moments and of the intimate connections made. We can see this totemic equivalence in the Hole's dress code rules: wear gear or strip to your underwear. Seeing the nakedness of others and the nakedness of yourself puts you into a different headspace.

This is why the consequences of people on safari are particularly dire. Such people break the spell. They disrupt the ritual space. Moments before a man was a leatherman or a puppy. The laughter of someone on safari dispels the illusion. When that happens, they become a lumpy middle-aged man in a leather harness, which is pulling their chest hair, or a twenty-five-year-old guy rolling around on the floor, drinking out of a dog bowl. The whole thing seems silly.

The physical experiences, the carnal details—the sights, sounds, tastes, smells, and touches—ground us in the body. Not just a physical body but a pleasurable body. Rejecting the inner charmed circle might be shameful, but it feels good.

In reminding us of our pleasurable bodies, naked intimacy not only binds a group together but connects them to a sense of shared humanity as well. While we might be in hierarchies of race outside the Hole, crossing the threshold uncrowns us, as the philosopher Mikhail Bakhtin described it in his writings on humor.

Bakhtin is most remembered—when he is remembered at all—for his writings on "dialogics": "The meaning of a word is determined equally by whose word it is and for whom it is meant.... A word is a territory shared." For Bakhtin, everything is a dialogical conversation, including and especially this book. You, the reader, help shape the meaning.

Therefore, when Bakhtin looks at humor, he asks why readers react differently to the same material. For instance, in one of his works, he asks why modern readers find the medieval work of Rabelais's Gargantua and Pantagruel—a parody of elite French society—so offensive and disgusting.

Sociologist Michael M. Bell summarizes Rabelais in this way: "Many people have found his writing distasteful and obscene, plainly offensive to basic sensitivities. Rabelais's novel ... follows the fabulous careers of Gargantua and his son Pantagruel, both fantastically obese and vulgar giants. They live an outrageous life centered wholly on bodily acts—eating, drinking, excreting, copulating, giving birth. Rabelais spares no detail in describing these acts. In a word, Rabelais is gross."[12]

Bakhtin argues that we find Rabelais offensive because he draws attention to the grotesque body over our modern civilized body. For Bakhtin, Rabelais is not gross, despite long passages describing shit. Bakhtin argues the gross differs from the carnivalesque. The gross, or offensive, makes fun of others, placing them lower than the speaker. A carnivalesque joke, in contrast, might use the same material attempting equality. The jokester is also laughing at themselves. They confirm our common humanity. As Bakhtin sees it, Rabelais is reminding us that we all eat, shit, ooze, and have sex. Furthermore, when the powerful are the targets of carnivalesque jokes, they are uncrowned. They are brought down from on high, but, because the clown is also laughing at themselves, they are not brought low. The joke attempts to level social relations.

Using a carnal sociology lens on pleasure, I argue that the erotic is carnivalesque, a reminder of our shared humanity. In the Hole, we are uncrowned, stripped of our clothes and identities and left momentarily outside of ourselves. Seeing the naked, or near-naked, bodies of our fellows and seeing their lust reminds us of our own body and our own lust. The collective moment of sexy community not only binds people together but binds them across boundaries. Rooted in the body, we are uncrowned. The high are brought low; the low are lifted high.

Just as totems serve as continual reminders of sexy community, carrying sexiness outside of erotic spaces, certain interactions can also act in this way, bringing erotic ritual with us into other spaces. The sexual joking of gay male communities serves this purpose, uncrowning us, drawing our attention back to the pleasure of the body, and, therefore, reiterating a shared sense of humanity and intimacy, even outside of places where radical sex has transpired.

On Mondays, Big Chicks, a queer bar in Uptown on Lawrence Avenue near Argyle Street, serves one-dollar hamburgers. It's a popular night: an excuse to get out of the house, have a cheap dinner, and drink a few beers.

Big Chicks is a bar that wears many hats. It hosts events for the bear community. It hosts FKA (Formally Known As), a party and art space for the queer community. Its proximity to Hollywood Beach—well, the closest gay bar at a fifteen-minute walk—means that I have wandered there with friends from a white wine fueled beach day.

While it might not have a backroom, Big Chicks is still a queer space. Since the people that frequent Big Chicks often also frequent more explicit places as well, the erotic power taints the place slightly, like the scent of a room after someone with too much perfume has left.

The interactions at Big Chicks serve to reinforce this association. One Monday night in the spring of 2014, Austin and I walked to Big Chicks from our apartment in the liminal zone between Boystown and Uptown. We still had our toughest, warmest jackets on and reaching Big Chicks felt like a victory. We had earned our cheap burger and beer.

We didn't come every week, but we went often enough that the burly man behind the counter smiled when we walked up.

"Hey guys, are you hungry?" he asked.

"Yeah! I'm feeling great tonight," I responded as Austin smirked behind me.

"Well, I'm here to feed you," he said.

"And, you have hamburgers," Austin quipped.

We all laughed and the joke bound us together. Austin wasn't attempting to cruise him, but the sexual nature of the joke referenced the body in a way that created intimacy between us. Jokes, mannerisms, and references queer space. The bar was gay, but we were queered together. The ritual reenacted the moments of collective effervescence we had previously experienced.

These moments of solidarity create intimacy between people. A naked intimacy unadorned with the barriers that many of us keep about us every day. Once people are reminded of the sensuality of their bodies, they are similarly unabashed about sharing their troubles.

Those who have not experienced sexy community might be surprised to learn that there are a lot of nonsexual moments that occur within erotic spaces. If the image of the Hole that you have taken from these pages is one of a sleazy orgy, people having sex everywhere, then you might have emphasized the wrong aspects of the text in your mind, perhaps because of the difference the spaces have from heterosexual and homonormative community spaces. There is a lot more talking than sex. Naked intimacy isn't exclusively sexual, and the erotic isn't exclusive to the sexual act.

For instance, the conversation I shared with the nameless white HIV+ cyclist at Men's Room isn't unusual. We might not have shared our names, but we talked about our families, our troubles, and our fears. He might have been getting his dick sucked one moment, but he was also talking about his nonsexual life. We never had sex, but sexual intimacy existed between us.

It also isn't surprising that I became friends with Marcus after spending night after night downstairs at Jackhammer. The erotic ritual of the space, with our bodies adorned in totems, created naked intimacy between us.

Naked intimacy made ethnography in sexy communities much easier than in the rarified air of other, more assimilated, Boystown spaces. In Minibar, people are closed off from others, out for a night of talking only with their friends. In Jackhammer, while people similarly come with friends, the naked intimacy widens their circle of who they are willing to talk to, a sexy community.

Tim Dean, in his book *Unlimited Intimacy* about barebackers and their reasons for having anal sex without condoms, similarly observes in an aside that he's noticed this easy intimacy at sex parties.[13] In the moments between sex acts—a group sexual encounter is never one uninterrupted sexual experience—people talked with each other and shared their stories from their everyday lives.

Dean argues that a sense of connection exists among barebackers—and, indeed, the HIV+ community more generally, with whom barebackers share a Venn diagram–like overlap—that he calls "viral kinship." They see themselves as having a shared history, and a shared body, because of their association with the disease. They are connected together into a shared viral family. Although he doesn't make this connection, I argue that viral kinship is forged because of the naked intimacy these men share.

Sexy community is this kind of alternative kinship. The concept of viral kinship conceives too narrowly. Sexual kinship is the tie that exists between people that are connected within a sexual network and is rooted in erotic spaces, reinforced through sexy interaction, and embodied in totems.[14]

Sexy community forms around erotic spaces, connecting those that frequent those spaces through moments of collective effervescence. Uncrowned, naked intimacy binds people across boundaries because they ground in a shared sense of the pleasure of the body. It is not quite a family, but it is a community. Not the nuclear family that other conceptions of kinship often imply, such as "family of choice," but family as clan, with connections and obligations to one another even if you're only distantly related.

4

Sexy Community

"I can suck a dick, cook collard greens, and speak Chinese," Deveaux said. We called Chuck that name when he was at Jackhammer even when he wasn't in face.[1]

She[2] looked back at me and fluttered his eyelashes. "I'm that good, honey. OK!?"

Deveaux took a sip of her afternoon tea. Chuck, a Black man in his mid-sixties, retired after working for the city and now comes to Jackhammer most evenings to have a "nerve tea," a.k.a. cheap bourbon straight up, and a glass of soda water. She was well connected in this community. He lived in a property owned by one of Jackhammer's owners. She plays madame/herder to the drag queens scrambling around to put on Monday night's show, what the bartender Omar affectionately called "the most tragic drag show in the city." Although later, Deveaux disavowed this role, claiming, "I don't herd those cats; I just watch them collect."

Gurl also advertises for Jackhammer more than they do.

"It's Sunday Funday at Jackhammer today!" Chuck's Facebook status would exclaim, "I'll be on the patio with all kinds of grilling goodness going on. [Rob] will be behind the bar slingin' your favorite cocktails, featuring our famous $7, 22 oz Long Island Iced Tea, our $4 Arnold Palmer, and our $3 PBR for you hipsters. Bar opens at 2, nerve tea will be flowing! See ya there!"

She has a stake in the bar doing well. Jackhammer is a community nexus for him. On Sundays, in a tradition going back to the Sunday tea dances of the seventies, Deveaux cooks up a different meal each week. I dream about her jambalaya.

This particular evening, Austin and I came to Jackhammer for their dollar-drink Wednesdays. Rob, the midthirties Latino bartender, kept feeding the two of us free tequila shots. He knew how to get a good tip.

Figure 4.1. Men hang out inside the Hole

Deveaux sat in her usual stool at the end of the bar, too big of a queen for the metal bar chairs that lined the rest of the bar, both figuratively and literally. The placement of this stool is meaningful. It is near the entrance behind the bar where the stereo system also resides, the de facto "family" part of the bar where the bartenders and off-duty employees would stand with their phones, resting between customers.

Although we parked our jackets down at the other end, I would always come stand next to him, listen to his stories, and talk to his friends about their lives, the latest gossip about the bar or their opinions about Boystown, a place few of them ventured anymore.

"I'm so glad that you two are getting married." Michael, a white man in his fifties and one of Deveaux's close friends, told me. "Do it now. Don't wait. You never know. Have I told you about Juan?"

He had, but that didn't dissuade him from pulling up his sleeve to show me the tattoo of Juan's face. Michael had already had a couple drinks, and clearly wanted to tell the story again. I didn't interrupt.

His partner, Juan, died ten years earlier, just before they were able to go to Massachusetts to make their relationship legally official. Their marriage wouldn't have been recognized by Illinois, but the symbolism would have been important. His partner's family didn't even know about him. He felt left out.

Deveaux broke in to lighten the mood with stories of his childhood in

Louisiana, although that too quickly took a somber turn. He was raised by his grandmother and began talking about her life.

"Slavery has still touched my family," he sighed.[3]

We toasted to better days ahead. Deveaux finished another nerve tea, and I took a shot of tequila, before he started to talk about the oldie show on the television above him.

Thankfully, Jeremy, a Black massage therapist in his late forties, looked at me from across the bar and held two fingers in front of his mouth, waving them in and out, raising his eyebrows suggestively.

"Sure thing," I said and followed him out back to smoke. It's not a habit, but something I will share after a few drinks if someone else is lighting up.

The back porch is a line of wooden cocktail tables built into the deck looking out over the back alley. Another of the bartenders, preparing for a shift later that night, came over, lit a cigarette, and joined us.

"What are you and Austin doing for dinner tomorrow? You should really come over," Jeremy said. "I make the best Italian."

Austin and I already had plans, but Jeremy and I talked about making fresh pasta and tomatoes, passions of mine as well, as our smokes slowly burned to the end.

When we came back in, Larry, a quiet older Black man that works as a mail carrier, was talking about health, the perennial complaint of elders, with Deveaux. The night was starting, with younger people trickling in for the dollar drinks. Not all of them talk to Deveaux, Michael, Larry, and Jeremy, but many do. John, a midtwenties white salesman, always makes an effort to come give Deveaux a hug, paying his respects and ordering him a nerve tea. Often, he does so to ask forgiveness for the mess he's been the previous night, drunkenly arguing outside or falling asleep in the bathroom after one too many.

At nine, Rob's shift is over, and the next bartender takes over. Usually, Rob would head home, but this night he stayed behind to hang with us a little bit, perhaps owing to the tequila he himself had been drinking. At Rob's coaxing, Jeremy and I started dancing with him in the middle of the nearly empty room, slipping our shirts off as the fading light came in through the front windows. Amid the clapping and the laughing at us dropping to the floor, our asses bobbing to the music, I could hear Deveaux calling to us from his stool, "If I go that low, there's no way I'm coming back up, baby."

■　■　■

That night was a moment, a snapshot, of sexy community. No one was having sex at that moment, but the spirit of the night had settled into the space, infusing even the day with intimacy of the night. A community formed in the space, with disparate people, of different races, coming together to talk about their triumphs and their terrors or sometimes just a good recipe for pasta arrabiata.

We were together in a web. Elders connected to no-longer-baby-gays who had finally made their way up from Roscoe's to become regulars at Jackhammer.

It's not Cheers. Bartenders might not know your name. We might not even know each other's names, or go to each other's houses, or be friends, but there is a sense of community, in being in it together.

Naked intimacy doesn't end when people put their clothes back on or pull their pants back up and wander upstairs from the Hole when it's open on weekends. Because the space, the gear, and the people act as totems for the erotic connection and collective effervescence that people experience in the explicit segments of these spaces, they remain connected even when not engaging in sexual behavior. Furthermore, the hybrid nature of the space—a place for sex connected to a place for talking—infuses both with the sexiness and social togetherness of the other. Even people that you haven't had sex with, and that you never would have sex with, are connected to you through sexy community.

Sexy community is a network of people, connected through naked intimacy that results from spaces that have erotic potential—a group based on sexual connection, erotic possibility, and sexual kinship. Sexy community doesn't require sex to always be happening. In fact, these spaces must be hybrid, with sexuality taking place alongside swapping stories or menial gossip. Sexy communities have real consequences. They connect people across boundaries such as race. Sexy community is a lesson straight society could learn from queers.

■ ■ ■

What is a community?

Sociologists have many answers to this query, and even more questions. Community has multiple aspects, some of which sociologists emphasize more than others. Community can mean spatial proximity, togetherness, identity, people bound by common characteristics and shared understandings. Community can mean the physical space, the place-ness of a group. People in a community might be interdependent, whether emotionally or economically. Community might just be people feeling like there is a community.

As Robert Sampson, a sociologist, discusses in his book *Great American City* about Chicago's neighborhoods and the Chicago school of sociology, a community can be all of these things, but some communities don't have all of these properties, so those properties must not be essential to the definition of community.[4] A community can be diffuse and still be a community. Its members might not share physical space, togetherness, or identity but still be communities. Internet communities, for instance, sometimes have none of those attributes.

I observed many of these properties in spaces of sexy community, but I also saw them in spaces that I wouldn't label sexy community—spaces that were interdependent, for example, because friendships had been built up over a long period of time from having been around one another, like the older men at Buck's. Thus, in this way, community can be similar to a group or a scene. In what sense do people "show up" to a place to interact with one another? People might be bound together in a web of social relationships connected to a space whether they realize it or not. We tend to move in similar patterns when we go out—going to this club, then this one, before ending the night in a third—what sociologist Adam Isaiah Green calls "circuits."[5]

However, Sampson says, communities do have something in common: they have a shared set of understandings. To return to the parlance of Erving Goffman's dramaturgical analysis, a community is a group of people with a shared definition of the situation. They share similar interpretations of what is going on. Their understanding of the space might be slightly different, but in general they agree on some basic facts.

In later chapters, I will discuss the concept of habitus, which I also consider to be part of the shared fabric of a community. For now, consider community, especially sexy community, to be a group, whether they realize they are a group or not, that has a shared definition of what is happening, a similar set of values concerning how to act in that situation, and shared criteria to judge whether others are acting appropriately in the space.

Therefore, by sexy community, I mean a community bound together by sex. The sexy community that I discuss in this book is queer, and I'm not sure that you can have a nonqueer version. I mean this not in the sense of sexy community containing homosexuality and nonheterosexuals, but that sexy communities reject the sexual shame dynamic that exemplifies the inside of Rubin's charmed circle. Perhaps queer straight people—that is those who are queer heterosexual people whom I discuss in the conclusion of this book—can also have sexy community.

Boystown, as a neighborhood, had multiple communities overlapping within it. One of these was a sexy community of queer men bound together through sex. Another was gay men who had been pushed out of straight society against their will but were desperate to return. However, before we consider how Boystown's landscape of communities has changed, I want to discuss further the aspects of sexy community, so that the stakes are clear.

■ ■ ■

Family is a complicated, fraught concept for queers. Family is frightening.

Queer people are pushed out of their families and into the world, often on their own. As Jeanette Winterson, a British lesbian novelist, writes, "Home was problematic for me. It did not represent order and it did not stand for safety."[6] No wonder. Many young homeless people were kicked out of their homes for being queer.[7]

Queer people carry with them the scars from this fight for their lives—for their dignity, and their morality, and their soul—with their families. They carry these scars with them even after they've patched up the initial damage and have good relationships with their family. They will always remember the moment they realized a family's love was conditional.

Consequently, many queer people have what researchers call a "family of choice." As opposed to the "family of birth" that comes from being born into a family, or brought in through adoption as a child, a family of choice is quite literally a family made up of the friends that you have selected to be close to. This family is the "brothers from another mother," the drag mothers, and elders such as Deveaux who dispense advice to those who will listen, and even if they won't.

In a beautiful speech given to the 2014 Queertopia Conference, anthropologist Naisargi Dave explained why family is a concept queer people have tried to get away from.[8] She argues, based on her research in India and experience in her own Indian queer family, that friendship is often proposed as the alternative to queer families, "opting for something entirely new rather than forever tinkering with a structure preexisting." However, queer family, she argues, is also marked by the "dumb fate" that blood families have.

"Queer family is built of loss, necessitated by deaths figurative and literal," she said.

In describing her queer family, she said:

> This was a space of openness to all who might turn up. And so I wouldn't call it philoxenic [a love of strangers] exactly, because this was not a love for difference as much an indifference to it: same or different, strange or familiar, we are ready to be made more ourselves or something new. Likewise, this family made itself a successful presence, as it occupied space in our hearts and lives, exerting a pull that felt sometimes like an embrace and sometimes like a sticky, troublesome grip. But this is where we come back ... to the intimate space of friendship, where we understand that to love is most of all to let be, to exist uneasily but sure in the

space between absence and presence. We turned up; we stayed; we left; we cried; a few months would go by, a year, sometimes more; studies were undertaken, romances explored and abandoned. But the stranger at the door was always welcome, and we would do it all over again.

Queer family is this kind of binding together, a "sticky, troublesome grip" for people that you didn't choose but rather who showed up out of the ruins of disconnection from straight life. Contrary to both researchers' and queers' depictions, it isn't a family of choice.

However, sexy community is something different, and compartmentalizing all queer connection into the bag of families of choice undercuts the many kinds of inventive relationships we have built out of the rubble of shame.

Family carries baggage. Family is tight-knit, not diffuse. However expanded or nonnuclear the definition we try to devise, family binds us to think about relationships in comparison to queer people's birth families and those structures that have shaped the American family.

People in a community, however, might not even be that close. They might not share more than a few words. They might not even know each other until you point out to them that they do. Although "community" is a term often invoked to describe an entire class of people—"the gay community," "the Latino community," "a working-class community," and so on—community can more aptly be described as a network. It is a network of people that have some connection to each other, occupy the same space, and rely on a shared culture or system of social mores. A sexy community is a specific kind of community. Sexy community is a network of sexual kinship, infused with naked intimacy and connected to spaces of erotic potential.

Community doesn't have to mean a "primary group" that involves "face-to-face intimate, affective relations."[9] A community is wider than a group of friends and a family of choice. Sure, communities exist that involve a high degree of that kind of togetherness and collectivity, but not all communities do. There are always those of us that move through community, are a part of it, even if we don't know each other's names.

Sexy community is obvious at Marcus's house, where his queer family—his leather family—also is rooted. Many families may exist within a given sexy community, but, just as with straight communities, it is only when those families occupy the same space and impose a shared culture—a collective sense of what is going on socially—that a community is truly forged.

I arrived a half an hour late to Marcus's party, and I was still the first person to arrive. GST.[10] Although both Austin and I had been invited, Austin was sick, so I had ventured out alone.

Figure 4.2. The back hallway inside the Hole

While Marcus's partner was in the kitchen getting ready, Marcus and I sat on the front terrace with giant goblets of wine that could barely be considered wine glasses. With the wind coming off the lake chilling us even in June, Marcus had thrown a warming candle in his small clay oven. I curled up on the bench, and he sat in the chair perpendicular. We drank wine, laughed about events at IML, and waited for the rest of the crew to arrive.

Over the course of the next hour and half, the house filled with people that, before that night, I had never met. Most of them didn't know each other either. The front porch held a large wide-ranging and unlikely group. An interracial couple in their early twenties held hands and leaned against each other the whole night in the limerence of young love and offered to sell me pot no less than four times. A Latino nurse who worked at Howard Brown Health Clinic sat next to me. He wore a preppy outfit that looked like he had just come from a boat trip with the plastics. A fifty-something white bisexual biker, who spoke little, mostly enjoyed his cigar while observing the room. A self-described "Buddha bear" with a big beard, a belly, and a smile to match climbed the terrace wall and sat perched like a leather-daddy gargoyle.

Although I hadn't met any of these people before, I began to notice they had always been around me. And I began to see them, from then on, whenever I was at Jackhammer, Touché, Cell Block, online, and out in Boystown on Sunday Funday. We had always been in a community. I just hadn't known it.

We weren't friends. I'm still not friends with some of them, but we are in a community, a community closer for having spread the indignity of sex around.

Although everyone knew Marcus—he had invited them to his home after all—many of them weren't in his "family," according to him. That was easy to see; only one of the people I mentioned above attended his "family leather nights."

Family is important. Queer families pull people together. But sexy communities are wider. Even if we aren't in the clubs, we carry community with us.

■ ■ ■

Sexy community isn't a new phenomenon, just now emerging in opposition to Boystown's assimilation. In the seventies, gay men experimented with these alternative communities built through sexuality, connected through sex. Patrick Moore, in his book *Beyond Shame*, memorializes the "sexual experiment."[11] Gay men used sex as a form of art "in which the artist did not wait for the audience to show up."

The sexual experiment is a history that Moore argues we haven't remembered: "We will, I believe, remember our institutions, the legislative battles, the fiery speeches, and the marches. It is our cultural, sexual legacy that is most at risk and needs to be reclaimed."[12]

The reasons for this collective forgetting—assimilation, terror of HIV, and shame—I discuss in more depth in a later chapter, "One of the Good Gays." For now, I want to focus on the connections between the radical gay sexual culture that developed before HIV, and the sexy community that remains, increasingly outcast from the mainstream gay clubs in Boystown. Before we can understand the changes to Boystown and the costs of assimilation, we have to understand what came before, and what now remains in the erotic periphery of BDSM and leather clubs, late-night hookup joints, pleasure cruises on Lake Michigan, and sex apps that gay men use to recapture this community.

Gay men pioneered sexy community and naked intimacy in the seventies in port cities like San Francisco and New York City that had built up substantial gay populations from soldiers returning from World War II.[13] For instance, Moore discusses the Mineshaft, a seventies gay BDSM and sex club in New York's meat-packing district, and the Saint, a private gay club in the East Village, in similarly ritualized terms to those I have used in discussing naked intimacy. He also unknowingly uses dramaturgical analysis, the metaphor of the theater. Moore argues that, like actors on a stage, gay men took on characters in these spaces, performing art with their bodies that put them on the sexual frontier and extended the boundaries of sexuality.

Boystown is often neglected in these stories of early gay sexuality. The focus is always on the more iconic gayborhoods of the Castro, Chelsea, or the East Village. However, these sorts of places also existed in Chicago.

One night, while I was standing in the Hole, an older man trudged down the stairs with his cane, then held his massive body upright by leaning on the bar. He told me about the scene in Chicago when he was younger.

The entire time we chatted, I was made slightly uncomfortable by the way he regularly touched me and rubbed my back while he was talking. In the space of the Hole, his caress was a reminder that not all kinds of naked intimacy are wanted. However, a gentle pulling away, a repositioning of my body, and he took the hint and continued with his story without making advances. The social rules held. I didn't act offended at his touch, as though he was below me, and he didn't enact possession of my body, as though he deserved to touch me.

"There used to be plenty of places like this," he told me. "When I was younger, I would walk into this place off Michigan Avenue."[14]

He took a slow sip of his beer.

"And someone would already be taking my cock out of my pants. I would be in a crowd of people, and someone would be on their knees," which sounded to me a lot like what I've described as having happened at Manhole night at Hydrate or Men's Room.

"You went down there to that part of town because no one else was there. No one could see you, but you were around your brothers," he said.

The two factors are difficult to extricate from each other. Were these spaces intimate because of the sexuality that coursed through them? Or did people feel safety in numbers, an openness with others because they couldn't be open about their lives in other circumstances? Although he felt intimate with these people, were they in a community, I wondered?

Moore's descriptions of Mineshaft, the Saint, and the Saint Mark's Baths in New York City indicate the men that frequented those places felt community. They grew to know each other, even if only in those spaces. They provided social support.

In terms of sexy community today, it's possible to answer those questions. Although erotic spaces have receded from Boystown proper—located on the periphery of the city, on the periphery of the night, or in the periphery of the physical world—they still exist, and those within them feel a connection with each other akin to that "old style club," as Sam said.

Many gay men are now out in their daily lives. The stigma of being gay is much less than back when this older man was young and getting blown in that club off Michigan Avenue. However, the stigma of the rest of the charmed circle still remains. Today's sexy communities are still stigmatized. They are still found on the outskirts of the charmed circle.

5

Sexual Racism

Sexy communities are built through webs of sexual kinship, crafted through moments of collective effervescence, reinforced through totems, leveled through uncrowning. These processes have the potential to bridge the divides that seem engrained in Boystown. Sexy community is queer radical community with people of different races and bodies coming together.

A foundational question of social psychologists is: how do groups connect, compete, and cohere?[1] On an individual level, we've seen how naked intimacy brings people together, binds them through erotic moments. How does naked intimacy influence the groups in those moments, beyond the individuals?

When I come to the Hole, I'm not just Jason. I'm white. I'm a man. I'm able bodied. I'm gay. I'm an academic. I'm married. I'm cash-poor and in debt, but from a family in the top quintile with a socioeconomic trajectory that will likely take me back into the middle class.

When I go into the Hole, or into any club, these groups, these hierarchies of power, come with me. They are part of who I am. What does naked intimacy do in the face of these hierarchies? It bridges power and connects groups into a sexy community.

I study axes of power through the lens of intersectionality: oppressions cannot be fully disentangled from one another. They overlap, transforming the experience of other social locations. In this book, race is the key issue I want to address concerning the ability of sexy community to connect people across power relations. However, while sexy community bridges some boundaries—such as race, age, and education—other boundaries, such as class and gender hierarchies, entrench. This chapter addresses this intersectional knot through the strand of race.

Moving from a focus on individuals to one of groups requires looking at the connection between people as, to use the term social psychologists use, "intergroup contact." How do members of different groups interact? How do their opinions of each other change? How do they draw on cultural scripts as group members? How do their structural positions shape, enable, and constrain their interactions?

I've discussed the Chicago school of sociology in previous chapters regarding the importance it places on ecological context. This research lineage also concerned how groups interacted and how they would eventually be absorbed by American society. For one of the founders of the Chicago school, Robert Park, intergroup contact followed a "race relations cycle."[2] Although it failed as a predictive theory, the race relations cycle has served as one of the basic models for intergroup interactions. Park theorized that as different groups—in his case races that had been brought together through immigration—interacted they went through a series of stages: contact, conflict, accommodation, and assimilation.[3]

At first, the groups made contact as the new group arrived. Then, they would come into conflict over scarce resources. Eventually, a hierarchical relationship would develop between them, as the more-powerful group accommodated the less-powerful new group. Finally, the new group would assimilate into the mainstream.

Park saw assimilation as inevitable because friendships and romantic relationships would develop across the group boundaries, eventually undermining all forms of discrimination. Scholars have used these intimate relationships as a barometer of race relations ever since.

Intimacy as a social barometer makes some sense. Researchers found that white partners in interracial relationships have greater racial literacy and are less likely to occur in areas that have strong racial boundaries.[4] Unfortunately, this metric tends to be misused, with researchers only looking at whether interracial relationships have occurred, rather than whether those relationships actually indicate a change in prejudice.[5]

This focus on intimate relationships turned into a foundational assumption of race relations: the contact hypothesis. Meeting different people, by virtue of exposure to them, helps break down the stereotypes that we have about them. After all, proximity is one of the basic rules of attraction: repeatedly being in the same room with someone is more likely to lead you to be involved with them. The contact hypothesis says that two groups interacting are likely to notice that the stereotypes don't fit and that the people they are interacting with are unique, but also that they are more like one another than different.[6]

The problem is that this isn't true. Even in the realm of romantic attraction, you could be attracted to someone despite or because of their group status. You might think of them as an exception to the rule. You might change your definition of the group to not include them—"well, he isn't like those Black guys"—or change your stereotypes such that they are about a more narrow subgroup that doesn't include this person.[7]

To really change someone's mind, you have to go beyond mere contact. Simply being in the same room with one another isn't enough.

Moreover, mere contact can actually make things worse. In what scholars call entrenchment, having superficial contact with another group can confirm your stereotypes.[8] Because your knowledge is based in stereotypes and you are not interacting with them intimately enough to disprove those stereotypes, you can interpret evidence around you in ways that are consistent with the beliefs you already have. This is a kind of confirmation bias, such as noticing bad drivers when they are women but not when they are men, thereby confirming the stereotype that women are bad drivers.

To change someone's views about a group, it is not enough simply to be in the same space with them: you have to connect with them intimately. You have to go beyond mere contact.[9]

We can see an example of mere contact at Roscoe's. Roscoe's is one of the most diverse places in Boystown. On any one night, many different kinds of people, especially people of different classes and races, come through Roscoe's because it is a place for people new to Boystown.

When I first came to Boystown, I went to Roscoe's fairly regularly, getting a sense of the space, mapping the racial dynamics in Boystown. Initially, the racial mix in Roscoe's led me to believe that maybe I had chosen the wrong place to study racism in queer communities.[10] But I had the wrong view of racism.

Roscoe's is one of the older bars still around in the neighborhood. Similar to other bars of that period, such as Sidetrack, Roscoe's is a very "nineties" club, with several distinct spaces, each with a slightly different feel. Roscoe's has three such spaces: the main bar, through which patrons enter, the room with the pool tables, and the dance floor with its immediate bar surroundings. Though Roscoe's appears to be racially mixed, it is segregated. Not formally, but through networks that tend to hang out in different parts of the bar and do not mix. This is segregation of circuits. The front bar tends to be where white men congregate. Black men tend to hang out near the pool tables in the room immediately next to the main bar. The one place where there is any kind of mixing is on the dance floor.

One time, my friend Nicholas came to visit me from Texas. We had been friends in college but hadn't seen each other for years, since we always seemed to miss each other when I came home to Texas during the winter. Nicholas is a pretty boy, a plastic, and a true good friend. He wears Burberry scarves, long, elegant trench coats, and fine leather shoes.

Figure 5.1. Friends pose outside Progress Bar

Because the crowd in Texas that he fits into is like the one at Minibar, that's where I took him most nights during the week he was visiting. One night, though, we decided to go to Roscoe's since we had a different group of people with us. We'd met up with our mutual friend Melanie, who had moved to Chicago a year before me, part of the same University of Texas–Austin to Chicago pipeline that also swept up several other people I knew. We were having a reunion of sorts: even an ex-boyfriend, also from Texas, came down from Madison to visit.

We met at Cesar's on Broadway Street, south of Diversey. Though everyone else loved the margaritas, I found them too sweet. I preferred my tequila be only slightly marred with lime juice, rather than brought to its knees with sickly sweet sour mix and fruit flavorings. Given that the restaurant's website is called Killermargaritas.com, I wasn't surprised when after three margaritas, we were ready to go dancing.

We stopped by Spin, but they were conducting the Friday night shower strip contest. No one was dancing. Instead, all eyes were on the nine contestants as they stripped down to their underwear and danced underneath the water from a showerhead on stage. We watched for a while, but got ready to move on. I gave Christian, the skinny white bartender, a kiss on the cheek, thanked him for the drinks, and headed out the door with my friends for Scarlet.

That, too, was overly busy. We took one look at the line extending down half the block—and at the additional dozen people smoking outside, and thus likely to skip the line to get back in—and said, "No way." By the time that we would have made it in to dance, it would have been nearly closing time.

With luck on our side, firmly believing in a third time being a charm, we headed to Roscoe's. No line at all, and no cover on Fridays.

I shouldn't have been surprised that we would end up at Roscoe's that night, considering the diversity of our group, which included a white woman, a Latina, two Asian men, and me. All of us LGBTQ.

The clientele at the front bar looked much like us in terms of makeup. We ordered drinks from the right side of the oblong bar, where many of the other white and light-skinned men stood. We came for dancing, though, and quickly proceeded to the dance floor.

The pool table room on the left side of the bar looked like it normally did, too, when we passed by. Black men and women played pool, stood up against the bar, where no bartender was present, and looked out the front windows, talking about the people walking by on Halsted. Though none of us went in there, I could see people I had hung out with before.

As we approached the dance floor, walking past the corner bar where Cliff, a Black bartender, stood vigil over people taking shots of Jäger, I could see that the room was starting to get more racially mixed.

Pushing onto the dance floor, we were able to find a patch where we could dance without as many people around us. We danced in a group, the kind of circle vaguely reminiscent of eighth grade that people form when they don't want to dance with each other. The music was nothing special; I later wrote in my field notes, "generic electronic dance music." No interesting remixes of Rihanna's "We Found Love," the current hit, just vaguely thumping beats and dance classics.

Soon, the floor got crowded, and we had to close up our circle to continue to dance together. Between the growing crowd and the drinks starting to make us feel woozy, Melanie and her friend had had enough, leaving the rest of us on the dance floor as they made their way to the stabler confines of the front bar.

Nicholas later told me he was originally making eyes at the daddy dancing behind me. However, the guy behind Nicholas grabbed his hand. Nicholas turned around, thought the guy was cute, and went for it.

I was left alone on the busy dance floor while they made out. Alone in the sense that the only person in our group left to dance with was my ex.

As we danced, looking away from each other at sixty-degree angles, I counted the room. At the time, I was interested in whether Boystown spaces were racially diverse. Counts of public spaces, as a version of an establishment survey, don't provide very accurate estimates of the number of people in attendance, at least not in a statistically relevant way. However, such counts can give a rough estimate of who is there.

Fifty-three groups of people stood around me. I judged whether people were together in much the same way anyone might. How are they standing? How are they interacting? Rather than counting specific racial compositions of these groups—I was counting in my head, not with a sophisticated tally sheet—I looked only at whether the group was same-race or interracial.[11] I didn't count the number of people in each group, although usually the groups were of two to three people.

The dance floor was diverse in the sense that there were many people of different racial groups. But of those fifty-three groups within eyeshot on the dance floor at Roscoe's, only seven were racially mixed. And that includes my group, with the interracial pairing of Nicholas and this white man making out less than six inches from where I was dancing.

Whereas the front rooms were largely same race—whites on the right, Blacks on the left—the mixed atmosphere of the dance floor with its erotic movement might lead sociologist Robert Park and others using his foundational assumptions about interracial romance to think something different might be going on there. The space might be "more diverse." However, even on the dance floor, mere contact rules. Only a handful of people interacted across racial boundaries.

And Roscoe's is the most interracial club in Boystown.

That's why, when looking at something like racism in a place like Boystown or comparing the relative diversity of sexy and nonsexy communities, we have to move beyond "diversity by numbers."[12]

Instead, I look at racism as layers within an arena of experience. In this case, I examine the sexual arena, the erotic intergroup encounters thought to erode other areas. Sexuality does reduce sexual racism, but only within intimate situations like sexy communities. Like mere contact, mere romance or mere sex is not enough.

Sexual racism is a system of racial oppression, shaping an individual's partner choices to privilege whites and harm people of color. It manifests itself on three levels: structural, cultural, and interactional. On all of these, sexy communities are more integrated.[13]

Structural sexual racism has to do with the availability of partners within the environment. How segregated is the community, city, or space? Who is around? This seems to be the only way most people look at diversity. Let's make sure a representative from every race is present, and then we can declare the space diverse.

However, we must also examine where people interact within nominally diverse spaces. Are the circuits segregated? This is the kind of structural diversity I was measuring when discussing the within-venue segregation at Roscoe's. Even if many racial groups are present in a space, nothing changes if they don't interact.

Racism is more complicated than segregation. There are cultural components as well. What images are around? What understandings of race construct our definitions of what is happening? What kinds of beauty are favored? How do we determine who the hottest people in the room are?

For instance, earlier that night when we were at Spin's shower strip contest, nine contestants were on stage. The first contestant was a Black guy. Barely anyone yelled out that he was cute as he danced. However, the next man on stage, a white man who by my estimation not nearly as fit, received a ton of noise. Another Black man danced under the water, followed by a white man. The pattern was the same: white guy receives attention, the Black man doesn't.

Two more white men stripped, but then a Latino guy broke the pattern. While he received attention from the crowd, he was also supposedly straight, or at least that was what the announcer told the crowd. The last contestants were a thin muscular white woman able to lift herself onto the shower, dangling upside down, her bouncy firm breasts visible through her sheer white tank top, and a Justin Bieber look-alike who would have done better had the crowd been full of lesbians.

At the end of the show, the contestants lined up on stage for judging, earning placement by stepping forward as the judge listened for the audience's reaction. The Black men received conspicuous silence, leading two men in the back of the bar—one white and one Latino—to shout, "Racists!" Most of the crowd clearly used a Eurocentric white standard of beauty.

In the end, the straight Latino man won, the allure of his heterosexuality overcoming the drawback of his color.

Or, maybe he'd just brought more friends in order to win the hundred-dollar prize. I discarded this alternative explanation through the process of triangulation because this wasn't the only time I'd seen such an outcome at these kinds of contests.[14] Many of the people I interviewed discussed Boystown's—and often, by extension, all mainstream gay spaces—white standard of beauty.

In my interview with David, a Black man in his early forties, he discussed the way perceptions of beauty within Boystown were focused on white bodies.

"We make decisions," he said. "Not everyone has to have a Black boyfriend, I'm not saying that. But we make decisions to put a headdress on a woman.[15] We make decisions to have Hong Kong night at Minibar without Asian people. We make decisions to put white strippers in the window or white models on placards. We make decisions to put heavyset Black women next to them, laughing and singing. These are strong images that have a—sort of—you know?"

"They're not incidental," I said.

"A good-time Black woman ain't something they just dreamed up at Spin," he said.

Versions of beauty, cultural images of how different races are going to be portrayed—these are also elements of diversity. These are also ways of gauging racism as a system of power that privileges whites and denigrates people of color. Often, these stereotypes rely on racial gendering, gender implications based on race that connect to presumptions of sexual prowess. Breaking these stereotypes—for instance, Black gay men who bottom or Asian gay men who top—results in lower sexual capital. Quite literally: in a study by economists Logan and Shah they found escorts on RentBoy.com commanded a higher price when they presented themselves in ways consistent with racially gendered sexual stereotypes.[16] Furthermore, white individuals dominate this sexual hierarchy; they are seen as the best, hottest sexual partners.[17]

These cultural images don't float in the ether, people use them. Examined though culture, we can see how these images shape sexual racism. It isn't enough for a space to have the mere presence of people of color.

I saw cultural sexual racism in action on the first night I took Nicholas to Minibar. Three months into fieldwork, I had been to Minibar several times before, to sit at the bar alone, occasionally talking to the bartender, who would tell me explicitly racist jokes about patrons standing only feet away. However, Nicholas, as someone from this kind of social scene elsewhere, was a helpful guide to the dynamics of plastic culture, since I had yet to interact with any of the plastics in Chicago yet.

Minibar is designed to give a "hotel lounge" feel, according to the owners. After the bouncer—a young Black man dressed in all white for the Wednesday night White Party—had checked our IDs, we walked past some couches up front to the bar stretched along the southern wall. Behind us, a row of cocktail tables hosted groups with bottle service.

One method I used to integrate myself into spaces was to use the same bartender every chance I could. I learned a lot from the servers who worked these spaces every night, doing their own form of fieldwork to gauge the customers, manage social scenes, and meet expectations for the kind of night groups wanted to have at the bar. However, the midthirties muscular man I usually frequented—his head full of jet black hair, skin a unique plastic taut from tanning sun damage that had been mitigated through rigorous moisturizing regimens—was busy with a mixed group of men and women. The group's hostess was handing out green glow sticks. The bartender was convincing them to take shots.

So we sat, instead, at the other end, where a white woman in her late twenties with blond hair and wearing a skintight low-cut T-shirt served us. Behind us, a group of five men stood around a table sharing a bottle of vodka.

Bottle service was confusing to me. Every table in the bar was reserved for bottle service, apparently a popular option. Bottles are $180, at least. Given the amount of drinks one can squeeze out of a 750-millileter bottle of vodka, a cocktail would be $10.50. Buying the same drink at the bar would run $6.50. Why pay more? To sit at a table? To pour your own?

Confused, I asked Nicholas, who looked concerned. "There's more to getting a bottle than the alcohol," he said, then laughed. "It gives you status. You get a table. You get your own place in the club. You have a place to put your coat. I mean if you have the money to throw away. Well, not throw away, but if you have the money, then that's something you can spend it on."

He sat for a moment thinking, "It's like those people that drop two hundred dollars to leave their car at the door. Sitting at the table, you also know that you have it reserved. Other people will be sitting there all night going, 'Oh, I wonder who's going to come for that. Oh, it's them! It's that bitch.' Ha, you can quote me on that." He winked. I wrote it down.

I didn't take much notice of the five men behind us until they started to dance around the table. A tall Asian guy in an oversized black oxford shirt danced with a shorter, bearded white man, wearing his white-and-red winter jacket indoors. They seemed out of place because the fashions they wore weren't the same. Their friends must have brought them, the three of whom seemed more in line with Minibar's fashion, even following the White Party theme. One of the three, a white man at the table, wearing a tight, white two-button Henley and jeans more expensive than my whole outfit, was trying to prevent another Asian man in their group from dancing into other people. The latter was that plastered.

The fifth man—a tall Black man in a white oxford, short cropped hair, and brilliant white teeth—danced up behind us, set his drink down, and moved away slightly to keep dancing. Step one.

Step two: five minutes later, he cuts between us again and turns to Nicholas. "Are you drinking my drink?"

I've noticed these accusations before as fairly common pick-up lines. The charge forces the person to talk to you and gives you the upper hand. The tactic is a version of what straight frat brothers call "negging."[18]

Of course, Nicholas flatly responded he wasn't. I looked over and joked, "Yeah, you have to watch him," to continue rather than cut off the interaction.

I should have taken my cue from Nicholas, who must have sensed from experience the negative turn coming.

A few more minutes passed, and he was back. "Asians are crazy," he yelled at Nicholas over the music.

Nicholas and I looked aghast for a moment, before he finished, "Crazy hot!"

Although Nicholas largely ignored him, giving him minimal interactional feedback, he continued to make sexual overtures. His comments mostly leveraged racially gendered stereotypes, both of himself and Nicholas, to couch their mutual attractiveness.

For instance, he told Nicholas, "You should take a ride on me. I'll give you an experience you've never had. Open you up."

Nicholas laughed dryly, responding, "You don't know what I've had."

"Each ride is different baby. Some are bigger."

The interaction relies on cultural stereotypes of sexual position. This Black man uses the lingering figure of the "big black cock" to construct himself as an aggressive top. Similarly, Nicholas is the chaste Asian bottom, feminized through racial stereotypes.

When people interact only through stereotypes, they objectify. They dehumanize. For instance, Lawrence, a Black gay man in his late twenties, told me over drinks at Daddy Night at the SoFo Tap in Andersonville that whenever he's online he can't get away from men of all races messaging him about his BBC.

However, out in the clubs? Some of these same men won't acknowledge him. They don't want their friends to know that they have sex with Black men. He feels that they use him like a sex toy, a big dick to play with, but one that you ultimately hide in a drawer when your friends come over. You certainly won't be caught dead with your mother seeing you with it.

Cultural sexual racism creates the environment, the context, in which interaction takes place, the scripts people use to flirt, and the metrics they use to determine who is hot.

On the other end of the scale, some only see individual prejudice on the interactional level as indicators of racism. Is someone actively being discriminated against? Are people using epithets or slurs? Less overtly, how are people interacting? Are they interacting in ways that indicate hostility, indifference, fetishization, or other indicators that they are basing treatment on group membership?

Individual prejudice is perhaps the easiest to see. It is the "no fats, no femmes, no Asians" of an online hookup ad. It is the manager of a nightclub who instructs the DJ to change the music because "the room is getting dark."

It is in the warnings from other white men about attending Circuit, a club for Black and Latino LGBTQ people in Boystown. I went to Circuit with

Figure 5.2. Circuit Night Club

JJ and his friends. It wasn't their typical haunt, but they agreed to take me there when I expressed interest, having never been inside.

We started the night off as we usually did, at Cuna, a sports bar in Wrigleyville that also hosted a mostly Latina lesbian night. After choking down another shot of Jäger with JJ, we decided it was time to leave.

Tamera and her fiancée drove to Circuit, while JJ, Flo, another friend of theirs, and I walked over, giving us a chance to talk. JJ's friend—a Latino baby gay, barely twenty-one—was also a newcomer, living out in the suburbs for work but wanting to experience gay life in Boystown for once. Circuit that night was hosting Urbano, the self-described "hottest Black and Latino Gay/LGBT/SGL parties in Chicago!"[19] Even though we had walked, we arrived first—Tamera and her fiancée likely making out in their car nearby. I paid my ten-dollar cover, the most expensive on the strip, and walked quickly ahead to catch up with JJ and the others, who had already started to march toward the back of the club.

The interior of Circuit is much darker than the other clubs on Halsted, in lighting and demographics. Once my eyes adjusted to the dimness, I saw that the center right-hand side of the room had a large dance floor about half-filled with a mix of men and women, mostly Black. Outside the dance floor though, leaning along the black railing that ringed the floor, there were about four or five times as many people. A good hundred people total. A giant crowd compared to the smaller spaces in other Boystown clubs.

As at almost every bar in Boystown, JJ had a bartender that he knew. This one was an white guy in his early thirties, which I found surprising given that he was the first other white person that I'd seen in the club. Grabbing the gin and soda that JJ bought me, I took a moment to survey the club.

I expected to be one of a few white men, but I didn't expect to be the only one besides the bartender. While a "white club" like Minibar might still have a presence of people of color, Circuit's status as a club for men of color deterred any other white people from attending. About fifteen feet from me, a man was leaning up against the railing in a gray trench coat clutching a brown paper bag. And I saw that I was wrong: there was one other white guy there.

"It was you and the creepy guy in the corner," JJ told me the next morning when he called to check on the status of my hangover. We laughed. "I bet you were scared they were going to eat you up."

"I can obviously handle myself."

"OK, *loca blanca*."

This was the third time someone warned me about attending Urbano. A few nights earlier, I made arrangements to hang out with someone I had met on OkCupid. He was busy Saturday, but I was busy Friday for these Circuit plans.

"Lol. O they are going to love you. Watch out =)," He texted. "Those boys love me but they might eat you."

Each time I was warned about Circuit, the obvious inference was that because I was white, I was vulnerable to an aggressive Black and Latino hypermasculine sexuality. "Those boys" were going to manhandle me, and I should protect my vulnerable white body from their assault.

However, that doesn't fit the experience I had that night at Urbano. While we were dancing in the main floor of Circuit, JJ, Tamera, and I had the space mostly to ourselves. A few men stood around the railing looking at our group. However, most, unsurprisingly, were interested in the moves and bodies of the group of slender Black men dancing a few yards away. No one was eating anyone else up.

As the night wound down, around 2 A.M., we left the dance floor and headed to the front late-night bar, Rehab. JJ and Tamera both got another drink, but I wanted to switch to water. JJ wouldn't allow it and pressed another vodka soda into my hands.

Clearly already a bit drunk, I stood up against the bar with JJ to watch the crowd. I certainly wasn't in the mood for an Asian American man in his early twenties to come up and dance against me, pushing his hands into my shirt. I wasn't interested, and tactfully brushed him off. However, he wouldn't stop and kept grinding into me, slightly slurring his words as he asked whether I wanted him. I had to be more forceful, pushing him off me and moving farther away to stand with Tamera at the other end of the bar.

As I typically did, I pulled out my phone to take notes: "I'm not sure whether what was communicated in that moment was that I'm not interested in him specifically or whether it was read as not being attracted to Asian guys in general."

He was the only guy that tried to eat me up. For the others, I was leftovers.

Unlike the warnings I'd received about Circuit in which Black men were characterized as sexually aggressive, the Black men I saw at the club stood and waited for others to approach them, almost as though there was concern on their part they would be misconstrued. From my new vantage point away from my unwanted dance partner, I could see three Black men standing together drinking beers near the front entrance, each bicep more bulging than the last. I was struck by several instances in which smaller framed men, mostly Latino or Asian men, came over and danced at them, not with.

At Urbano, in that moment, it is possible to see how each of the layers of sexual racism supports the others. The club was structurally segregated—with virtually no white people there—because of prejudicial warnings based in cultural stereotypes. At the club, the scripts of flirtation were also rooted in racial gendered expectations. The sexually aggressive men, however, were largely Asian, not Black. The former weren't counteracting stereotypes, though, as their actions still relied on the cultural scripts and racial gendering of Black men as masculine tops and Asian men as feminized bottoms.

Sexy communities are less sexually racist on all of these levels. I realize this is probably the strongest, most controversial claim in this entire book. Instead of assessing the claim through a diversity by numbers approach, using establishment surveys, gut reactions, or stories about when someone experienced prejudice in a certain bar, let's apply the framework of sexual racism.

Spaces containing sexy communities are more diverse than their assimilated counterparts in their structural segregation, in the availability of partners to choose from. For instance, Roscoe's appears diverse when comparing Boystown bars with each other. However, the segregation within Roscoe's is significant. Black men tend to hang out in the side near the pool table, while white men are near the front door. They exist in different sexual circuits. They are in the same space, gazing across the divide, but the divide exists.

However, at Jackhammer, men of different races are in the same circuits. Downstairs in the Hole, Marcus, Owen, Derek, and I, along with many others, all share stories together at the door. We exist alongside one another, not separately with sidelong glances across the invisible divides as at Roscoe's.

One might argue that Jackhammer is more racially diverse because it is in a different neighborhood. Rogers Park has a higher percentage of African Americans than does Lakeview, where Roscoe's is located—26 percent and 4 percent respectively. However, I discovered through fieldwork in both locations that there wasn't a difference in the residential or travel patterns between the two locations. Both bars had patrons that lived in the neighborhood. But both also had patrons that traveled, sometimes significant distances. Chicago is a notably segregated city already. Jon, who lives in the South Loop, drives to both Roscoe's and Jackhammer, because it would take hours to get there by public transit, but he goes nonetheless.

Regarding cultural markers of sexual racism, sexy communities are also different. People within those communities have sex with people of multiple races, but, as discussed, that is a facile approach. Race is still used as a source of pleasure, exclusion, and fetishism in these spaces. However, race doesn't foreclose other possibilities.

Consider Owen. Because people are within the same circuits, they apply racial stereotypes unevenly and inconsistently, often as a shorthand for other attributes. They still use stereotypes. For instance, someone at Jackhammer might say that they want Owen's "big black dick" as a way of expressing attraction for him that is consistent with racial gendering and cultural images of Black bodies. However, Owen does not perceive them as attracted to Black men exclusively, mostly because they do not indiscriminately apply that criteria to all Black men in the Hole. Nor do they only reference that attribute when flirting with him, instead using a constellation of allusions. Therefore, Owen does not feel compartmentalized by race within this space, dehumanized as only a big black dick.

He can be more than the image of the big black cock because a wider variety of racial sexual presentations are possible in sexy communities. While Owen enjoys getting his dick sucked in the back hallway, there have been plenty of times when he would emerge from the back hallway with a different kind of smile on his face.

"Damn," he said to me and Derek once, as we were enjoying our drinks at the bar. "Needed that."

He had just been fucked, he bragged. We both gave him a slap on his muscular ass, which hung out of his jockstrap.

That flipping of racial stereotypes concerning sexual position was much more common in the Hole, where sex happens just down the hall, than at Roscoe's, for instance, where sex was literally a more distant prospect. In terms of cultural markers, sexy communities draw on a wider set of possibilities.

Not to say that sexy communities are devoid of racist interactions. No space is immune from prejudice. At one party, for instance, the room was, using the shorthand Boystown managers would use, "looking dark." While Jackhammer usually has a higher percentage of people of color, this day was unusually Black dominated because it was the annual CD4-Chicago party celebrating the HIV/AIDS community and allies, which disproportionately affects Black gay men.[20] I was standing at the right side of the bar, in that small "family" portion near where Deveaux sits. A bartender leaned over and whispered to me in disgust, "I didn't know this was going to be a ghetto party." I didn't know what to say. So I merely stared at him as he went back to work.

While that instance was explicit, the prejudice expressed at Jackhammer was usually much less blatant than the kind of racist statements coming out of the mouths of servers and patrons of Boystown bars. Regardless, the presence or absence of racist words is a poor indicator of racism.

If diversity is not a product merely of location, why are these radical sexual spaces more diverse? They bring people together into an erotic ritual space that brings them out of themselves, creating the kind of intimate connections—like naked intimacy—that sociologists have shown reduce discrimination.

Michael Warner has suggested another reason: "Queer scenes are the true *salons des refusés*, where the most heterogeneous people are brought into great intimacy by their common experience of being despised and rejected in a world of norms that they now recognize as a false morality."[21]

Queer spaces, by virtue of being on the outside of the charmed circle and stigmatized by society, Warner argues, bring different kinds of people together. They don't have the choice of whether to be friendly with each other. They can't afford prejudice.

This explanation, however, misreads the situation. Stigma pushed queer people together against a world that hated them, but plenty of queer spaces have prejudice.

Queer spaces, though, contained sexy communities. These spaces, having rejected the false morality of the inner charmed circle, had naked intimacy through their moments of collective effervescence. Spaces with erotic possibility, where people can experience naked intimacy with each other, form sexy communities. Sexy communities are not just diverse in a paint-by-numbers sense. The people within them have experienced connection beyond mere contact.

Warner goes on to explain that dignity and shame infuse everyday relations, identifying as "Bourgeois propriety" what Rubin referred to as the inner charmed circle.

He writes: "In what I am calling queer culture, however, there is no truck with bourgeois propriety. If sex is a kind of indignity, then we're all in it together. And the paradoxical result is that only when this indignity of sex is spread around the room, leaving no one out, and in fact binding people together, that it begins to resemble the dignity of the human."[22]

This "dignity of the human" is the connection that results from the naked intimacy of erotic encounters. When everyone acknowledges that sex is possible, that sex is human, then people are able to break free from the partitioning between moral and immoral, good and bad sex that the charmed circle embodies. When the ignominy of sex is "spread around the room," coming to the space begins to embody the stigma and indignity of the immoral, despised sexuality. A sexy community begins to form.

"Shame is the bedrock," Warner explains. "Queers can be abusive, insulting, and vile toward one another, but because abjection is understood to be the shared condition, they also know how to communicate through such camaraderie a moving and unexpected form of generosity.... The rule is: Get over yourself.... You stand to learn most from the people you think are beneath you."

Because people in the space have had naked intimacy with other people in the space, they've experienced a transcendental headspace in which they felt connected to each other, and they imbue others with this connectedness, even people that they haven't had sex with or felt those moments. The space, and the people that frequent that space, are connected into community. A community of sexual kinship beyond a "family of choice" that they can carry with them as an alternative to the precepts of the straight world.

This kinship erodes other forms of discrimination, loosening a strand of the intersectional knot. Park's original insight into romantic attachments was incorrect—not in totality, but in part. Park incorrectly thought, and sociologists ever since then have been assuming, that romance produces intimacy that can erode boundaries. But not all sexuality moves beyond mere contact. The mere existence of sex, romance, and attraction doesn't move people to reconsider their stereotypes. People continue to use them as cultural scripts, moving within segregated sexual landscapes, to attract others, sometimes explicitly evoking racist stereotypes to make themselves more attractive.

However, the framework of sexual racism doesn't imply we shouldn't use race within the sexual realm. I do not advocate for a world in which race has no sexual meaning. I find that to be dangerously close to a color-blind ideology that would only favor assimilation to the white norm of beauty rather than dismantling white sexual privilege and the denigration of people of color.

Neither do I agree that we must, to use David's words, "all have Black boyfriends." We choose from the partners around us—structural sexual racism.

We find certain attributes attractive because of our social conditioning—cultural sexual racism. We do have control though, over how we interact with others, whether we will consider partners that don't fit within our narrow racial frames of attraction, and if we will list a "White Only" or "BBC Only" preference on our profile.

Rather, we should explore the pleasure of race. We should follow what I call Schilt's dictum, after a similar commandment from sociologist Kristen Schilt to find "the pleasure in gender."[23] Gender is a site of not only sexism but also pleasure. Similarly, race is not only an oppressive construct, harming those placed on the wrong side of the hierarchy, but a site of identity, culture, and pleasure. I believe it is possible for race to be a site of sexuality that is pleasurable, without being fetishistic. In sexy communities, I see that exploration, that attraction that uses race in a way that neither excludes nor fetishizes.

6

New, Now, Next, Not

I watched a lot of *RuPaul's Drag Race* for this book. Hard work, I know. I sat at Spin, near the beer taps, talking to Christian, a waifish white bartender who would tell me bawdy jokes and hand me the occasional free beer for laughing along to his stories about some recent all-night coke binge. *Drag Race* was a regular activity, a reason for me to be in the space observing, week after week.

Traditional advertisements didn't play, since Spin was designated as an official viewing party. However, occasionally the Logo TV channel would plug their website NewNowNext, a gossip blog and entertainment website featuring the work of previous drag queen runner-up Pandora Boxx. Much later, after Spin shut down and after I stopped watching *RuPaul's Drag Race*, I realized how useful the conceit "new, now, next" is for thinking about social life. Except, I would add one additional word: "not."

New, now, next, not. These four words are as useful for talking about the latest happenings in the world of drag queen music videos and recaps of Tim Gunn's latest fashion show on Bravo as for the world of Boystown. They are a theoretical tool, a philosophical push to think through the dimensions of a concept.[1]

"New, now, next, not" fleshes out the limits of sexy community. Where does it appear and how does it form? What does a contemporary, perhaps unexpected, form look like? Where is it going? What isn't sexy community?

■ ■ ■

New.

Sexy communities don't have to have sex explicitly in them. They have to have erotic possibility. BDSM and leather spaces—both inside and outside of Boystown—better preserve the erotic possibility in their spaces but are worse at remaining viable as businesses in the face of gentrification. Without the money to remain open, many have been swept away.

However, there are nights we can see sparks of sexy community. Successfully resisting assimilation means being on the outside in some way. Outsider status can happen through exclusion of others, or from stigma and isolation. The plastics manage to keep sexy community on their boats out on Lake Michigan through money and strict body rules concerning attractiveness. Men's Room keeps sexy community rooted through exclusion, often of women, but also of anyone looking to be on safari via rules on clothing.

Juicy, a night at Hydrate, enabled sexy community through being a night for queer people of color. Although supposedly a night for Latinos, Juicy embodied the kind of racial diversity I argue is associated with sexy communities. Juicy did so by having an erotic dance floor and an atmosphere conducive to late-night hookups. People took each other home from the bar to have sex after the kind of physicality that fills the space with erotic potential.

I went to Juicy with JJ and his friends. I'm not sure that I would have felt comfortable initially going to the Latino night alone. First, I feared I would have been pegged as fetishist of some kind, which fits the initial reactions I saw from JJ and his friends when they saw white men alone at spaces like Circuit that are predominantly for Blacks and Latinos in Boystown. "Just you and that creepy white guy," as JJ said.

Second, and more importantly, I wouldn't want to go on safari into other people's spaces. I waited to be invited. A queer of color party wasn't mine to crash as a white man.

Although usually we went to Cuna first for the ladies, JJ's friend Flo thought enough women would be at Juicy that we didn't need to bifurcate the night.[2] The day before, I had proposed they come to my place first. I lived in Boystown, while they lived out on the west side of Chicago, in a Latino community as might be expected given Chicago's racial segregation. Why not come to my apartment to pregame?

"Hey babe so what's the plan tonight?" I texted JJ around eight that night.

"Well. The plan to hold the door open for u, buy u a cocktail, give u a hug, kiss ur hand, slap ur ass, then been u over so I can lick ur man pussy," he responded.

"I didn't say what was the plan for your fantasy once you got home. I meant for us all that are going to juicy =p"

"Oh wow. Fantasy for when I got home. Interesting. I was planning on doing it in public."

"Lol =p"

"Juicy papi"

"Yes. When? Y'all coming over to my place first? Or should I meet y'all there?"

"Only if ur in a jock strap"

"No promises"

"Lol . . . Ok all kidding aside. We running a lil behind schedule. Went to laundry so it kind of sort of thru us off a tad. We r home now abt to start getting ready. Might not make it to ur casa. We should meet at Juicy. I'm leaving my casa at 930 on the dot."

At 9:45, I got another text from him. He was running even later.

"As long as we make it before midnight when the cover goes up," I responded. I hadn't even dressed, since I knew he wouldn't be on time. I put on a black Iron & Wine T-shirt, gray jeans, and spiked my Mohawk.

Twenty minutes later, he texted me they were on their way, roaring down Irving Park in Tamara's car. I took my cue to leave, walking from my place on Pine Grove over to Broadway.

As I passed the Chateau Hotel on Broadway and Sheridan, I heard a honk behind me.

"*Loca blanca*," JJ yelled from the passenger seat. "Get your ass in."

No sooner was I in the car then Tamera hit the gas, throwing me back against the seat as I struggled to get my seat belt on.

We chatted about the night. They had all pregamed at JJ and Flo's house. Flo had just woken up from a nap, since three of them were up at 4 A.M. for work.

Miraculously, Tamera found a space right in front of Hydrate. I could tell that it was a different kind of night immediately. For one, people were actually already at Hydrate at 10:30 P.M., unlike every other night, when most people wouldn't come until they were drunk off their asses and getting kicked out of Roscoe's, Sidetrack, or the other main Boystown clubs. Hydrate was a late-night hookup bar, an atmosphere that, combined with the elements I will describe, enabled the ambiance of a sexy community, even if just for a night. About ten people were already clustered outside the bar smoking when we walked up.

As we walked in, I noticed the second difference. Their typical bouncer was not there that night. Instead of a butch, white lesbian with short spiky hair, a Latino man and woman collected our cover at the door.

We were still early enough that Hydrate hadn't opened the back bar, where the main dance floor was, when we arrived. To pass the time, we downed shots that JJ bought, as usual. After the third, I begged them off. Despite my Texas and Wisconsin university education, I wasn't used to drinking quite that much in a short time.[3] Besides, I needed to remember what was going on. As usual, being glued to my phone helped. While the group was talking, I took notes on my phone.

The front space didn't take long to fill up. Frivolity filled the room, not like a normal night at Hydrate, but unlike their Manhole night either. The atmosphere said "party," not "sex club." Two Latina women walked by in booty shorts, bikini tops, and green hand muffs on their shoes and wrists. Flo turned around to check them out as they walked by and then made a face at me, with her eyes opened wide and bugged out and her mouth agape.

So as not to feel like I was mooching on the group, I bought a round of Coronas, JJ's call, as we went to the back bar to dance.

As I discussed in "On Safari," where I described dancing on this same floor, only a few feet to the left, dancing creates the same effervescence that people experience in the Hole because they are rooted in the body. Dancing, like sex, is erotic. Or it can be: at Roscoe's, the kind of dancing I saw involved people keeping to themselves. Although JJ wasn't a big dancer, he stood near us, basking in the mood and holding his Corona. As I expected, Tamara and Maria were making out while dancing pretty much as soon as we got to the dance floor. I lost track of time, a good gauge for whether one has experienced a moment of collective effervescence.

At 2 A.M., JJ went to the bathroom, and I wandered up to the front room. The flirty atmosphere I'd noticed on the dance floor was especially evident there. Yet the differentiation between the spaces is important. While the dance floor was the dynamo generating the erotic charge, the front bar provided the social space to connect. Like the upstairs and downstairs differentiation of Jackhammer, the bar was hybrid: sexual and social.

I stood up against the bar, sipping a glass of soda water, and taking notes on my phone. Although Juicy was a Latino night, the makeup of the bar's patrons was the most racially and gender diverse I'd seen in Boystown, even more so than at Roscoe's. Next to me stood a Latina woman, a white woman, an Asian American man, and a tall Black man.

I must have been staring, because within five minutes, the tall man was talking with me and introducing me to his friends.

"Did y'all know that it was Juicy tonight?" I asked, as he put his arm around the small of my back.

His three friends pretended they didn't see this maneuver as they affirmed that they did. They came to Hydrate frequently but decided to head over earlier than usual because of the event.

I wasn't the only one being picked up in the room: the pairing up that usually happens at 5 A.M. when the club closes was beginning to happen three hours earlier, because of the atmosphere of erotic possibility. Thirty minutes had passed since I had seen JJ or anyone else I knew. I thought JJ had fallen into the bathroom, or perhaps scored some ecstasy and was back on the dance floor, like I knew he did occasionally. I didn't want to ruin his buzz.

"Let's get out of here," the tall man said.

The next day, I got a text from JJ: "Not a happy camper here."

"Not feeling well?" I responded. "For some reason, although I slept late, I'm not hung over."

"No I'm not hung over at all." The period the text equivalent of a curt tone.

"Oh that's great! Why are you not a happy camper?" I texted back, oblivious.

"U disappeared on me. I went to the bathroom waited in this long ass line. Used it. Then u were gone. Looked for u all over the club. Waited outside for 30 min n nada. Sad sad face. Couldn't call u or txt phn died. U asked y am I not happy. I was worried. Cause I knew u had a buzz going n I couldn't locate you. Thought something happened but obviously ur ok."

I vigorously apologized. He was concerned. I had been a jerk to not make a bigger effort to tell him good-bye.

At the time, I wrote in my field notes the incident indicated we were close. He considered me part of their group. He was worried about me, that I had been put in an unsafe situation.

Later, I wondered whether his concern was really about the fact that I had hooked up with someone else. Two months later, JJ confessed feelings for me. His admission cast doubt on the erotic talk we'd had by text earlier in the night, and in many other cases throughout our friendship. The erotic talk that maintains sexual kinship can provide a cover for other feelings.

Not all erotic possibility is actually possible. Romance can come at the expense of sexual kinship. The strain of unreturned feelings taxed our relationship. We kept hanging out, but that night changed things for us.

Overall, that was the problem with Juicy as well: it didn't last. A community can't be built on a few nights. Oscillating nights, leaving you unsure if the place you're going to will offer a fun night with the energy of sex or a darker mood of meth, makes it hard to keep community going.

After that night, JJ's group and I never hung out at Juicy again, although the event happened one additional time to my knowledge. Instead, we went back to hanging out at Cuna before going to Spin, spaces that didn't have the same kind of sexy atmosphere Juicy managed to attain. Juicy had potential, but its sexy community didn't congeal. That is surely part of the interpretation, but it is also possible that JJ kept me from the space and the possibility of watching me flirt with someone else.

■ ■ ■

Now.

Sex is physical, rooted in the body. Doesn't a space that is defined by so much physicality simply have a different hierarchy? Beauty can be as harmful a dynamic as class or race. Patrick Moore discusses this criticism of the seventies New York scene, paraphrasing his critic suggesting that "the young and the hung rank highest regardless of financial, social, or intellectual standing."

Moore reminds us, however, that "despite the inherent cruelty towards those who are not traditionally beautiful, the gay bathhouse (and other sites of gay male sexuality) brings together different classes and enables interaction between them. While it is true that that stockbroker might only approach the cabdriver in the bathhouse because of his penis size, it is also true that they would have an intense physical, and, perhaps, emotional interaction. They might also talk afterward and actually come to know something about each other's lives. . . . Beauty is no fairer than birth in determining access, but at least different determinants were at play."

Moore's defense is inadequate. It isn't enough to say that "different determinants were at play," as though that's any better. I'm unwilling to trade one form of oppression for another.

Rather, beauty—especially as traditionally seen in American society as a particular white, muscular, masculine flavor of male physical attractiveness—is not especially influential to developing sexy community.[4] There are sexy communities where traditional beauty is a major factor in who is accepted, there are those who break with tradition and favor other hierarchies of beauty, and those that do neither, instead taking all comers or favoring several at once simultaneously. Sexy communities, as spaces developed through sex, interact with notions of attraction, but that doesn't mean a particular kind of beauty or body is necessary for them to form, maintain, or cohere.

More forcefully, while sexy communities are queer in their radical sexual orientation, not all are built through queer means. Sexy community is built through exclusion—through protective fostering of a sexual atmosphere. And some, it is true, are made possible through enforcing strict hierarchies of class, beauty, or other boundaries.

Rather than viewing sexy communities as trading one form of oppression for another—beauty instead of race, gender instead of class—sexy communities must be examined intersectionally. Oppressions cannot be examined in a zero-sum environment. Instead, the intersectional knot suggests that our understanding of oppression changes as strands loosen and tighten, but these strands are always present.

The sexy community of the plastics—or "the boat people," as some people call this group of plastics that take boat trips on Lake Michigan—is an example. Protected through class, the members are leveled through meeting the access requirements to the space. While politically conservative—or at least more conservative than the average gay man, that is, with values aligned with their class—their spaces are queer, for those who can get in.

There are two ways to get on the boat: be young and beautiful or rich. Since I am neither of those, an invitation was hard to come by.

I had heard about the boat trips from many people. I had seen these guys hovering off the coast when at Hollywood Beach, their ships scattered out of reach, but close enough that those on shore could see tanned muscular bodies lounging on decks. The boats are little private clubs, a Boystown on Lake Michigan, floating away from the women and ugly people running around the Boystown of Halsted Street. My original intent was to observe them as an example of racial exclusion. I did not expect to find a sexy community there.

I had squeezed my way into several different groups of plastics. Their groups had a similar milieu: upper-class, mostly white men, drinking vodka sodas at Minibar or Sidetrack. Most didn't maintain or frequent spaces of sexy community. Sexy community was not in the frat-esque Pride party I attended, trash strewn about the yard, where a group of white men laughed about why they would never have sex with Asian men. Minibar isn't queer or radical or sexy or intimate, no matter how many TPAN functions or Black Pride events it hosts. These spaces have all the exclusion with none of the sexual intimacy.[5]

Not all plastics were like this, though.

I hung out with this particular group—those on this boat—at the Bar on Buena in Uptown, just after I had met Austin. He introduced me to his friend Clinton, the rich variety of boat party attender, whom he knew because they both used to live in Hyde Park.

I drank whiskey, while most of them drank vodka soda, but despite our differences, we had a good time. Trent, the boat owner, and I discussed my work. He gave me his opinion about changes to Boystown and he offered to take us out on his boat at an unspecified future time.[6]

The following summer, I was able to cash in on that offer. Before Trent's inaugural cruise of the summer, he posted the event to his Facebook friends to join if they wished to get on the list. This is perhaps one of the more accessible boats for this reason.

I flaked out a few times because of work, signing up through the personal link e-mailed to me, only to cancel a few days later. I knew this trip would need to be the one, otherwise I might stop receiving the invitations. Austin agreed to go with me, since he'd been on this boat with Clinton years earlier, when he was younger, fresher meat.

Luckily enough, Clinton noticed I signed up, and agreed to come too. The Sunday Funday cruise had already filled up, so we signed up for Saturday, which had fewer people. Nine men signed up online, but we wound up with thirteen, which is much less than the twenty-one possible occupants. This lower number, though, was probably more because of the projected cloudy weather than some other factor.

Austin and I came by Uber, worried we would miss the castoff time and be left on the dock. Clinton sent me the pier number and the code for the locked gate, but it didn't seem to work when we arrived. I jiggled the handle like an idiot, trying the code over and over, until someone working on a boat nearby called out the code for me so that we could get in. Thanking him, we hustled down the otherwise empty dock, looking for the boat number when Clinton called out to us from the next pier over. He had sent us to the wrong place. I'd made an excellent first impression.

When we arrived to the right ship, I realized I might be wrong about who goes on these voyages. Clinton brought his friend Margaret with him. She carried a handle of Fireball whiskey in one hand, clutching her purse in the other. Two men were already there, a giant pack of Bud Light cans at their feet. Each of them had a beard and lacked the muscle-beach bodies I associated with the space. At first, I thought, "oh well, my information is wrong."

I am not wrong. Not by half.

Ten minutes later, as the rest of our motley crew made small talk, the captain arrived with four white muscle boys in tow. One was clearly the first mate, since I had seen him out with Trent numerous times before, and had an easy familiarity with the boat's operations. He immediately set about prepping the boat for departure. Two others introduced themselves to the rest of us. Newbies. Only one of these four muscular men otherwise acknowledged my presence after this. It's no coincidence I later learned that he was the newest person on the boat besides Austin and me and the one with the least-developed abs. Midway through the outing, though, he seemed to realize that we were outsiders, and didn't speak to us again. I never learned any of the others' names, despite all of us sitting on the same boat for hours.

Two other muscular boys had actually jumped aboard the boat just prior to departure, one Black and one Asian. They were even more buff than the four white muscle boys that had arrived earlier. Austin and I sat, exchanging a word or two with the newbie, while everyone else was silent. The two last-minute arrivals knew the rest of the attendees, hugging Trent, saying hello to Clinton, the first mate, and the other long-timer.

At just about the same time, a middle-aged woman came over from two boats down and asked, in true Midwestern fashion, "Can I offer you all a sandwich or some pasta salad? They are left over!"

She climbed onto the boat, carrying a tray of finger sandwiches of unknown variety.

The boat's occupants remained silent, everyone staring at her as she tried to push the sandwiches in different directions. I saw a few people subtly looking from person to person, trying to get a sense of what the others were going to do before offering a response. Inner monologues, mine at least, asked, "Am I going to eat carbs in front of these guys?"

Moments passed before Trent came back to the front. His "no thanks" dissipated the awkwardness and sent her further down the dock.

After we left the dock, my jottings got more sporadic, because we stripped down to our swimsuits as soon as we left the dock, the clouds blocking the sun but not our desire for it. Clinging to my phone looked increasingly awkward.

And anyway, the spray, as we skipped over the water, was noisy, so we didn't do much talking until we started floating off the coast of Hollywood Beach. Drinks poured, shots taken. We started to settle into our respective beach rhythms: tanning, talking, or just relaxing and letting the lake breeze refresh us.

I continued to feel moments of heightened body awareness—verging on policing—throughout the trip, but, I wondered, "Am I doing this to myself or is the space doing it to me, or both?" I noticed, for instance, that I have some dark hairs on my upper arms that I should have shaved off. At lunch, I took not only a second helping of grilled chicken but also a bun for my sausage, bread I feel certain was left as a trap. Gotcha.

I usually feel uncomfortable in plastic spaces. Leather spaces make me feel attractive. In plastic spaces, I'm made aware of not being in the "right" social class—that is, of not having the leisure and money necessary to produce the kind of body the other men have. That's not to say that down in the Hole or on the dance floor of Hydrate, no one has six-pack abs or biceps that look like they could tear through shirt sleeves. There are plenty. It's that this isn't the only kind of body image present. I don't feel like I stick out as much.

And it is about class, not just genetics or wanting it bad enough. Producing the kind of body the plastics favor—the muscular clone—takes time and money.

Simon, a plastic gay man I hung out with several times, has a regimen that's instructive. He wakes up every day about two and a half hours before work in order to go to the gym first. Every day he walks the fifteen minutes to the Lakeview Athletic Club, one of the gyms in Boystown. He learned how to be effective at the gym because he hired a trainer, someone who taught him a routine and the proper way to lift weights. His preworkout breakfast is an egg-white omelet. For lunch, he takes a tub of food to work. His meals are monotonous: chicken breast, hard-boiled egg, and boiled broccoli. He makes them ahead of time and puts them into Tupperware so it is easy for him to pull out quickly later. Even with these time-saving tactics, he still spends a large amount of time and money preparing and buying healthy food.

Not everyone can simply "go to the gym" or "eat healthy" because these things cost money and—that even bigger indicator of class—time. Such that social theorist Pierre Bourdieu argues that the rich often engage in the conspicuous consumption of time rather than money.[7] Preparing a lavish meal using techniques requiring hours can be another way of showing your freedom from wage work. Similarly, a gym habit demands money for a membership, but the schedule to attend for hours every week is an even more onerous requirement.

However, it's more than my body. I don't have the right clothes. My swimsuit was all wrong. I chose the one I thought would be most like the ones they'd be wearing: black short trunks with a few zippers that came to the midthigh. However, you could tell by the slightly faded black and the out-of-style zippers that mine were out of fashion. Compared to their new, even shorter trunks, boy-shorts really, in a variety of bright colors, my swim trunks looked sad.

I don't have the right interests either.

Standing at the back of the boat, drinking a Bud Light that the bearded men had brought, I talked with these rich men, since the pretty boys were at the front sunbathing, where they remained for most of the trip. The ones that were on the boat because of their literal rather than embodied class stood at the back, which is where those of us out of place also stood, mostly silent. Clinton, Trent, the two bearded men, Margaret, Austin, and I stood at the back of the boat drinking. They were all very nice, and despite my tone here, I did have a fun time.

I just didn't know what to talk about really. After the boat anchored off the coast, the boys settled in the front and the rest of us settling for the back, the two bearded men handed out beers to the rest of us and started talking about cars. Tell me, what are the relative merits of different BMW models? One mentions he enjoys his 3. His friend chimed in he should upgrade to the 5 like he did.

What am I supposed to add to this conversation? Austin, at least, knows a bit about cars, and was able to follow along, knowing, for instance, unlike me, there are different numbered classes of BMW. The conversations that they had were about topics, and objects, and concerns—Clinton often discusses the drama of his condo association, for example—that I don't share. They are an elite group.

In short, I have the wrong tastes. Without the taste to fit in, I was easily excluded.

However, other sexy spaces are elite in other ways, excluding those that don't have the right tastes. Hydrate requires hours of drinking, dancing, and, for some, a familiarity with drugs, all skills requiring cultural knowledge and patterns of consumption. Online communities, like Grindr, require an iPhone or Internet connection and use specialized lingo. At the Hole, one must be willing to absorb the stigma, as well as handle raunchiness and nakedness without being self-conscious, both of which are also skills.

Nothing got better when another boat, owned by Trent's friend, arrived with more people. Everyone on the other boat was male, but more men of color were aboard. They tied the boats together to make it easy to pass between, but by this point I was just sitting against the side of the boat, drinking beer and passing the time with Austin, observing, comparing the space to others I followed. Could a space so exclusive be sexy?

The space had the same kind of intimate sexy joking, the shedding of clothing to reveal the body, the same acceptance of sexuality as an indignity we all share. While no one was having sex, the space had naked intimacy and kinship, at least among those that met the requirements for the space and had the right tastes to fit in.

Moreover, the sexual racism I expected to find—that's why I was there after all—wasn't present. Not only were many men of color present—in much higher numbers than I'd seen in other plastic events—but the cultural and interactional aspects of racism were lessened. The attractive men of color were seen as attractive neither because of their race nor despite it. The other men on the boat engaged in the same sexual banter and touching I otherwise described in "Naked Intimacy," just with tight V-neck T-shirts and Gucci sunglasses instead of leather harnesses.

The presence of Clinton's friend Margaret on the boat actually highlights the absence of women on the boats. The boating set isolates themselves from the women invading Boystown. Barely anyone but Clinton talked to Margaret the entire trip. To be fair, whenever someone did try, she would end up telling a story about her boyfriend that seemed slightly homophobic. For instance, he won't own a hatchback car because he doesn't want to look gay. Another case of homophobia feeding gay misogyny, the intersectional knot.

Also, despite the belief on the part of some that older people disappear or die by the time they turn thirty, sexy communities, even the sexy community of plastics, clearly disprove this notion. The plastics, too, had plenty of older individuals among them, who, while they don't appear to be at the same age as, say, Deveaux at Jackhammer, that's because they are better preserved, able to afford the kind of food, health care, grooming products, and time-consuming health activities that would keep their skin taunt, their hair black, and their bodies firm. That is, as long as they provide the money that enables the pretty boys to suntan on the decks of their boat, they are granted access to the space. Age isn't as big an influence on acceptance by the group as having the right kind of body or money—namely, their taste, or what I will later call habitus.

The boat people use capital—erotic and literal—to buy places on boats to recapture some of the classic gay environment. These are the men who can still afford to live in Boystown, despite gentrification. However, they don't have enough money to buy a club space on par with what they can create privately on their boats: a place away from women with strict requirements for getting in. Although not queer in the political sense, these spaces are still queer in their sexuality and their separatism. Despite belief on the part of other queers that these spaces are especially racist, they are actually fairly egalitarian, as long as you are within the tiny 1 percent of humanity that has the right kind of class to gain entrance. As Boystown assimilates, we're going to see more of this kind of space that doesn't use separatism through stigma to achieve sexy community, to recapture what they feel has been lost.

■　■　■

Next.

When sexiness leaves the clubs, why not bring the sexiness back with you?

Online applications and mobile programs let people carry sexy community with them back into clubs and into places in their straight lives where sexy community never had a presence before. Using a mobile phone, people can connect with others throughout the city.

In this way, sexy communities don't have to involve physical spaces. The spaces can be virtual. While sex can occur in many forms, and masturbating with someone over the Internet can produce a community—just go to a fetish website like PupZone or chat rooms at Gay.com—I am focusing here on place-based online communities. Such spaces are connected to physical places and locations and help lay the groundwork for people to have sex physically, not just virtually.

In a place-based online community, you can tell if someone is physically nearby or indicate your location in some way that ties you to Boystown. For example, Adam4Adam is a website that allows you to select your location to find other people with whom to hook up. Since users self-select their location, they don't necessarily have to indicate a place accurately reflecting their physical position. Just as JJ and his friends piled in a car to head to Boystown from their neighborhood on the west side, gay men can virtually travel to Boystown on Adam4Adam. Through the web, they can re-create

Figure 6.1. Sidetrack nightclub

some of the sexual atmosphere they might not find in Boystown or, alternatively, might be easier to find in the anonymity of home.

In my conversation with Ginger—a name he selected with a laugh, pretending to flip his hair, "It's like I'm on *Gilligan's Island*, Professor"—we started discussing the relevance of online spaces after he expressed a sentiment I found surprising: you go to Boystown only when you're single.

"If you're meeting someone, don't ever take them on a date to Boystown. I think that it's a place you go when you're single or want to get drugs or sex or you want to dance," he said.

We sat in the back corner of the Argo Tea Café on Broadway. He took a sip of his tea, hot despite the summer weather.

"When I first started going there," Ginger said, "it was really because I just wanted to dance and have a good time and feel like I could be a sassy diva if I wanted to."

I had been studying Boystown for almost two years when we first talked. This seemed to go against the discussions I'd had with others.

"It's interesting that you mention it's a place to go if you're single and want to find sex partners, if you want to find hookups. A lot of people are saying the other thing. That they are going to go online if they're going to find a hookup rather than go to Boystown," I said.

"Well, if we're talking about prioritizing, I don't think anyone's choosing Boystown at this point over sitting at home in your boxers and having your five tabs open," Ginger said.

"I was just saying, was that your feeling?" I said, suddenly unsure if I had come across as being antagonistic.

If I did, Ginger didn't seem to care. Raising his voice and setting his tea down, Ginger brought out his sassy diva.

"But I would say that any of those gays would say that I was full of shit. When you set foot in Boystown, everyone is on point. Everyone is aware that you're being looked at, and everyone is giving a performance. Whatever it is. Whether it's butch trade or it's 'I don't care' or it's innocent schoolboy. Everyone's giving. People are really aware of their surroundings. Validation from other men is always part of that equation. It's not like that in Uptown."

Before I could ask him to explain more, he went on. "Boystown is a stage. Once you set foot—" he paused.

"I just feel like there is a sexual undertone to the whole Boystown. People who tell me that they don't think that are full of shit. Every other storefront is a sex store. You know what I mean? You have hot pieces in the window. You have dildos and you have a brunch spot. It's all about consumption. There's a lot of consumption. Whether that's drinking or eating or fucking. I don't know. Did I answer your question?"

Ginger certainly had a different take on Boystown than others I'd spoken to, though these conversations were connected to the same theme. He sees Boystown's consumption as about sex, but sex used to sell rather than as a point of connection. Why were the spaces in Boystown infused with sex for him when others didn't feel that way?

I had planned to ask him that question, but he'd already addressed it on his own.

Responding to Ginger's concern about whether he'd answered my question, I said, "You definitely did. I think it was really helpful for me to hear a different point of view than others. One thing that I have been really interested in—"

"That's why everyone—sorry," Ginger said, cutting me off. "That's why everyone signs on to Lakeview or is on Grindr! Those bitches don't live in Lakeview, but they're signing in on Lakeview because they want to be seen. If you're like, 'fuck it, I'm not leaving the house tonight,' then I'm going to keep it on Uptown," with "it," here, being Adam4Adam's location view, which lists where you are and therefore who will see you in the feed of pictures. Although he uses the example of Adam4Adam in his description, he also mentions Grindr's ability to locate you, which I will return to in a moment.

Ginger continued, "Keeping it Uptown. You know what I mean?"

I nodded. I knew what he meant. I didn't need a translation, even though it meant writing this section with more intercessory notes explaining.

"If you're feeling a little low," Ginger said, "and you've been sitting in the Uptown section for like an hour and no one is hitting you up, you sign in to Lakeview."

These place-based online communities let you travel to Boystown—sign on to Lakeview's section—much like people would have traveled to Boystown for sexual encounters back when those were available in Boystown.

Why does Ginger think Boystown has a sexual atmosphere, when others don't? Grindr.

Ginger is an avid Grindr user. Of course Boystown is going to have a sexual aspect, because when he is in the area, even though he may be experiencing the clubs in a similar fashion to others, the use of Grindr layers over the space, giving the places a sexual atmosphere otherwise missing.

Augmented reality enables sexy community to form through these apps because people can use them to meet in person or to transform nonsexual meet ups, in person, into erotic possibilities through meeting later on the app.

Many times, while out doing fieldwork, I would see people meet after having both been on their phones, alone, at other parts of the club. This happened especially in places like Minibar, Roscoe's, and Spin—places that removed the erotic possibility in their spaces as a result of so many people coming there on safari.

If you see someone out in Boystown enjoying a drink alone, then he is also on his phone. One might think that he is entertaining himself in the same way you might while waiting for the train, reading Facebook or the latest news. One might assume that he is using his phone as a replacement for carrying a book or a newspaper, something to read instead of stare blankly at the television.

He is probably doing those things, but interspersed with replying to threads on Facebook, updating Secret, or reading their Feedly, they are on Scruff, Grindr, or another app. Rather than sit around waiting for someone cute to catch his eye from across the bar, he will "woof" on Scruff, or send that person a message, "Sup?"

Because if you see that someone's location is less than five hundred feet away from you, on one of these applications, there is a chance he is in the same bar as you, or at least at one nearby. I've played a game with friends several times out at the clubs called "Spot the Grindr." Pull up Grindr and see if you can spot the first person on the list—the nearest person to you—in the club. If you say hi to them in the flesh, then the rest of our group of friends will buy you a drink.

One night out at Minibar, for instance, I saw a white man in his early forties chat with people on Grindr while sitting a few feet away from me down the bar. He would sip on his drink, type a few words into his phone, and then set it down for a while, looking around or enjoying the ambiance.

After quite a while—I didn't mark down the exact time—another man approached him, younger, in his thirties maybe. From their body language, it was easy to see that this was their first time meeting in person, but they had spoken before: they confirmed names, there was no hugging, but they both had a friendly demeanor, an indication they'd conversed. By all signs, they had met on Grindr that night—first on their phones, but then in person. They had augmented Minibar with an additional back channel of sexual information.

Men can use Grindr the opposite way as well.

In an upstairs corner of the Bourgeois Pig, a coffee shop near DePaul University's Lincoln Park campus, Frank, a midtwenties-ish white gay man who is part of the politically queer social group I followed, told me quite a few stories about moments in which he met someone out in the bars and then followed up with them over Grindr later.

"Jeremy was drunk. He comes up to me at Hydrate and he tells me that he's really sad. He and his boyfriend just broke up. He would really like to come back to my house and just cuddle. And I said, 'Well, my boyfriend and I just broke up too. I know how you feel. If you want to go back to my house and cuddle and tell me about it, then absolutely we can do that.' Then, he wandered off in a drunken stupor," he said.

He turned to put his feet up on the bench next to him, laying himself out for the long haul.

"Then, then, I saw his profile on Grindr and I sent him a message. And I was like, 'Hi Jeremy.' And he was like, 'um, who are you?'" Frank laughed. "I was like, let me tell you a story and I told him about all of the stupid things that he said and he was like, 'oh my god, I don't remember any of that.' So I immediately—I wasn't doing anything, so I met him for lunch and I told him about everything that happened, which he had no recollection of. And he was sweet and he was hot. So we started hanging out."

Hanging out.

They didn't hook up in Boystown. They didn't use the clubs as a site where they could build some naked intimacy between them. Rather, they connected using a different channel, following up in the sexy atmosphere of the online chat, the sexual app.

This is the kind of hybrid interaction needed to develop sexy community: connection to others through sex. Sure, people might use the app to find sexual encounters, meeting someone at their apartments, bypassing any community space at all. However, people also layer over existing places that have lost sexy flavor with a virtual space enabling that kind of connection or for following up later on an encounter they had in Boystown, turning a nonsexy encounter into a sexy one.

Not everyone sees this as "community" for two reasons. First, it's important to distinguish what people are trying to get out of such connections. While people can be together in a space, and those people might be racially diverse people, reveling in the naked intimacy in the space, if that space doesn't connect to a social space, creating a hybrid, then it can't truly be a sexy community. That is, sometimes people are just looking to fuck.

Ginger described moments like this. "I'm a lot more controlling," he said of his perspective on hooking up. "And I'm also okay not getting it. So it's like, if it doesn't happen, I'm fine."

I nodded.

"But I'd rather get, kind of, more of an experience that I want out of it," he said. "Because when I first started hooking up online, that's what I was doing. All these one-on-one experiences that would make me feel really shitty about myself. Or like I did too much or I went too far or we did have the boyfriend experience. And I was like, 'I hope he's going to call in the morning.' And he would spend the night and that was it. There was no investment anything more than it was to be fucked."

He emphasized the last word, "fucked," with a long hard *K* and a hint of malice. "And I think being a bottom—and I'm really just a bottom. Not like a vers bottom. And I've had a discussion with my friends a lot that they, you know, I think when most guys are horny who are versatile or tops, they're just looking for something to fuck. So I recognize in that moment, I'm just a hole for them to fuck."

He said smiling. "I'm a cute hole." He laughed and then grew serious. "But I'm a hole for them to fuck, right? So I'm like, well, I'm going to be extra cautious for how I'm going to allow that experience to happen for myself."

Ginger controls the online experience, knowing that some people are not looking for connection, just looking to fuck, with the long hard *K* and the slight malice. However, sex can be important beyond the physical act and the moment of orgasm; sex can connect even when the other person is just a hole, but only if they continue to connect through ritualized interaction.

Frank, for instance, wakes up every morning and checks his Grindr and Scruff. Logging on, he can see if anyone messaged him from the previous night after he went to bed. He can carry on the conversation. He can message a "good morning" to someone he has been talking to. He can message someone with whom he's been flirting or say hello to a fuck buddy with whom he has both a sexual and friendship relationship through the app.

He carries these conversations, this community, with him into the straight world. Standing in line at Starbucks, he can see who is around him. Eyeing the person across the room, he tells me, he might not know if the person is gay. If that person is on Grindr, then he knows. He can say hello. He can flirt with him. He can invite him to fuck in the bathroom if he wanted to, because he has a back channel. He has the Hole he can carry around with him in his pocket. The gay bar might not be sexy anymore, filled with straight women and turned into a tourist trap, but he downloaded a gay bar into his phone.

However, some still don't see this as community for a second reason. Sexy spaces must include a social element, but they also must be place based to generate a community. They can't remain solely online without social feedback. Someone must be able to observe.

Mark Nott wrote an essay on finding community through Grindr for the Chicago-based *In Our Words* queer blog, in which he discusses his own ritual of going on Grindr through the day.[8] A commenter with the screen name Insecure 'Mo responded:

> Is it really community if all it does is perpetuate a bunch of directionless small talk? Speaking from personal experience, there's almost always a snub from one side or the other when randomly confronted with a Grindr acquaintance (the type mentioned in your ritual) in real life. You recognize him. He recognizes you, but god forbid either of you acknowledge the fact that you actually seem to have something in common; the fact that you met on Grindr precludes that.
>
> The ritual you speak of? It's a ritual of avoidance, a knee-jerk reaction to every not-so-subtle averted glance while actually trying to connect with someone in the real world. Grindr is a pseudo-community at best, and in fact the ONLY thing that legitimizes it is the "homonormative" predilection of frequent, random sex. Without it, you've got Facebook chat with a bunch of insecure'mo's.[9]

One of the difficulties of ethnography is making sense of these disagreements. Mark Nott, and many of the participants in my study, like Frank, Ginger, and others, have found friends in the community of Grindr. I've seen people meet in Boystown clubs after using their phones to find sexually interested people in their immediate vicinity. Insecure 'Mo disagrees. In qualitative methodology, we call this a "disconfirming case," a situation in which something is wrong with the emerging theory.

Insecure 'Mo saying Grindr doesn't have community doesn't prove it doesn't, any more than Mark Nott saying that there is community proves it does have it. People say a lot of things. However, an ethnographer can't discount disconfirmation. No outliers exist in ethnography. Why might Insecure 'Mo feel this way?

This person has engaged in many of the same behaviors: going on Grindr, having directionless small talk that may or not lead to more personal discussions, the glimmer of sexual possibility in the subtext. Why does the same chain of events produce different responses? Why hasn't it produced naked intimacy, sexual kinship, and, ultimately, sexy community for this person?

Without any more information on Insecure 'Mo, that's hard to say. However, I have heard responses like these before from people of color.

Although this may be a next direction of sexy community, people of color routinely report that they receive explicit discrimination and prejudice in these online spaces, not the kind of intimate connection beyond mere contact that I see in sexy community.[10]

Why? After all, I argued that the sexual realm is an "augmented reality." The Internet is not some special space that is devoid of racism. The Internet has the same kind of racism that the rest of our everyday lives have. People don't treat the online and offline differently.

However, the different modes of interaction enable different interactional expressions. These spaces are different social structures. Online, you interact one on one with the people you are talking with. Offline in a bar, you may be talking to only one person, but you are in the context of observation by others. Similarly, the written versus verbal modes of community enable different contexts for conversation. For instance, online profiles encourage people to construct a perfect partner, which people use to list preferred attributes, "preferences" that they do not necessarily see as racist, even when race is listed.[11]

Participants believe that one of the reasons people are willing to be so explicit about their "preferences"—the most common way to code racism— online is because the social mores of Internet interaction are still forming.[12] People still believe the Internet affords them a degree of anonymity to their interactions, even when photos and other identifying text is present.

Sam, a biracial Black gay man, described it to me this way: "Well, I think that in real life if somebody approaches you at a bar and starts talking to you, even if in the back of your head you're thinking that's not going to happen, you may end up having a conversation, being a civil human being."

He paused, then laughed, "I mean, I really haven't seen somebody come up and be like 'Oh sorry you're Asian!' and walk away. Everyone around you would look at you like, 'Oh my god that guy is such a big asshole.'"

The face-to-face interaction today has social mores against explicit racist statements. Sam went on, though, to say that, "when it's just pressing buttons in your darkened bedroom, you can get away with this shit." Online interaction, in other words, doesn't have those same rules.

However, it would be a mistake to think one has to declare a racist sentiment explicitly for it to matter. Samir, an Indian American gay man in his late twenties, points out the absurdity of that argument, "Sure, the Internet gives you more anonymity so you can be an asshole. But I think in a club, you can still be an asshole to someone. I know that many of myself and brown friends and Black friends feel invisible. And that is sexual racism."

He sighed, "You don't need to be told I'm not into brown people to know you're not into brown people."

The kind of connection happening for many people—especially when they are "just looking to fuck," as Ginger put it—is a kind of mere contact. A furtive fuck where no one else can see you doesn't create naked intimacy in the same way as the hookup cultures of Men's Room or the late-night cruising at a bar event, such as Juicy.

The racial consequences of sexy community—sexy community itself—doesn't work if people don't observe you doing it. If you can keep a bifurcated life, sexualizing Black men in private while in public not acknowledging their existence, then you haven't had any kind of connection, you haven't been in a moment of collective effervescence. When some place is filled with observers, giving positive feedback, in a moment when they are experiencing the naked intimacy of feeling more than themselves, then that will result in something stronger than mere contact. Going online and finding a hookup in your darkened room is an individualized meat market, filtered to your current pornographic interests, not a sexy community.

However, these online apps play an important role in building sexy community when they are tied to physical spaces, when people use them to augment their realities, meeting physically through the app, following up with people that they've already met, or layering over the straight world with the sexiness they used to only be able to get in the gay bar. When they use them, that is, to create hybrid spaces. As carnal sociology would predict, the physical body facilitates emotional engagement. Interaction alone doesn't produce sexy community.

■　■　■

Not.

Places like Steamworks, the gay bathhouse in Boystown, although obviously sexually oriented, don't necessarily have sexy community because they are built around a code of silence. As is the case online, the anonymity of offline cruising can't build a sexy community without also including a hybrid space for people to talk.

Although I include discussion of my own sexuality, I didn't want this book to become an erotic novel, a voyeuristic look at the exploits of a gay man out in Boystown. I was unsure about fieldwork at a bathhouse, much less talking about my own experience there. After talking with another gay sociologist, I decided I would use Steamworks's less prominent feature: the gym.

Steamworks purports to be a "sauna and gym." Judging by online reviews from Yelp and Gaycities.com, it isn't uncommon to go to Steamworks to only use the gym, even if I wouldn't find anyone in my three years of fieldwork that actually admitted to using Steamworks for this purpose. Steamworks even sells "gym-rat" packs of tickets for shorter periods of time than the typical locker rental. For eighty dollars—they were on special in January of 2012 because of New Year's resolutions—a man could buy a pack of twelve coupons, which would grant two hours access to a locker. Looking over their website, I found out that on Tuesdays, as a student at the time, I could get a free membership and five dollars off a locker rental, a marketing ploy to get more young people to come use the facilities on what otherwise would be a slow night.

For the uninitiated, most bathhouses are able to host sexual activities by being private health clubs. Anyone—read, any man—is eligible to join for a cheap monthly fee, five dollars for a month or twenty dollars for six months. Then, you pay per use of the club's facilities.

The cheapest level is a locker rental. For slightly more, you can get a "standard" room with a twin bed on a pallet covered in a plastic sheet, making cleaning the room between guests easy. Larger rooms, or rooms with extra equipment like sex slings, cost even more. Although people don't typically stay for the full time, rentals are for eight hours each. The two-hour gym-rat rental is much shorter in comparison.

After finishing my field notes on the previous night, around 5:30 P.M., I walked over to go work out. When I left the house earlier that day, I brought a pair of gym shorts. As soon as I put my laptop into my bag when leaving Caribou Coffee, seeing my shorts served as a reminder that I needed to get this done, despite my nerves.

I had never been to a bathhouse before. My knowledge up until that day had been entirely theoretical. I knew only about their history within the gay community from my studies, my friends, and, frankly, my fantasies.

I knew about their growth from places where men would gather to literally bathe, use the sauna, and soak, into places where men would cruise for sex. I knew about their fall from grace, no longer popular venues due to that intertwined sense of sexual shame and fear of disease that arose with HIV/AIDS. Many had been shut down, or boycotted, as vectors of disease. I knew that some, like Steamworks, clung on, popular among the older crowd, the sexually libertine, travelers, and, on holidays, everyone else.

Outside of select groups—namely, the poz guys, whose disease puts them on the outside of the charmed circle already—openness about going to Steamworks was limited. It is a sex club in a culture of sexual shame.[13]

Figure 6.2. Steamworks Baths

That same sexual shame created the nervousness I was experiencing on my first trip. It almost got the best of me.

Steamworks is about three blocks from the Caribou Coffee on Halsted on the same side of the street. Yet I crossed to the other side so that I could look at the place as I walked by before I approached.

Steamworks is located in a fairly nondescript building. There is no sign, just two inset doors facing sideways into a steely metal exterior. There are no real windows, only frosted glass. Two large flags list the building number. Those that frequent Boystown know the building and its purpose.

I worried: Would someone see me walking in? Would they think I was a sex maniac? Would a future participant in my ethnography see me walking into the bathhouse? Would they have a negative impression of me later when we met?[14]

It is impossible to tell the thoughts of others. I can't read minds. However, I can tell that sexual shame and fear run through the heads of others based on their actions.

People always get a kick out of my pantomime of someone walking into Steamworks. A man will be walking down the street as though he is a man on a mission, someone important with places to be. Looking straight ahead and walking fast, full of purpose, he will be marching by Steamworks as though he is on the way to the gym, work, or the pet store just down the street. Then, suddenly, he will dart sideways, scrambling to get out of view inside the building.

With those thoughts of sexual shame running through my head, I walked right by the door the first time. At first, I was going to walk home. I started making rationalizations: Did I really need experiential data from Steamworks? Could I get that information from interviews? Must an ethnographer experience everything?

Two blocks away from Steamworks along Halsted toward home, I turned down a side street. I needed to clear my head and give myself a dose of self-reflection. Why was I so resistant to going in?

Partly because of research worries, but also because of my own reactions as a gay man. I'd never participated in this part of gay life. I didn't know what awaited behind those steely doors with their frosted windows. Was it going to be a raunchy *Queer as Folk* orgy on the inside, men climbing over each other, their bodies writhing together to electronic music? Or was it what I imagined to be the stately bathhouse interactions that Truman Capote or Michel Foucault engaged in? Would I mess up, by not knowing the rules? Would I look like I was on safari?[15]

I walked all the way down a side street, reaching the train tracks before turning and following Clark Street down to Belmont again. I turned on Belmont, nearly at Halsted Street again. I took a left at Spin, walked past the Fitness Formula Club gym, and...

...walked right past Steamworks again.

My nervousness infuriated me. An ethnographer should be a little bit uncomfortable. That's how you know that you are doing your job correctly. My brain wanted me to get a firsthand account of the place, but my gut felt butterflies at the prospect.

I circled around one more time, approached the door, and ducked in.

The corridor was dark. Dim. Dusky. Immediately one is faced with a turn into a long hallway meant to help prevent a line from forming out the door. No one was present when I arrived, no line.

I walked down the hall into the opening on my left that was, by comparison, flooded with light: the membership desk. Behind glass, two cashiers stood waiting in front of a large colorful sign listing the rental prices. A young Black man stood at the counter being checked in by a young Latino man with a short-cropped beard and a beanie. I walked up, pulled out my student ID, my driver's license, and my credit card.

"Can I get a gym-rat twelve pack?"

The cashier was a tall, skinny white man who looked about my own age. His face was covered in the patchy stubble of someone who hadn't shaved for a few days but can't produce a full beard. Perhaps I exuded nervousness or seemed like I didn't belong, or maybe because the gym membership is rarely bought, but he looked surprised. He claimed he was new to their system, and looking confused, took the materials I offered and processed my membership.

"I will keep your valuables in a lockbox behind the counter. Your locker will be on the third floor next to the gym. Your rental lasts for two hours, but you can come down and give us another coupon if you'd like to stay longer," he explained.

As he talked, two more people came in and were processed by the other cashier. I realized I had broken an unstated rule. I had walked up immediately. Both of these men waited around the corner to be called—"Approach!"— before coming into the light to be processed. They furtively looked my way as they walked up to the membership counter. The first was a middle-aged Latino man with slicked-back, short-cropped hair. The second was a heavy, older, African American man. His trench coat, pressed collared shirt, and slacks said middle-class office job, maybe a manager or banker. Soon, none of us would be able to tell.

Finished with my membership card, the cashier instructed me to sign it and handed me the key, a towel, and a "welcome pack" of condoms and lube. Then he buzzed me through the main door, which they keep locked to deny entry to people who they do not want entering the club.[16]

I would have until 8:15 P.M.

I plunged back into the dusky dimness. I followed the cashier's instructions to find my locker. I turned right, passing the first-floor locker room immediately on my left as I walked down the hall past the big screen TV, the entrance to the sauna, and up the stairs near the end of the hall. At the base of the stairs were two vending machines, one with lube and another with soft drinks and protein shakes.

I climbed the stairs. On the second floor, I saw an olive-skinned man in his midthirties clad only in a towel. He glanced my way before heading down another hall. I walked up to the third floor, where I found the gym, a small locker room, an open shower area, and two computers sitting on desks.

Surprisingly, working out in Steamworks was a pleasure. Unlike most gyms, there wasn't anyone else competing for the equipment. I was probably at greater risk of killing myself without a spotter, but I worked out there several more times.

The space is sexual, not sexy. There are parts of the building where sex is not taking place. Namely, the front space near the vending machines, which has couches and TVs for people to rest. You may see one or two people chatting, but most are sitting in silence, checking out the people that walk by, cruising in small glances.

Even the nakedness doesn't produce the same erotic intimacy as places like the Hole that contain sexy community. That first time, after I finished working out in the gym, I took a shower in the nearby open shower. Two people stopped while walking by, standing, staring while I lathered up. The encounter was uncomfortable, not because I was unnerved by their gaze, but because the way they looked at me seemed tentative yet possessive.

That doesn't mean that no community exists at Steamworks. As dramatized in *Steamworks: The Musical*, an uproarious production that Austin and I went to on our second date, regular attendees do recognize one another and sometimes talk. Naked intimacy still exists in such places. However, the strict differentiation of space, the setting aside of almost all space for sexual contact, and the context of cruising mean these interactions are the exception.

You have to bring the community with you.

For instance, Austin and I went with a few of the poz guys over Market Days, one of the gay high holy days of summer in Chicago. We met Brandon, Karl, and Matt for a few drinks beforehand at the Lucky Horseshoe Lounge, avoiding the clubs in the main section of Boystown, which were overrun with Market Days revelers coming in off the streets. The Shoe was packed.

Sick of battling for breathing space, Karl turned to the rest of us after a single drink and said, "Ready? I'm ready."

Brandon, Karl's boyfriend, had only been to Steamworks for the first time a few weeks before. He, too, seemed eager to get there.

Steamworks is only a block away from Lucky Horseshoe. Unfortunately, Halsted Street was closed at Belmont, the police pushing people out of the street and into the intersection, supposedly for street cleaning after Market Days. A likelier explanation: they wished the large group of Black people gathered would get lost. The police had closed that section of the street in the hope that the crowd would leave the neighborhood for other pastures.

Most, like us, instead walked one street over to Clark, circled around on Buckingham, and approached Halsted from the side street. Slipping past a barrier—many people were still on the street—we could see the police at the corner of Halsted and Belmont preventing others from coming in.

The line at Steamworks spilled out the door. No surreptitious slinking in this time. A midtwenties white guy, in flannel shirt and black-rimmed glasses, stood against the bike rack outside smoking. As we waited in line, Karl struck up a conversation with him.

When we were almost at the entrance, Karl turned to him and said, "I'll catch you inside."

"I'd follow that ass anywhere," he replied.

Most of the men standing in line inside were silent, but pockets of laughter erupted intermittently among people there with their friends.

A half hour later, after waiting in line to get lockers, since they were the only rental available on such a popular night, the four of us, minus Matt, went to go get changed in the first-floor lockers. Matt, as was a habit of his, had disappeared as soon as we walked in the door, although I would spy him periodically through the night as we walked by each other, occasionally stopping to chat a bit about how things were going on either of our ends.

While each of us went off on our own at times—some, like Matt, for longer periods of time than others—we did gather together to sit in the hot tub and chat, make terrible jokes about the people around us like catty queens, and play a bit of grab ass underneath the water.

Places like Steamworks aren't conducive to the kind of discussion we were having; they aren't designed for it. First, much of the club is lit in the low twilight that, while bright enough once your eyes adjust, is meant to inspire cruising.

Second, most of its spaces are designed for sex, not talking. The only real space that might qualify as a hybrid space would be the front lounge near the lockers, where people tired from the action, but without a room of their own, often retire to watch TV on the big screen, while also watching the new people walking into the baths. Even this space, though, doesn't have much talking because of the low tones culturally prescribed.

If you don't believe me, and you have some kind of access to the space, go try to talk to someone. Be your own ethnographer.

Most of you, though, don't have the kinds of identities that would grant access—or even desire—to go to Steamworks. So, try this comparison experiment. By yourself, ride a city bus. Sit next to someone and try to talk to them. It's awkward! You may be in a public space. There may be plenty of people around, but the social rules are different. Conversation between people who know each other is fine but frowned upon between strangers. Steamworks is this kind of public space. While for some people the idea of a place where people have sex that also has the public social mores of a bus or other public space might seem strange, consider the history of bathhouses: public spaces transformed by closeted men coming to have sex.[17]

While bathhouses, like Steamworks, are obviously sexually oriented, they don't have sexy community in them because they are built around silence. Some people build some community there, or bring some community with them, but the anonymity of cruising can't build the kind of connection that occurs outside of these spaces when they have hybrid areas.

■　■　■

New, now, next, not. Properties of a concept: how does it develop, what does it look like now, where is it going, where is it not?

Sexy community is network of people, bound together through sexual kinship, connected to a hybrid erotic space where they experience moments of naked intimacy. These spaces are racially diverse because they connect people beyond mere contact.

These sites of sexy community are wider than families of choice. In Marcus's home, there were people connected to the community that were not considered bound tightly enough to be in his family. You might not know everyone in your community, but you know your family.

Sexy communities don't have to involve people having sex in the space, although many do. When I hung out with JJ and his friends at Juicy, the hooking up that occurred at the end of the night had the erotic possibility that allowed for sexy community, making the space diverse with many kinds of people outside of the ethnic group the night was meant for.

Having explicit sex doesn't make a community sexy. The space must also be social. Without the hybrid space, a community can't form. In a place like Steamworks, although people are having sex, there isn't community.

Sexy communities, although queer, aren't all BDSM leather-bound sexually stigmatized spaces. Sexy community forms because it is separate, a space set aside from others. Made sexy through segregation from everyday life. For the boat people, that separation happens through access, the periphery of class. The hookup joints are on the periphery of the night, with flashes of sexuality just before the lights turn on at closing time.

Similarly, sexy communities can be on the periphery of the physical world. Sexy communities don't have to be rooted in physical locations, although many are. Such apps as Grindr and Scruff enable people to carry communities with them. They have to be tied to physical spaces, though, have to become place-based online communities.

Many of these spaces won't always be sexy communities, just as Juicy only developed briefly. Places disappear. Even the Hole won't be the site of sexy community forever.

"These places have come and gone," Marcus told me over red wine on his front porch, on a night when Austin and I came over to have dinner. He had recently stepped down as the guard of the Hole. "It is time to move on for me. Let some younger people have it."

In his midfifties, he's seen many of the leather, BDSM, and radical sex spaces transform over the years. Cell Block, for instance, used to have a more explicit backroom before new owners came in and shuttered it, part of the assimilation of Boystown's spaces.

Or as Marcus put it: "And then they came in. They weren't leather people so they painted it tan and turned it into Bennigan's."

Like a loveless marriage, without the sex, the attraction faded. As people found other spaces that would give them the ritual thrill, they stopped going as often as they used to.

Similarly, after the Hole closed briefly in 2013, Jackhammer's attendance became more staccato. Men's Room parties syphoned off some of the customers in its absence; Cell Block experienced a bit of a resurgence; and Touché, next door, gobbled up a few of the people coming late night to play in the back.

Similarly, the hookup joints are having a hard time maintaining that erotic possibility in the face of those on safari and makeovers meant to render them more attractive to those kinds of clientele.

New spaces also sometimes emerge, though you can never tell if they will stick around, opening and closing again quickly. Near the end of writing this book, Manhole went from being a theme night at Hydrate to its own club again, to closing completely.

As the places shift, new spaces opening, old places gentrifying and assimilating, the people move between them. As things have changed, assimilation hasn't destroyed community, it has shifted it, split it from occurring only in one space, where everyone is pushed together. Queers carry with them their community connected through sex, tinged with the lingering energy of the spirit of the night.

MIDNIGHT

The night teaches us about the day. The night has a spirit, its own rules breaking with those of the day. The workaday world gives way to the terror of darkness, the fright of what exists around the corner, but also the carnival, bright lights, and shady characters. With the veil drawn over the world, we feel as though we release our true selves, the parts that we keep hidden from employers and family. We revel in, or recapture, our youth, the spirit of the night sacrificed on the altar of adulthood.

Queer culture embodies the night. It's scary. It breaks with the traditional, with the family that we came from, and with the rules of respectability. Queers are dangerous. To be queer is dangerous. Breaking the rules has consequences. To be separate is to be alone, apart, free from stricture but also from support.

Queers built that support for themselves. We spread the indignity of sex around. Uncrowned, we connected, not merely, but truly. We became gay and queer at once, shared spaces indistinguishable.

Perhaps not anymore. The spirit of the night lives in shadow, on the periphery of the everyday world: in the darkest hours, in the raunchiest dirtiest spaces, in the most select venues, in those online back channels and backrooms hidden in plain sight. Can the shadow survive contact with the light?

Boystown is changing. New people arrive. New residents move in. New money changes hands. We can be one of the good gays now. Our stigma will no longer protect us.

How little it protected us then.

I want to live in twilight. I want the legitimacy of the day, and the spirit of the night. I want to romance the shadow, but the light corrupts. Boystown is fracturing; businesses fracking the depths of queer culture to sell to the surface dwellers.

I fear the consequences, but welcome the dawn.

7

Gay Disneyland

David, a Black gay man in his midforties, stared at me across the table at Starbucks in Rogers Park. He looked a bit dumbfounded at my question.

"The bars have changed in the last ten years," he said. "More of a themed—"

He stopped. "It's sort of like Disney World or Disneyland. Every bar has a theme to it."

■ ■ ■

"Gays are great at gentrifying areas." Ginger, a multiracial Latino man in his midtwenties told me over tea. "That is, white gay men, sprinkle them anywhere. They're like fleas. They get in, they transform it. Soon you get flowering plants and brunches. Cultural events. And then all of a sudden, the yuppies move in. And then all of sudden it's not a gay area anymore. And I think Boystown is that place where—this is not even from me, there's a lot of queer folks who don't feel like it's their community anymore."

He looked at me dead in the eye.

"Boystown is wilting. And there are actually not—it's become so ridiculous that there's not a lot of the gays with money living there anymore. They're moving up. You've got to start moving up more. Because it's not—"

He paused to breathe, starting again more slowly. "It's a tourist trap, in a way. It's like a fun Disneyland park. That's what I like to think of it as. And I think that there's a lot of hope given into it with young people who are disenfranchised and who want a space to grow."

■ ■ ■

I had talked with Ryan, a young activist, about those young people before.

"Why don't we start at the beginning," I asked. "What, in terms of Take Back Boystown, what do you know about that story?"

"To me, Take Back Boystown is part of something that was going on way before summer," he said.

"Great, let's start there."

"I—" he paused before even starting. "Like Boystown," he hesitated, as though to preface his critiques. "There's been a battle in Boystown over property. They are trying to make Boystown this sort of gay tourist—like Disneyland. Historically, the LGBT community has had strong, you know we've had, there's been periods where we've had a strong sense of self-community care. We've had Howard Brown. We've had the Broadway Youth Center. We have the Center on Halsted. The Take Back Boystown stabbing was a way to vilify those services. Because those services bring in people that are seen as undesirable by real estate developers and business owners. If they could eradicate them—eradicate those services from the neighborhood— that would be a gain for them."

■ ■ ■

Nearly everyone I talked to about Boystown would at some point, unprompted, compare Boystown to a theme park, a gay Disneyland. Assimilation transforms gayborhoods. Boystown has become a tourist attraction, a destination. Boystown is a place for people to visit and consume, rather than live. Boystown is like a section of Epcot in which you can eat gay foods, drink gay drinks, wear gay clothes, all of which are available for purchase in the gift shop.

"It's kind of everything that you would want if you were going to visit a gay neighborhood somewhere," Jackson, a Black gay man in his midtwenties, told me over coffee at Dollop Coffee in Uptown. "There are like fifteen clubs and everyone is looking adorable. People are roaming in groups, looking good. It's like, you know, a TV gay neighborhood."

Boystown is a fun night out drinking before you leave the fantasy of fabulousness to go home to the real world. Boystown isn't a place where you live, or a place where gay men to go to meet other men to date, to dance, to fuck. Boystown is a neighborhood to consume. To Adam, it's a mall.

"I was long out of high school before I realized that people actually lived in Schaumburg [a Chicago suburb] and Schaumburg wasn't just a place to put Woodfield mall." Adam said.

"You mean there is more than an IKEA there?" I said.

"Right? Boystown has that kind of mystique now. You come to the mall when you want to go shopping, and when it is time to go home, you get in your car and go home, but there's no need to live at the mall." Adam said.

As a real estate agent, Adam knew quite a bit about the changes to the

Figure 7.1. Outside Roscoe's bar

neighborhood over the last thirty years. He lived through them. Now, he made his living by knowing the right spot in the city to suggest. We were having coffee at New Modern Grill, a greasy-spoon diner at the corner of Halsted and Belmont.[1] Adam is a big man with a big personality. He filled the side of the booth opposite me, looming over me, telling me in a booming voice about the changes to the neighborhood.

New Modern Grill looked neither. It looked as though it had lived since the neighborhood was straight. The aged menu was displayed with black letters on a yellowed, lighted background, prices in red. The old cook shuffled behind the counter in a stained once-white apron. The waitress in gray sweatpants and a long blue T-shirt that fell to her knees wagged the coffee pot at us, but we waved her off.

"Yeah, I'm good. I'm feeling a little jittery. So, that's a good sign," he said.

Then, with little additional prompting, Adam continued the story of Boystown. "Lakeview [the designated community zone containing Boystown], and I know this demographic from being a realtor, the gay and lesbian population continues to decline in Lakeview, but unlike in past situations where people have been priced out, people have been simply choosing to move away. Whether it's better prices, or more space, or they want to raise a family, which is something that they didn't necessarily have gay man and women actively and openly doing so much. There isn't really a reason to live in Lakeview for safety or comfort levels. There's no real reason to feel more safe in

Lakeview than, let's say, Lincoln Park, Edgewater, or any other middle- and upper-middle-class area in Chicago. There's no real reason to live in the gay ghetto."

What is the point of a gayborhood? Gayborhoods were once about safety. A place to escape to, away from the hateful eyes of the rest of society. A place for, primarily men, to live out an alternative life, unlike their fathers and brothers who got married and had children. For straight people, a gayborhood was also a corral, containing the aberrants and their sexual deviance from infecting (somewhat literally) the rest of society.

According to Adam's explanation, we don't need Boystown anymore. Accepted in straight society, gay men don't need to live in the ghetto. We've assimilated. Gay men can live anywhere, only returning to the gayborhood for fun. Amin Ghaziani, in *There Goes the Gayborhood*, argues that the flight away from gay neighborhoods represents a postgay era for American society. We've won, now we can live anywhere.

Not everyone wants to live in Disneyland, after all, as much as you may have wanted to as a child. As Adam says, there are many reasons queer people might not live in Boystown today. Many queer people do not live in Boystown for two interconnected reasons. First, while Adam's realty business may not work with them, Boystown is too expensive for many queer people. Second, its party atmosphere is not conducive to raising a family. Thus, Boystown occupies a youthful stage in the lives of some gay men—a theme park to party in before settling down, growing up, and moving to Andersonville, or what Ghaziani calls "Mandersonville."

"I would hate to live in Boystown." Raazia, an Indian American queer woman in her late thirties, told me.

"Why?" I asked, but I already knew the answer, from other participants. "Sometimes I ask stupid questions just to get it on tape."

"Because it's neurotic," she said. "It's absolutely noisy, it's neurotic and it's mostly party people in their twenties, barfing in the alley behind there. And I'm beyond that. I never found that attractive. And I think that it's also very expensive. I think price is a huge factor. It's too expensive for people even to rent. So really most of the people who can afford it, right, either you live in a really tiny Podunk apartment there or you happen to be somebody who's relatively well off, goes to DePaul, whose parents can afford to subsidize your rent."

Now the only people who can afford to live in Boystown are DePaul students, upper-class gay men, and straight families. Boystown underwent what sociologist Japonica Brown-Saracino calls "late-stage gentrification."[2]

Gentrification, she argues, has two phases, making up the life cycle of a neighborhood. The first phase, early gentrification, is more recognizable, what many of us think of as gentrification, full stop. Gay men, artists, bohemians, hipsters, and other white people with few economic resources but a lot of cultural capital move into an area predominately home to poor people of color. Gradually, the character of the neighborhood changes. Instead of being known as dangerous, it is hip. Prices rise. The neighborhood's previous residents can no longer afford to live there and move to a different cheaper, poorer area of the city. Over time, this results in areas of concentrated poverty, neighborhoods so Black or Latino that no white people will move into them.[3]

The gentrified neighborhood now isn't a "Black neighborhood" or a "Spanish neighborhood." White people live there. Without the dangerous specter of color haunting the neighborhood's reputation, more white people move to the area, except this time they have more money. These people begin to "improve" the neighborhood, turning it into a hotspot of activity. Eventually, prices have risen so much that the early adopters—the artists and bohemians and gay men—can no longer afford to live there. Privileged upper-class white people move into the area, and the cycle begins again with a new neighborhood. This less-discussed second wave of displacement is late-stage gentrification.

Boystown initially followed this pattern. In the late 1970s and early 1980s, queer people began coming north into the area known then as New Town, a Puerto Rican neighborhood, from areas in Lincoln Park and Old Town. Some groups that still exist in Boystown from this time make reference to the area as New Town, such as the LGBT writers group the New Town Writers, the Belmont Alcoholics Anonymous group known as New Town Alano Club, or the dry cleaners on Broadway and Cornelia, New Town Cleaners.

"The location of Boystown has changed. Traveled north," Adam informed me.

"Tell me a bit about that then." He didn't need a lot of coaxing for the history to spill out.

"A lot of gay migration, gentrification. Seriously, if you look at the nicer, nicer areas of Chicago that have gentrified over the years and become hotspots, you'll look at the gay migration of Chicago.

"When I first started making a foray out into the world, the gay area was moving from Hubbard and State area to what was then called New Town. And New Town was east and south Lakeview—Lakeview and Lincoln Park."

"So right on the northern edge of Lincoln Park?" I asked.

"Right, but on the Diversey side. But as that became more expensive..." He trailed off and switched directions. "Lincoln Park was initially down there, State and Hubbard—that area. A lot of us lived there but more so because we worked there. You know that was a little funky, nasty part of the Loop that nobody went to so it was safe to open gay bars where people would never look to find anyone because nobody went there."

That part of Chicago, known now as the River North area, still bears the mark of those times. Two holdouts, Downtown Bar and Second Story Bar, survive because of the revitalization of the area, mostly as a result of business people going there after work and also travelers. Today, River North is one of the most expensive, touristy parts of Chicago.

That touristy spirit, though, also has been creeping north. Adam continued: "And this goes way before the eighties, into the sixties and seventies before, you know, I was old enough to go out or anything, but Lincoln Park was kind of a ghetto."

"Mm hmm" I agreed. "Ain't a ghetto anymore."

"Right! There were really terrific houses and cheap stuff that nobody wanted to live near really. Gays moved in and started gentrifying. Other people followed and priced themselves out of the market and started to move north into what is now Boystown."

As people moved, Adam explained, the bars began to follow them.

"The bars south of Diversey closed as things got more expensive and tastes changed.[4] New bars, things moved from Broadway, south of Diversey to north of Diversey. Late seventies and early eighties, you had Christopher Street. You had Little Jim's there. You had Men's Room."

As these bars began to materialize, Boystown's street culture began to take hold. While some richer gay men would jump into a cab as soon as they left the bars, many of the older gay men I talked with told me about how they would walk in groups between the gay bars that began popping up along Halsted Street because they felt unsafe in what they described as a homophobic area. These jaunts developed into a street culture of hanging out on the street, walking up and down Halsted, that continues to this day among Black and Latino queer and trans youth, who congregate along the streets at night.

When the millennium turned, Boystown entered late-stage gentrification as straight people began moving into the area. George, a white gay man in his late thirties, told me that he moved back to Boystown, after being away since the early 2000s, "because it was a fun place to hang out and to fuck. But my husband and I were looking, and we're like 'Oh my god. It's become fucking Lincoln Park!' It's the demographic that I do not want. You know? It's not the neighborhood that it was ten years ago. It's less gay. It's less diverse. It's more of a tourist's stop."

George explained that, twenty years ago, a bar owner would have "all seventy-five of their staff lived in the neighborhood and would walk to work. And then today, one of seventy-five lives in the neighborhood, because the other seventy-four can't afford it because rent's gone up.

"I mean, you walk around the neighborhood and see the shops that are here now and see the people who are shopping here now. It's not what I imagine a typically gay neighborhood to be. It's not the place for . . . the transients to come in. It's not the place for students to live. It's not the place for..." George paused to consider his words.

"Um, uh." He sputtered, unsure how to put it. "a more mixed atmosphere. You know?"

I did know. George was lamenting a gay neighborhood, perhaps a neighborhood that never truly existed, that was more mixed. A neighborhood that he would see out in the bars in the late nineties when he had last lived there. A neighborhood in which there were many different classes and colors of gay men pushed together against the rest of Chicago.

"I'm fine with straight people living in the neighborhood but not... but I also want like, a significant gay presence," George explained. "And there still is, but I feel like the gay presence, I don't know, but I feel like a lot of the gay presence leaves when the bars close. You know?"

"Mmm." I did know.

I lived out on the edge of Boystown at the time, at Irving Park and Pine Grove. Barely in the neighborhood, people would tell me. The apartment was the closest I could get on my graduate student salary, working remotely on a project at the University of Wisconsin–Madison. Even then, I mostly slept on my couch. I rented out the bedroom on Airbnb to afford the rent.[5]

I would walk into Boystown proper each day to write, or do fieldwork, or conduct interviews, like this one with George at the Caribou Coffee on Halsted Street across from Hydrate and Little Jim's. The neighborhood had a completely different vibe during the day than at night, when people from all across Chicago would begin to trickle into the neighborhood to party at the bars.

During the day, George went on to explain, "it's a lot more baby carriages and strollers than it used to be. And it's not necessarily the gays with baby carriers. They all live in Andersonville or out in the burbs."

These are the straight families who now come to community meetings in Boystown to complain about the noise level from gay bars on the street. Parents telling the owner of Tulip's Toy Gallery that the sex toys displayed in the store window are inappropriate for children to see. Residents attempting to shut down the Broadway Youth Center or The Crib, a shelter for queer homeless youth. These are the straight families whose demand for amenities in the neighborhood is so high that a giant day-care facility began construction in 2014 on Halsted Street, in the space that a gay bar previously was going to be built.

The kind of gay man that used to live in Boystown—working class, service industry, students, young, white—now lives farther north in Uptown or Edgewater. Many gay men and queer people, especially white people, live in neighborhoods farther north. Ryan, a white, formerly homeless, queer college student, told me that he lived just north in Uptown because Boystown had been taken over. "There's straight people who have moved into Boystown and like, you know upper-income, heterosexual families that want to raise families in Boystown now. It's getting to the point where even, like, single gay people can't live there anymore."

We were sitting in the student union of the local college he attended. It was quiet, both of us talking in hushed tones, such that the recorder had a hard time picking up parts of the conversation. At his last statement, though, we both laughed, perhaps at the absurdity of a gay neighborhood where no gay people could live, causing the table of students nearby playing League of Legends on their computers to turn and stare at us.

"Yeah," I agreed, again more quietly.

"Like, now it's usually the people that go there don't even live in the neighborhood, they just go to the bars." Ryan said.

"Right, where would you say that people, do they just live anywhere else in the city?" I asked stupidly. I wanted to know if gay men truly did live anywhere now, or "Is there some other spot where people have been pushed to?"

"Wait, say that again?" Ryan said, confused by my artless and leading statement of the question.

I tried again. "So if they don't live, if young single gay men don't live in Boystown anymore, where have they been pushed to?"

"Oh yeah. Well there's been like a bunch of new places. I know Pilsen has a few gay clubs. Logan Square.[6] There's a lot of gay people who moved there. Um, a lot of [members of an organization I am involved with] live in Logan Square. Rent's cheaper. Um, Uptown. Of course, there's some issues of gentrification around these, too. People are constantly having to move and direct the city."

Ryan's explanation fits with Ghaziani's analysis of residential movement patterns. Even from a postgay perspective, gay men still follow a pattern. They don't spread evenly across this city. There are many places, many different neighborhoods where one could live. While white gay men might live in places other than the gayborhood, they still tended to cluster, like other white men in their income brackets, in neighborhoods like Uptown, Edgewater, Logan Square, and Lincoln Square.

However, if we expand our conception of queer people beyond the traditional white gay male residents of gayborhoods, it becomes evident that many people of color never lived in Boystown to begin with. Pauline, a Black lesbian in her late thirties, told me that when she was young, in the late 90s, she lived on the south side of Chicago. JJ and his friends, a primarily Latino group, all live on the west side of Chicago. These arrangements are typical. Chicago is a segregated city. Boystown is no exception to that. The census data, although notoriously unreliable for neighborhood demographics for Lakeview (the designated community zone containing Boystown), show that, since 1990, Lakeview has consistently been 75 percent white.

Yet, all of the queer people who have never lived in Boystown, or who newly can't afford to live in Boystown, or who can newly afford to live safely and openly in other parts of Chicago—all of these people still come to Boystown. Boystown is the gay destination. The place to party. Rather than focusing solely on neighborhood residence, we have to pay attention to a carnal sociology of pleasure: where do people go when they consume?

Because, despite being the gay party destination, Boystown should have followed the pattern and moved north. Usually, a cycle of early and late-stage gentrification would mean that Boystown wouldn't be the gay neighborhood anymore. The bars would close down and relocate to the parts of the city that young, white, queer people now reside. Others would join the bars in Uptown and Edgewater, like Crew or Big Chicks: gay businesses following gay dollars.

Boystown didn't move north, though. The gayborhood remained in Lakeview for reasons that set the stage for its transformation into a gay Disneyland. First, the city of Chicago formally declared Boystown a "gay village." This was the first officially designated gay area in any city in the United States—surprisingly so, given the perhaps greater notoriety of the Castro, West Hollywood, and Chelsea.

This designation led the city to award a beautification grant to the neighborhood, along with several neighborhoods of color: Bronzeville, Chinatown, and Humboldt Park.[7] This beautification project created public art that visibly marked the area. In Boystown, large rainbow pylons—what many call Boystown's golden phalluses—were erected. Today, these pylons hold plaques for the Chicago Gay and Lesbian Hall of Fame, honoring famous LGBTQ people throughout history. They are literal stakes in the ground, marking this as the gay area of Chicago.

Second, cementing the area as the destination and official gay area for LGBT people in Chicago, the Center on Halsted opened in 2007. This multimillion-dollar community center offers social services and community events for Chicago's queer community. Similarly, in 2013, Howard Brown Health Center, an LGBT health nonprofit, opened their second clinic in Boystown. Despite continued troubles, the Broadway Youth Center remains in Boystown as well, providing drop-in services to queer youth, many of whom are homeless. That these services were put in this neighborhood—rather than opening smaller centers situated throughout the city as was once proposed when the Center on Halsted opened—marks Boystown as the gay destination of Chicago.[8]

As George said, "We just happen to have golden penises and the Center on Halsted that will hopefully help it [Boystown] last."

But there is one more reason: economics. The major bars and entertainment conglomerates on the street own the buildings in which they reside. Formerly, moving a gay bar was a matter of letting the lease run out in response to a rent hike. The new bar, perhaps with a different name, would open up in the cheaper gay area. Today, the business owners in the area have to figure out a way to protect their investments.

Those that do not own their buildings are far more transient, opening and closing regularly. Circuit, the Black and Latino club across from the Center on Halsted, for instance, has closed several times for brief stints over rent arguments with the building's owners. Cocktail similarly closed several times over rent arguments with its building's owners, who also owned competitor Roscoe's across the street. Eventually, Cocktail permanently shuttered, replaced with a more upscale bar called Progress. Sidetrack, Roscoe's, and Minibar all own the spaces in which their bars are located. Owning a location means they are rooted in a way that discourages moving.

Like others, when Austin and I moved in together in January 2013, we felt that we couldn't live in Boystown anymore on our student salaries. Sleeping on the couch and renting out my bedroom on Airbnb wasn't going to cut it anymore. We didn't go far though, only moving three blocks from where I used to live, across Irving Park into Buena Park, a subset of the Uptown community zone.

Did we move to Uptown because we felt that we were integrated into straight society? We may not have felt forced to live in the gayborhood, but that didn't mean that we stopped venturing to Boystown to shop, eat, and drink. People go there from all over Chicago to hang out. JJ and his friends, as I've said, live out west. Yet, they still pile in the car several times a week to come out to Boystown for an afterwork drink (or five). Frank's white queers live in Edgewater, Rogers Park, Logan Square, and Lincoln Square, but I still see them around Boystown on a regular basis, having coffee in Caribou, using the services at the Center on Halsted, or going to an event at Sidetrack.

Is that assimilation?

Assimilation is the acceptance of a minority group, the process of blending them into the mainstream. One interpretation of the residential movement away from Boystown is that American society is becoming postgay, moving beyond gay identity because of the rising acceptance of gay people. Scholars like Ghaziani rightly argue that we should look at the factors that produced gay neighborhoods initially. We should not assume that they will always exist essentially in the same form.[9]

Gayborhoods, as mentioned earlier, initially formed in the aftermath of

World War II. Port cities, such as New York City and San Francisco, experienced an influx of men separated from their families and the forms of social control exerted by them.[10] New economic forces also allowed these men to live without wives, because they could get their household labor through the marketplace instead of requiring a family homestead to support the family as an economic unit. These freedoms were specific to gay men. Lesbians and queer women were generally not similarly free to leave home or have the economic capital to support themselves without men, with Andersonville being the notable exception concerning formation of a community of queer women—and worthy of its own book.[11] These new realities meant that gay men could come together into gayborhoods.

However, there was still a general antipathy against gay men. Gay men could not live anywhere they wanted in cities. Gay bars were routinely raided by police. Those bars that could stay open did so under the protection/extortion of organized crime. The "gay ghetto" was the dirty forgotten place, as Adam the real estate agent chronicled earlier, where no one went and thus gay men could be marginally more open.

The gayborhood was born of these two forces: newfound freedom to live separately from a heterosexual family unit and a hatred forcing gay men together spatially. This separate space created separate cultures from straight society, queer cultures with different sexual values than the heterosexual majority, which relied on the subservience of women to maintain the home.

The second of these forces—bias against gays—is breaking down. Assimilation punctured the membrane of the gayborhood, sending gay men to live in other parts of the city.

In my conversation with George, he called the mixed blessing of assimilation the "classic dilemma," as in the question posed by Joshua Gamson in his famous essay, "Must Identity Movements Self-Destruct?"[12]

"It's the challenge with normalization of queer lifestyle," George said. "Well, the gay partnered lifestyle. I don't know if you can say queer lifestyle is still normalized, but um, as it becomes easier to be out in other places, there's less need for the gay..." He trailed off again, struggling with how to express a complex connection.

He began again: "It's the classic dilemma. It's, like, we want equality. We want acceptance. We want affirmation. But at the same time, as someone who is very involved in the community, and wants affinity, and is working at [community organization], it's disheartening to see. We're losing part of that because there's not as much to fight for. There's that complacency"— the postgay era, according to some scholars.[13]

If you can live anywhere, what meaning does the gayborhood have? Boystown may not be the residential neighborhood that it once was, but it remains the consumption capital of Chicago for gay people. More gay people may live in Edgewater than in Boystown, but the Pride Parade still happens in Boystown.

I argue that, instead of hastening the gayborhood's disappearance, assimilation changed Boystown and our relationship with it. Boystown's continued popularity as a gay Disneyland is evidence not that we are beyond gay identity but that gayborhoods remain extremely relevant. The gay men who frequent such neighborhoods, though, while still identifying as gay, are different from earlier populations there. Acceptance brought great things to gay people, but it cost something, too. Boystown is so accepted that everyone now comes to Boystown to have a good time, for better and for worse.

8

Becoming Gay

No one is born gay.

Whether desire is biological, or social, or a bit of both, we learn how to be gay. What do gay people like? What do gay people do? (Even how to have gay sex isn't apparent on first glance.) In *How to Be Gay*, noted sexuality scholar David Halperin remarks, "Gayness is not a state or condition. It's a mode of perception, an attitude, an ethos: in short, it is a practice."[1] More than a culture or identity, gayness is a habitus.

Barbara Streisand, Madonna, Lady Gaga. Diva worship isn't genetic. You weren't born this way, baby. It's an acquired taste. So, how do we learn to be gay? How do we learn this practice?

For many queer people in the Midwest, the answer lies in Chicago.

When I first came to Boystown in March 2011, I was about to celebrate my decade gay-iversary.[2] Through movies, friends, bars, and pornography, I had already learned how to be gay.

Boystown was something altogether different. Like many of the queer people that I have talked to, the sights and sounds of an entire neighborhood in which I was the majority were intoxicating. In Austin, Texas, where I had lived before, as long as you stayed within the city block surrounding Oilcan Harry's on Fourth Street, you felt safe. In Madison, Wisconsin, I rarely strayed from the isthmus, near the city's university. In many cities, that aura of safety extends no farther than the parking lot surrounding the tavern where everyone queer in the surrounding counties is forced under one roof.

That's if you're lucky. Many places have so much less.

From that first exhilarating visit to Boystown, I knew I wanted to move there. I had plenty of gay friends, but I wanted to move to a gay place. I wanted to live where I would see gay people, do gay things, and feel a kinship with the space.

Figure 8.1. Roscoe's bar, viewed from Progress Bar

When I finally moved to Boystown, I did what most baby gays—those new to gay culture—do when they come to Boystown: I went to Roscoe's.

"Roscoe's has a great reputation and I think people from out of town, it's kind of their first stop." Adam told me. "Even if you are coming from, like, Butt Fuck, Kansas, you've heard of Roscoe's."

Standing at the corner of Roscoe and Halsted, at the epicenter of Boystown, Roscoe's earned that reputation over the last twenty-five-plus years. The inside is murky. No matter the time of day, the dim light comes mostly from the floor-to-ceiling front windows, which seem unremarkable now but which were considered brash when Roscoe's first opened. Roscoe's was the first bar in the neighborhood to uncover their windows, when faces were an act of defiance. Most gay bars, when Boystown was developing, had covered or tinted windows to prevent patrons from being seen by passersby, the only tell that it was a gay bar being an upside-down neon beer sign in the window.

Walking past the imposing and offensive cigar "Indian" statue standing at the front, I sat down at the oblong bar and watched *RuPaul's Drag Race*. The happy-hour crowd was clearing out, so the bar was sparsely populated at 8 P.M., I took notes on my phone, laughed along to *Drag Race*, and waited for the crowd to pick up. I felt awkward by myself, nursing my whiskey ginger and waiting for someone to talk to. The bartender, a Latino man with a gray cowl sweater and a trucker cap that said "MEAT," would occasionally walk over to ask me if I was doing alright. I may have been there by myself, but no one is left alone for long.

Weekdays, gay bars give you something to do, a reason to be there. Berlin brings you in with theme nights to dance, Scarlet with college nights and fake frat boys, Cocktail with dancers. Sidetrack has videos, both comedy and musical. On this night, Roscoe's had karaoke.

Live band karaoke is the most intense. You have to know the song by heart. Holly, the hostess—large at over six feet tall even before her heels, with big hair and an even larger outsized booming voice—would hand you your lyrics on a laminated sheet and the band would play. You could barely hear yourself over the band, but the rest of the bar would hear every note.

"I'm just a girl in the world." I bellowed in the style of Gwen Stefani from No Doubt. I left the stage so full of adrenaline I had a stomachache.

"I like your energy," Holly told me, beaming, as she posed in her black pantsuit. We didn't talk much for the rest of the night. We didn't need to: telling me "come on back," her words made me feel welcome and cautiously integrated as a newcomer.

Returning to my spot at the bar, two young men were squeezed into the space at the bar beside me: Darrin and Jon, who had come from watching *Drag Race* at Spin. Darrin, a twenty-five-year-old Black gay man with a big smile and close braids, ordered a pitcher of Long Island Iced Tea, some of which Jon, a Latino gay man in his early thirties with a scraggly beard, promptly offered to me.

Two glasses later, they dragged me out into the night to see the rest of Boystown. We didn't land too far away, winding up at Sidetrack across the street. They were playing show tunes on the screens adorning every wall. Drunken queens bellowed songs I had never heard before to grainy videos of some Broadway diva from the seventies. Occasionally, a tune would come on that we knew, and the three of us were suddenly "Defying Gravity," our voices and the camaraderie carrying our feet just off the ground.

Sexual joking—all the better cover to explain away flirting gone awry—is always present. Darrin grabbed my ass. I told them both I was writing a book and asked to follow them around, but they didn't care. It's OK to get manhandled a little in these bars. It comes with the territory. It is an engagement with each other's bodies that lets us tell each other we belong.

This is how people get introduced to gay culture and integrated into the web of relationships in the bars, clubs, house parties, and coffee shops that Boystown has to offer. You head out nervous into the night, perhaps with a few friends if you're lucky, and hope to meet other gay men who can show you how it is done. They introduce you to a community, to spaces filled with expectations and culture, to moments that instill within you a gay habitus.

Throughout this book, I've discussed the sociological evidence that our spaces are important to whom we are, one of the central tenets of the Chicago school of sociology: that ecology, space, and place matter. The kinds of spaces we move through and the places we go are the community structures shaping who we are. Indeed, for the German sociologist Georg Simmel, neighborhoods are the way in which we maintain the "village mentality" of community in the face of the atomization and loneliness of the big city.[3] This is particularly true of the nightlife spaces that I've been discussing.

When sociologists discuss neighborhood effects, though, they mostly focus on the spaces in which we live. I want to shift the attention to the spaces where we consume, those places of pleasure. As Oldenburg has written, these are the "third spaces," where we connect with people outside of our home and work environments, which he identified as our first and second spaces, respectively.[4] Third spaces influence the character of a community. A place like Boystown may have fewer gay men living in it than before, but they still come from across Chicago to consume in it. To learn what our spaces teach us, we have to be attentive to these spaces of consumption. Spaces contain social psychological lessons of culture. They don't just reflect that culture, though, they teach it. We must see the culture that consumption teaches us. From these "third spaces," we learn a habitus. If Boystown changes, the habitus it teaches changes. The people we become changes.

Habitus is most associated with the French sociologist Pierre Bourdieu. He describes the connection between social class, culture, and consumption. Bourdieu's habitus comes from the class dispositions of one's youth and proceeds to form an internal logic by which one judges and makes choices of taste, of distinctions (as his book was titled), and between cultural objects. Class is more than a social position to Bourdieu. Class is an embodied status coming with unconscious rules telling us why some things are better than others. How many operas can you name? How about reality TV shows? Which one is better to watch? The answers to those questions relate very much to your social class. Habitus is your understanding of the rules by which you generate capital within a field. Put another way, habitus is our social understanding of taste, so ingrained that the distinctions feel natural to us: what do we like and dislike?

Loïc Wacquant, a student and collaborator of Bourdieu's, developed the concept further, elaborating on what he sees as the four central features of habitus.[5] First, habitus is acquired. No one is born with a habitus. It must be learned over time. Second, habitus is beneath the level of consciousness. Habitus is made up of the mental structures from which people make their decisions, particularly consumptive decisions of taste. We do not consciously have habitus. It is the unconscious set of principles that one uses to reason, forming opinions that seem natural from one's perspective. Third, habitus varies by social location and trajectory. Habitus is not the same for everyone across a culture. Rather, different social positions have different sets of tastes that seem obvious to them.

Refining the concept, Wacquant, through a focus on carnal sociology, a sociology focused on the body, added a fourth feature: habitus is malleable and transmissible because it results from pedagogical work. That is, habitus is taught as well as acquired. Habitus is embodied in but also results from bodily practices that instill social structure within our mental life.

Some might ask: If habitus is taught, how can it be learned unconsciously? The lessons aren't explicit; they are learned through social interaction. True, sometimes one explicitly learns the rules of the game ("You shouldn't do that"), but social learning theory shows us that even though we are learning from other people, we aren't aware of that which we are learning. We are picking up our everyday lessons of taste. To use Wacquant's boxing example, we learn to put our bodies in a particular configuration sometimes from boxing lessons but also from having put our bodies in particular spaces, which require certain configurations, and sometimes slowly changing ourselves to dodge blows or get in a quick hit and feel the rewarding rush that comes from it. The nightclub teaches as effectively as the boxing ring.

Why should we care about a philosophical concept like habitus? Outside of a few academics that use the term, why should anyone else care about it?

Habitus captures the connection between who we are and the structures that we live within without being rigid or predestined. Habitus shows us how parts of ourselves that seem natural are shaped by our environments, the ecological contexts and the social structures that we move through as we are taught the social relationships of taste.

The original concept of habitus, though—which did not include Wacquant's fourth feature—was restrictive, top-down. Like Freud and Marx, Bourdieu envisioned an extremely top-down structure to social life: our social arrangements instilled within us a habitus that led us to make decisions that would prop up that structure. We have little agency, according to this concept. We follow the instructions given us by our social position: habitus forced upon us.

Like the Chicago school, I take a more symbolic interactionist approach to my interpretation of habitus. We learn a habitus through our actions. As Wacquant explained in *Body and Soul*, others teach us a habitus to correspond to the social positions we place ourselves in or into which others constrain us.

Wacquant's elaboration, the version I build on here, is more didactic and iterative. We make choices that feel natural to us in our daily lives. We make these decisions from a set of choices that have been handed to us through social structures and then use a framework for decision making and taste to choose (habitus), but they don't seem like decisions. They seem like the obvious choice because habitus feels natural to us.

Because social locations vary—the third feature—different social structures, what Bourdieuian sociologists would call different fields, instill different habituses within people that move through them. Habitus is a general mechanism that we then specify by field, much the same way that assimilation is a general process I have specified as sexual assimilation. Sexual fields produce erotic habitus: what *should* I find attractive? *How* do I become attractive? Racial fields produce racial habitus: what *should*, for example, a Black person do to embody authentic blackness?

As I explained in chapter 5, "Sexual Racism," sexy communities transform our *erotic* habitus through naked intimacy, expanding our set of choices about racial partners, but also the methods through which we think others can be attractive, moving beyond mere racial stereotyping. But where do sexy communities come from? What social process produces sexy communities in some spaces, but not within gay Disneyland? What has changed? The habitus instilled in these spaces has changed. *Gay habitus* has changed.

Gay habitus, then, is about learning how to comport yourself as a gay man, how to groom yourself, becoming comfortable with sexual language, and learning how to read, as the drag queens say. Gay habitus is developing a sensibility that is gay, a worldview that is gay, a gay way of talking. Gay taste.

Gay habitus is not only gay cultural knowledge; "habitus" is not merely a synonym for "culture." Culture is knowing the tunes in the musical theater videos that play on the screens of Sidetrack on Tuesday nights, that only the most devoted theater queen would know. Habitus is the intuitive sense, learned over many visits to Sidetrack, of how to discuss these tunes. Habitus is knowing the rules of the game so intimately that you make the right choices believing that those are the right choices to make. Habitus is knowing that when you are out with the plastics, you drink vodka soda, not because you feel forced to, but because it naturally seems the right decision to make. Gay habitus establishes the rules of the game for how to be a gay man with all of the right consumption, mannerisms, and physical details we associate with gay men.

I propose habitus as the mechanism for assimilation, social psychological changes corresponding to changes in social structure but communicated through cultural consumption. A change within social structure reflects in the changing organization of consumption and taste, teaching different habitus.

Figure 8.2. Sunday Funday outside Progress Bar

Gay habitus helps us see how the internal psyche that gay men have developed in their neighborhoods, and the structure that produces it, but is also produced by it. We can see the kinds of consumptive choices that connect gay men to a history of other gay men. The culture of gay men dies with each generation anew. To keep it going, there must be a way of transmitting that culture to each new generation.

To put it explicitly, habitus, for Wacquant, is carnal, not just rational rules, but also physical and located within the body. We learn it and teach it to others.

I argue we should add an additional layer to our understanding of habitus. Because Boystown instills a gay habitus that transmits gay culture, habitus is developmental, as well as forced on us by social structure. It is a method of cultural transmission and assimilation. Habitus is instilled within us by our social relations and social spaces. We learn to be who we are. We also shape ourselves by going to some spaces instead of others. Assimilation changes people by changing the habitus they acquire through the spaces they consume.

Furthermore, because habitus can be learned and taught, we seek out tastes, modes of perception, and consumption habits we believe to be superior. We want to be better people. Those on safari don't know these rules; they don't have the proper habitus, though they eventually might if they keep coming. As I will discuss, those on safari want for themselves the same kind of queer appreciation for sexuality and the body that is ironically driven out by their tourism. Similarly, baby gays don't yet have the right cultural knowledge because they haven't picked up a gay habitus yet. Straight women on safari in gay bars are problematic because they don't realize there are different sets of rules.

Of course, I don't mean to imply that gay habitus is uniform. There are subcultures within gay cultures. People flow between these spaces. Someone might be wearing a harness one night, and then put on their best duds to get bottle service with friends at Minibar on another night. A change of venue dictates a change of clothing: it won't do to come in a harness to Minibar. The kind of fine leather shoes that someone wears down in the Hole are much different from those one would wear at Minibar. People can have multiple kinds of cultural knowledge. Habitus is similarly not uniform and unchanging. Different material conditions, different social situations, teach slightly different habitus.

The idea of different habituses brings up another important point: no one is born straight either. If gay habitus is learned, straight habitus is as well. However, gay people first learn straight habitus as well. Let's examine the sexual expectations of straight habitus, as revealed in Gayle Rubin's charmed circle.

Gay men generally grow up in straight families. They grow up internalizing a straight habitus of what a family looks like, family being only another name for sexuality. We learn that a family is monogamous and heterosexual, that it circumscribes sex to only the home, that it limits sex only to procreation, that it barely involves sex at all. When sex does come into the equation, it should not involve toys, it shouldn't be kinky, it shouldn't involve more than two people. These are the lessons that we internalize about sexuality growing up. They form part of the straight habitus, the unconscious rules that our families teach us about how best to conduct our sexuality. These aren't merely cultural lessons. They are a set of judgments that we can learn, and they involve a set of cultural consumptions that are made as a result.

As Boystown transforms into a gay Disneyland, how does gay habitus transform? The habitus these spaces teach changes to be more respectable, to value the inner circle, to be closer to the straight habitus that gay men grew up with in their straight families. Boystown, these days, teaches us not to be queer, but to be one of the good gays.

9

One of the Good Gays

DEAR LADY A: *Where are all the good gays? Is it something about me, that they don't want to be with me? I want a serious relationship with a nice guy who is not into multiple partners. I want to get married some-day just like everyone else, and maybe even have some kids, but the men I meet are just up for one night stands or meaningless short terms. Even though I like getting meaningless sex on weekends, I'm also getting tired of that scene. I know I want a real relationship that might go somewhere and I don't know why I can't find those kinds of gays. Help me?*
—MANHUNT

"Good gays," I rolled my eyes, reading the letter to Lady A, the sex advice columnist at *Redeye*, a Chicago weekly newspaper, on the Red Line "L" train speeding toward the Belmont station.

Yet many gay men are hoping to be one of the good gays—not one of those shameful queers bent on disappointing their parents. Gay men, like every-one, are full of contradictions. They hook up, but find it shameful. They hate Boystown, but go to "dance."

This is a product of assimilation: taking on a straight sexual morality, which views sex as shameful. The transformation of a minority group such that they become less distinguishable from the majority.

Assimilation for gay men isn't the taking on of new values. Assimilation is the lack of transmission of queer values. The gay habitus taught in Boys-town's spaces changes. Without integration into sexy communities, gay men don't become queer. In many ways, they remain culturally straight.

Assimilation of gay men isn't about whether they hook up or not. As-similation is the set of values they apply to judge whether their sex lives are fun or shameful. For gay men, assimilation looks like trying to find—and be—one of the good gays. One of the good gays in a monogamous relationship, with middle-class respectability and a couple of kids.

As queer sexual spaces recede from places in Boystown, as the nightlife turns into a gay Disneyland, the queer values of the outside of the charmed circle recede as well. The gay habitus instilled within gay men frequenting these places is no longer sex positive.

If gay men come to Boystown at all, that is. As gay men are more accepted in everyday straight life, maybe they don't need to go to Boystown at all. Maybe they can meet men at work, bring them home to their families, get married, and live like their parents. They like men, but have they become gay or remained straight?

That is assimilation. That is Alexander.

■ ■ ■

Alexander could very well have written that letter to *Redeye*. I met Alexander through a mutual friend, Joel, while out at Cocktail. I was surprised to see Joel, since he didn't live nearby. Apparently, he had come into town for a date with Alexander, whom he had met on OkCupid.

Alexander is lanky, with dark, shaggy, almost stringy hair, not the short style typical among gay men.[1] While he was a few years older than me and—this is important—had been out for nearly as long, he always seemed younger to me, a youthful demeanor that seemed almost naive at times to my jaded eyes. His questions, his uncertainty, his carriage, his habitus read "baby gay" despite his literal and gay age.[2]

Joel and I hugged. We exchanged a few words, but I left them to get to know one another. I gave Alexander a card to contact me for an interview. I never expected a call.

Surprisingly, he did call. I had been in Chicago for less than thirty days at that point. I hadn't even interviewed anyone yet.

My years of interviewing experience couldn't prevent this ethnographic truism: your first interview for a project will be a disaster.

I scoped out the Center on Halsted a week before as an interview location, eyeing a few tucked-away locations within that space. The tables in the main downstairs lobby seemed too exposed for a personal interview. However, I thought I could take Alexander upstairs to the lounge, where comfy chairs and small tables dominated a tiny corridor.

When Alexander arrived, I took him upstairs, settled in, and, right as I popped new batteries in my digital recorder, a member of the center's staff rushed in to tell us that we were out of bounds. It turns out that we were in the senior center, which is only available to elders before 4:30 P.M., after which the center's staff promptly shut it down. We had to leave.

Figure 9.1. Progress Bar, formerly Cocktail Bar and Restaurant

I asked my contacts at the center later, why couldn't we use space clearly set aside for people to lounge? They told me the staff was told to police the space, to reduce the amount of available sitting space for the primarily Black youth to loiter around the center, perhaps forcing them to go to other locations. They were equal opportunity, though, telling us to go downstairs or find a spot in a local coffee shop.

With little choice, Alexander and I walked down Halsted Street to Caribou Coffee, talking along the way about his life. This screwup was a useful opportunity for someone studying Boystown, what's called a "walk along" interview. He discussed moving to Chicago a few years ago. He was now emerging onto the dating scene after losing a significant amount of weight, the reason he would later give for his lack of gay knowledge.[3]

"This interview brought to you by Caribou Coffee," Alexander said as we settled into this more exposed location and I switched on the recorder.

"I know! Maybe they'll give me some free coffee for the product placement," I laughed, not knowing they would be out of business in Chicago by the time I began writing this book.

This being my first interview, I was full of general questions. What did he think of Boystown? How often did he go? Did he have any good stories? These are the kinds of questions that I could follow up on, mining afterward for themes that appeared in later interviews.

Alexander hates Boystown, he told me, because "the gays" are all about physicality, about hooking up. That's not the kind of "scene" that he's interested in. He wants to find a relationship, preferring to flirt with people out at work, rather than jump "immediately" into sex.

This impression of Boystown, as a kind of free-for-all bacchanal, is common among gay men with assimilationist tendencies, just as the impression of Boystown as straightlaced, in both senses, is common among the more queer affected.

"Are there any places you do like?" I asked him.

"I like Sidetrack. It was more of the, like, just chill guys who were in their late twenties and early thirties type of thing. That's more my scene. But it's just ginormous and I don't really drink that much."

"Okay." I said, forcing him to explain more by letting the silence draw out.

"But it was awesome. I went there with my friend after this party, and she was wearing two layers of Spanx. She looked really good, had this bright red dress and a mink stole, and little lace gloves. She looked fabulous. This really pretty blond," he said, becoming animated.

"And there I was with my pants a size too small and a really bright red shirt that was too big, and I had eye makeup on, my nails were painted. So everyone was kind of like, 'what are they?' So, of course, everyone wanted to talk to us!" he said.

"Exactly, the most people people at the—" I said.

He cut me off in his excitement, "It was awesome! And everyone was making googly eyes at me and it was great. At the time, I was very much not comfortable being at a giant bar, but it was great having my friend there. She gave me this, it was so funny, she gave me this tour where she dragged me around. She just walked up to people and be like 'you're hot, you're hot, no, you're hot.' She'd just walk up to guys who were making out and be like 'Oh my God, you're so hot.'"

We both laughed. I suspect for different reasons.

His friend was doing everything I recommend straight women not do at bars, but in many ways, the roles were reversed. She brought him to a club where she had apparently been before—since she was capable of giving a tour of Sidetrack—and introduced Alexander to the sexual nature of the spaces. However, Alexander's introduction to Sidetrack was unlikely to instill habitus. He wouldn't learn any of the rules. He wouldn't get a sense of what it meant to be a gay man at Sidetrack. Instead, he got a good sense of what it was like to be a straight woman at Sidetrack, interrupting people making out to impose her gaze upon them. Given this experience, it isn't surprising that Alexander thinks of Boystown as just about "physicality," without a queer frame to understand the meaning behind that physicality or question the dichotomy of physicality and meaning in the first place.

"So why do you never go then? That sounded like fun." I prompted, leaning back in the wooden chair, scrawling a few notes into my iPad about issues to follow up on, like his friend's presence.

Alexander, however, took our conversation in a different direction. With a flick of his wrist, he dismissed his need for Boystown, echoing the fears of the Northalsted Business Alliance I would hear later. "I don't have a reason or purpose to ever go," he said, "especially because the industry that I'm in I'm always working and socializing and going out to parties, like really, really cool events where there's free wine, amazing catered meals, I don't need to go out. And I'll get on hit there."

Alexander doesn't need to go out to Boystown, with what he sees as meaningless hookups, when he can flirt with men through his job out in the straight world.

Or online. He frequented a number of dating websites catering to both straight and gay singles, like Match.com and OkCupid, which is where Alexander met Joel.

He sighed. "I don't know, I might meet somebody tomorrow, too, so, we'll see!"

"Okay," I agreed.

"I mean it's so easy. Everyone wants to meet. You know, and whatever else they want, I'm not giving them, so that's too bad," he laughed.

"Oh, so coy," I teased, unintentionally reinforcing a queer habitus of the sexual libertine, rather than a neutral interviewer's agreement with participants' statements.

"Well, I don't know," he picked up on my statement's ethics, changing his mind. "I shouldn't say that because, you know, like Joel drove here and then—hey! It's just like, I'm trying to make it sound like I have these standards, but then there's this guy that drove to see me and then within thirty minutes we're in bed. So it's just, you know."

"So, what was different about that situation then?" I asked.

"I don't know. I don't know. We had this great connection, or at least it seemed like it, I don't know. It's working out really well and it is kind of scary because we're basically the same person on a lot of levels. Like, we listen to all the same music. It was really funny, actually, so because that weekend that he came down, the first one, I had all this stuff planned. I was like 'you can come down, but I have all these things to do!' So I just took him to everything, and we ended up going to my friend's barbecue and having a great time," he said.

Despite being about to go on a date with someone else—getting pad thai together, his favorite dish—Alexander seemed genuinely animated about going out with Joel.

It seemed that way, too, when I saw them out again together at Cocktail. They were hanging on each other a bit, finishing each other sentences, enjoying the limerence that comes at the beginning of a relationship.

Three weeks later, Alexander and I went to the Dice Dojo, a board game shop in Edgewater, to play a few rounds of Dominion and Small World, since Alexander wasn't big on the club scene in Boystown. Joel and Alexander still seemed to be going strong, although Alexander mentioned going on dates with other people, a fact seemingly at odds with his monogamous attitudes.

I was surprised to receive a number of the frantic text messages two weeks later, just as I had returned from a trip. He "had a lot to talk about." Knowing I taught human sexuality classes, he asked me a number of questions about HIV transmission. He was concerned, almost terrified, about his chances of contracting the virus but wouldn't tell me more about the context. He seemed to calm down once I explained the basics.[4]

I invited him over the next night.

My apartment was sparsely furnished, an austere ethnographer's abode littered with IKEA furniture and old hand-me-down things that I had picked up from friends or thrift stores. As a point of reference, Austin's first reaction to my apartment was, "That's the ugliest couch that I have ever seen." That should give you a sense of the desolateness of the space that Alexander walked into.

I made myself a cocktail and invited him to sit at my computer desk. I sat in a red Queen Anne chair that my cats had nearly destroyed, fabric coming off the side in puffs.

Supposedly, he came over to play a board game. It quickly became apparent he wanted me to ask him what he came to talk about. He was relieved when I finally pulled out the recorder, asking me if I knew any available men.

I laughed, "Next time we're out, I can introduce you to a couple, I'm sure."

"Oh, I guess you're just good at keeping secrets then. Well, I'm also good at keeping secrets," he dangled his information in exchange for the names of some potential guys to date.

"Yeah, I am good at keeping secrets. Like the names of the people I interview!" I reminded him with a laugh to cover my discomfort.

"Yeah, like Joel's name I guess," he said.

"So, you told me you had stories?" I prompted.

"Well, so, when I messaged you I was having this really emotional moment," he said.

"Ah, I'm sorry," I said.

"No, it's fine," he said, and then hurriedly, "Now, it is fine, but it wasn't at the time."

He sighed. "It is just that you know that I'm so weird, and it's because, as you know, I'm just starting out on the whole dating scene and I don't know what I should be doing or like when or how. There are steps, and like every person is different and you just never know, and then, you know, you find out, and you know, people are just weird."

He seemed to be dropping down a rabbit hole of uncertainty. He didn't have the vocabulary—the culture—to explain. He tried to say that he doesn't know the rules of the game of sex and dating in the gay world. Gay relationships don't always follow the neat trajectory or rules popular culture says straight relationships follow. He hadn't learned a gay habitus.

"Like, what's an example?" I said.

"Like the steps to take. I don't know what constitutes—" he cut himself off and switched directions, finally about to say what he came to say. "So the reason that I liked Joel when I met him was that it just happened. It was natural. Like he was like 'alright, let's do this.' He set boundaries right away. Great! There was no guesswork. It relieved that pressure. It was wonderful, but um—"

Finally the other shoe seemed about to drop. I leaned forward in my chair, setting down my glass to hear what he was building to.

"Well, I just want to ask you. You say that you don't know Joel very well," he said.

"I've hung out with him in social situations, but we haven't hung out by ourselves before, just the two of us." I said.

"Because I'm going to tell you something that's like—it's just weird. I don't mind saying this, because this is what I signed up for," he said, looking straight at the recorder. "This is great because it's like I'm getting free therapy!" he said.

"It's really not," I tried to dissuade him, perhaps unsuccessfully.

"So, so, OK, so," he stuttered. From my point of view, he was uncomfortable, unsure with what he was about to say, a mixture of shame and indignation carrying through in a warble in his voice.

"I like everything about Joel," he lied, whether to me or himself I wasn't sure.

"Everyone has problems, stop beating around the bush and tell me. What's Joel's problem?" I said.

"He's—he's a whore!" Alexander said.

"Okay," I tried to keep my voice neutral.

"He actually doesn't know how many people he's slept with," he said.

"Okay," the neutrality more difficult, since I, too, didn't know how many people I'd had sex with, having made a commitment to not count at age nineteen when I began identifying as queer. Suddenly, his questions about

HIV the previous day made more sense, even if his chance of seroconversion hadn't changed.

"I mean, he was toying around with it, and told me that his number was fifteen, but turns out that's the number of people—the number of straight guys he's been with!"

I couldn't help but laughing. "Damn!"

"I swear, he must be somewhere in the triple digits, but I'm not actually quite sure. When I found this out, it was quite upsetting. Well, not upsetting, disappointing. Like, oh," he said, drawing out the "oh" and sounding more upset than disappointed.

"Why was it disappointing or upsetting to you?" I asked.

He sighed, loudly, loud enough for me to hear it later on the recording as a breathy wind, despite the recorder sitting well away from him on the table.

"Well, you know. That's a good question," he said. "I don't know why. Because, well, my experience has been so different. He got kicked out of his dad's house when they found out he was gay. Him being gay was a huge issue that I never had to deal with. My mom? She wasn't happy about it, but she didn't kick me out of my house!"

Appreciate Alexander's level of self-reflection here. Even as he was expressing ambivalence about slut shaming his former date, he recognized their different experiences, their different values, related to their different histories with being gay. Being gay for Alexander mattered, his coming out was an event, but it doesn't have the trauma he associates with Joel's identity.

"And at the same time, I asked him 'how do you meet these people?' and I saw on his phone that he has every app, Grindr, Adam4Adam, and every single hookup app ever. And that? That was just—" he made a noise of disgust. "Just for me, the concept of going online, and just getting a hookup not only is it something that I wouldn't do, I don't think that's OK."

"Could you tell me why?" I said.

"I think it's gross." He said simply, reaching for his glass of water, and changing the topic of conversation.

■　■　■

Alexander is gay but has straight sexual values. He's internalized the norms of straight society: how to meet people (at work), appropriate numbers of sex partners (few), or when to have sex (in a relationship). He associates violating these rules with disease and death.

Why wouldn't he?

It only comes as a surprise if one thinks gay men are essentially sexually deviant. There is nothing inherent to desiring someone of the same sex that also means desiring multiple partners, sex clubs, and one-night stands. Those are queer innovations.

Alexander grew up in a straight family. As I discussed in the previous chapter, gay men become gay through culture, located in our nightlife and the communities anchored in these spaces. If he hasn't experienced that culture, if he finds that culture deviant because he subscribes to the values of the inner circle—like say, don't make out with people in a nightclub or don't find a hookup on Grindr—then he hasn't become gay. He dates men. He fucks men. He has a gay identity, but he's not culturally gay. As Nate Silver, gay journalist said, he's "ethnically straight."[5]

Why doesn't he share those values? Alexander has assimilated, and assimilation is a problem of cultural transmission.

Sociologists like me apply theories like assimilation to LGBTQ people, but we seldom examine the differences between sexual minorities and the context in which assimilation, as a concept, was developed.

The concept of assimilation was developed to explain racial groups' transition into the white American mainstream. Sociologists frame assimilation as a problem of generational transmission, from parents to children, from ethnic immigrants to their second-generation children. For racial minorities, those often studied by American sociologists for questions of assimilation, the story often goes: the children of immigrants grow up in a household with one culture, then go out into American culture and learn another. Whether that's white American culture or Black American culture depends on the context and often how that ethnic group's skin color fits into the American racial schema.

For instance, Alejandro Portes and Min Zhou's classic paper discusses the expectations immigrant Sikh families have for their children. They expect their female children to marry at an early age, require that they obtain parental consent to date, and caution them to avoid dancing. These expectations run against such mainstream American expectations, as seen in popular culture, that women delay marriage until after they've completed their education, that they date, then introduce their partners to their family only after they are serious, and enjoy sexualized movement in nightlife and parties. Portes and Zhou saw the successful passing of family norms to second-generation children as evidence that these families were resisting assimilation to the American mainstream. Changing attitudes, in contrast, were signs of assimilation.[6]

In these cases, the dominant culture is on the outside. Assimilation occurs if the next generation accepts these outside values. If they remain in their immigrant enclave, following local community norms, then they have resisted assimilation. For racial and ethnic minorities, assimilation is a struggle against outside generational forces, bent on changing their children.

For sexual minorities, for queers, assimilation is the opposite. Assimilation for gay men happens quietly, because nothing changes at all. The outside force bent on changing the children of straight parents into gay men, with queer sexual values, is gay culture in the gayborhood, instilling a gay habitus through habits and practices of consumption within the bars and clubs. The outside force is the minority group.

Minorities don't have much power of persuasion compared to the majority's stigma. Acceptance, or even mere tolerance, of gay men in their families means they do not require a substitute family, a family of choice they find in the gayborhood, a sexy community where they can find connectedness.

The process of coming out made one gay, in part, because it caused a break not only in identity but in the family as well. Having left one family, gays find a new one, with new expectations, new rules, and new habitus.

You have no family. You have no friends when you start out gay. You have to seek these things. You have to become gay. You find sexual kinship with people and adopt a gay habitus by being in gay places and learning the rules.

Society's acceptance of gay men doesn't change them into straight men. They remain straight people, but homosexual straight people. In this way, assimilation for gay men is a lack of learning a new culture.

As we often have, let's return to Gayle Rubin's charmed circle. Although Rubin did not explicitly use the charmed circle as a metaphor for assimilation, her charmed circle is a good tool for explaining the changes that assimilation brings. As the barrier to homosexuality disappears, it is not that all queer sexuality is less stigmatized. Instead, gay men are welcomed into the middle of the circle, with the attendant expectations for stigmatizing the outside.

However, that, too, is not entirely true. Assimilation is partially a two-way street, a blending.[7] It involves the normalization of gay people, and the straightening out of queers, but also lessens the distinctions between straight and gay people such that they are indistinguishable. An assimilationist gay man would say, "Great. The only difference between me and them is the sex/gender of the person we're with." Full assimilation would mean that the groups no longer appear separate. Instead, assimilation often looks like some of the groups' traits are coming into the majority and changing their culture as well. Assimilation is the lopsided blending of two groups, one into the other: the majority changing the minority to fit their habitus but taking aspects of that group as well.

■ ■ ■

This is all very abstract. Let's pull it down to the concrete level.

Marriage is a conservative cause. Marriage, even same-sex marriage, is not queer. In America, it may be advocated by the left, but only in the sense that the American left is still to the left of the right on this issue. The right is so far to the right that even though the left is on the right, they are still only slightly to the left of the right. Right?

As the Against Equality collective discusses in their many books, essays, and speeches, marriage connects one kind of relationship to the state with its allocation of benefits and rights. Same-sex marriage only expands the definition to include, and contain, same-sex couples. Rather than disconnecting rights from the government's preference for one kind of relationship, same-sex marriage entrenches those rights.[8]

In the words of Yasmin Nair, Chicago queer activist: "There are suggestions here that the very specter of gay and lesbian and queer sex might trouble the normality of marriage, but surely no amount of fisting, fucking, fellatio, cunninglus [*sic*] or S/M—all of which are regularly and copiously engaged in by straight couples across the political spectrum, even if often covertly—actually shifts the meaning of marriage within the state itself." Nair's point is valid. Fisting won't change the relationship between the rights apportioned by the state, like health care, immigration, or social security. It won't change the legal arrangements required.

That said, marriage does more. Religious conservatives recognize this and have been against using the word "marriage" for these relationships, more willing to accept a second tier of "civil unions" instead. Similarly, gay conservatives—Andrew Sullivan, for instance—have been in favor of marriage, arguing that it will lead gay men to "grow up," a.k.a. assimilate, become straighter.[9]

The word "marriage" applied to gay relationships imports the expectations of straight relationships. Husbands might be expected by friends and family to have children. They might be judged by the same moral standards regarding monogamy or outside partners. Now that they are on the inside of the charmed circle, they will be expected to act like it. People might assume, and rightly so, a certain similarity to their straight families, a more cohesive transmission of other cultural factors down between generations. They might expect them to look a bit more like their parents. They will expect them to be normal.

Marriage legitimates. The backing of the state, along with the expectations of friends and family, says that marriage makes a relationship final, true, and legitimate.

Nair interviewed Mattilda Bernstein Sycamore, queer activist and writer of *The End of San Francisco*, about the changes to San Francisco and the queer civil rights movement.[10] Their conversation reflects this line of thought:

YASMIN NAIR: You talked about the nuclear family unit not necessarily being part of this queer radical space. But supporters of gay

Figure 9.2. Men holding hands in Boystown

marriage, about which you've written critically, would argue that same-sex marriages are different than straight nuclear family units. Couldn't it be argued that these do shift or even end the oppression of marriage because they're structured differently, with different or no gender expectations?

MATTILDA BERNSTEIN SYCAMORE: It's sad to me to see the ways in which gay people are propping up a failed system. If you ask most straight people in the United States whether marriage is working, people will say, "Hell, no." Anyone who has a brain that's working knows that marriage still exists as a site of anti-woman, anti-child, and anti-queer violence, historically and in the present. And I think for many decades, gay people, including mainstream gay people, have created love and lust that are not predicated on state acceptance.

I remember when the whole gay marriage thing exploded in San Francisco and Phyllis Lyon and Del Martin, who had been together for more than four decades, were the first people to get officially married. They said, "Finally, it's legitimate." And that was one of the most horrifying things I've ever heard. This was a couple that had been together for over 40 years, and now their relationship was legitimate because of a piece of paper from the state?

The fact that gay people can get married doesn't change marriage. It just makes that failed system stronger.

Should we be so horrified?

While I agree that the fight for marriage has come at the expense of resources toward universal access to benefits like immigration and health care, sometimes these expectations—these rules that come down from our parents and society about how we are to act in a relationship—matter. Legitimacy matters.

Marriage is about divorce.

Marriage changes how one splits up, from the method to the acceptable reasons. From a legal economic standpoint, marriage raises the barriers to exit a relationship. Bureaucratic barriers arise. Cost becomes an issue, in terms of both the money to pay a lawyer and the potential cost in property and income.

These barriers make marriage and divorce weighty decisions, the kinds of decisions that you mull over and seldom make lightly. When "partners" break up, you scream and fight—or cry and smolder. Then, you pull the U-Haul up to the apartment building and leave. There is no official negotiation of property, only a talk as you take what is yours and scrutinize who was the first person to suggest getting the dog. Debt incurred together doesn't even exist. That electric bill coming in the mail is the responsibility of whomever happened to put it in their name. It isn't a decision made lightly, but "partners" have no recourse.

When "husbands" break up, there's an official process. They get a divorce. Those same things happen—the fights, the dog, the electric bill—but they are subject to official negotiation. The possibility of divorce not only makes a marriage more secure, but it also provides peace of mind that you can do things jointly.

Of course, I owe some of this line of thinking to my lawyer-husband, Austin. "Marriage is more like a corporate merger," he likes to joke.

True, I got married for the legal rights. I'm staunchly against the state's apportionment of legal rights to married couples, a kind of discrimination against other relationship types and a penalty on single people. Health care, immigration, security in old age: these are rights that everyone should have, regardless of their relationship status. The government's intervention in this area remains a tie from our current era of "romantic love" marriages to the past "economic unit" style of marriage.

Nevertheless, marriage does give me peace of mind. It provides a cultural framework to show others how important Austin is to me. It provides symbols, like my ring, demonstrating our commitment even when we are in situations that break with traditional notions of married life. No one will be shocked that we are attending a party at Jackhammer's Hole, but open acknowledgment of our relationship challenges the notion that marriages must be monogamous.

Marriage also protects our relationship because there are no rules when you drive off the road. It can be rough going, avoiding obstacles and making our own path.

That's been part of the scary and wonderful part of being queer. Not being allowed to marry forced queers to invent our own rules, opening new relationship possibilities outside of the nuclear family. Yet there are risks. Though the risks may not be any greater than those in married relationships, given the high rate of divorce, they are risks nonetheless.

While not changing the relationship with the state's provision of benefits, same-sex marriage does change what it means to get married, but only if its participants continue to be open about the kinds of activities that they engage in outside of the charmed circle. As Nair points out, straight people do plenty of BDSM and fisting, yet marriage remains the same. However, that's not really true. When those acts remain hidden, divorced from their identity, then what does it matter? When they are openly acknowledged, then the scorn of the inner circle falls on them just as much. Heterosexual people are assumed to be on the inside of the inner circle.

Similarly, for gay people, queer relationship styles and erotic potentials are not removed, distanced, from what it means to be gay.

They are what it means to be gay.

■   ■   ■

Or at least they used to be. Perhaps now they more aptly describe what it means to be queer. The sexy communities of queers live divorced from the everyday life of gay people, pushed to the peripheries of Boystown, or out of Boystown altogether.

Today, when someone like Alexander says they are gay, what does that mean? What cultural traits come to mind, if any, when someone comes out to someone else? Because, of course, Alexander does identify as gay. He is a gay man.

But he is not a gay man in terms of where the charmed circle would place him. He is not on the outside. He doesn't want to be. He doesn't want to be involved in the naked intimacy of strangers. He doesn't want a sexy community built out of the remnants of shame, of failed families of birth. He doesn't want to be queer. He wants to be one of the good gays.

Can he ever be? Or, does the existence of the good gays make the rest of us bad?

On a beautiful, cool, June day, I saw proof same-sex marriage could change the expected relationship path for gay men. While the sun was out, the summer hadn't been hot, so it was the perfect day to go to the beach, such as they are in Chicago. Running along Lake Michigan, the city maintains a number of public beaches to let people lounge on the imported sand. The gays tend to gather at Hollywood Beach—officially, Kathy Osterman Beach—in Edgewater, staking out a section of sand near the pier. On the right summer day, it is like a gay club in the middle of the day, dance music playing from Bluetooth speakers and gay men standing around in as little clothing as law allows.

I had set up my huge beach tent. I inherited my mother's fair Irish skin, which burns in even the slightest patch of sun. I slathered myself head to toe in Banana Boat Kids SPF 50 sunscreen, giving my skin chalky white patches, even more so than usual.

Austin and I were hanging out with some of the poz guys, the group I'd most identify with radical sexuality as having been pushed into a sexy community through viral kinship and as a result of the stigma given them by the good gays. They were taunting me with their tans by wearing SPF 15 and lounging in direct sunlight on their beach towels. Mark was playing opera *at* the other beachgoers playing pop a few feet away, a veritable war of gay musical styles.

Our wedding was a few weeks away. I was complaining about last-minute arrangements. Illinois legalized same-sex marriage on June 1, 2014, automatically converting our marriage from New York into a marriage in Illinois. We were finally having a wedding to celebrate.

"So, when are you two getting married?" Sean said to Brandon and Karl, boyfriends of eight years.

The two of them looked at each other, a bit bewildered at the question.

Karl's mouth hung open a little, as he mulled over what words to choose. Then Brandon said, "We aren't?"

Sean seemed surprised at the answer. The expectation was committed couples would, of course, get married once it was legal.

"Oh, I just assumed!" he said.

We all laughed to relieve some of the tension.

"Just because we're getting married doesn't mean they have to," I said.

Then, Karl asked an even more surprising question.

"Are you two planning on having kids? I know you have a dog, but are you those kinds of gays?" he said.

"No," I laughed. "Just, no."

When I asked Brandon about this situation later—over a pot roast when Karl was away on a business trip and his friends were taking turns making sure Brandon didn't starve—he told me his mother had been pressuring his married straight brother for years to have kids. Now his mother was ramping up the pressure on him as well. Why won't he marry his partner? Don't they love each other? Why won't he make her a grandmother?

Luckily, Austin and I shut that down with our own parents. A dog is hard enough to take care of.

Yet even Karl, someone breaking the path of marriage expectations, expected us to fulfill those expectations once we joined the rolls of those married. These are the kind of consequences that scare me when it becomes expected that you need to get married in order to continue to have a relationship—as Sean's question suggested—or when gay couples that do marry are held to those standards—like Karl thought.

These expectations were always at the heart of the marriage movement. Same-sex marriage became an issue because of rising worries about gay men's adolescent culture. Same-sex marriage was supposed to make us grow up and put an end to the "sexual experiment."

. . .

I've frequently discussed Patrick Moore's history of the "sexual experiment" by gay men in the sixties and seventies. Sexual libertine values flourished, along with a dark side of drugs. It was an experiment in creating an alternative community, the kind that I've identified as "sexy community," spaces and networks infused with radical sexuality, connection outside of the nuclear family structure that continues to dominate American life.[11]

Gay men's sexy communities were in their adolescence. They had yet to be consolidated or synthesized with the rest of their lives.[12] The allure of drugs, alcohol, and the naked intimacy of sexy spaces was too strong for many, who were also experiencing rejection outside of these spaces in the straight world. It was easy to while away one's life when so little awaited outside the enclave. Moreover, sexual spaces were beginning to become stale, isolated from other institutions that also included women: "The wonder of sex palaces and dance clubs must have lessened after two or three years of almost constant attendance in them, after which the men had to consider them not as a novelty but as the central component of the rest of their lives. Because the lives that men lived at the time were so new, there had been no time to integrate the theatrical intensity into a fuller life that also included women and family."[13]

Moore argues that gay life was beginning to come out of this phase. In places like New York City and San Francisco, where sexy communities flourished, pushback against drugs and excess was already happening. Those in the scene for the longest, who were beginning to tire, developed ways of integrating these experiences into the rest of their lives.

If not for AIDS, these elders could have transmitted this knowledge on to the next generation: "An older man who has experienced a period of youthful intensity around sexual experience can tell a young man just entering the scene that it is possible to come out the other side into a balanced life." They were beginning to imagine integrating their community built beyond shame with mainstream society.

Instead, just as gay male cultures began to pull through the pain and exuberance of adolescence, the sexual experiment was halted by HIV in the eighties.

Moore asks, "Was this performance worth the risk? We cannot know, because the performance was never finished. It was a rehearsal that will be forever judged as opening night. And this, ultimately, is the cultural impact of AIDS."

If it was understood as performance, the experiment was a tragedy. The darkness gathered through a perfect storm of drug addiction and viral decimation. The advent of HIV made integration impossible because it inexorably linked radical gay sexuality and death. The experiment was over. The following passage resonates so deeply, allow me the extended quote:

> It was incredibly difficult to reconcile a sense of pride in our sexual culture with the overwhelming grief for loved ones infected with HIV through unprotected gay sex. For all of our bravado and sex-positive messages, we have carried with us a belief that we got what we deserved. For men of my generation there was the double bitterness of living constantly with death without having enjoyed an earlier era when sex was less associated with guilt and shame....
>
> Even though infection rates continue to rise in our young men, exhaustion and the empty promises of seeing ourselves represented in the mass media have lured us, despite American statistical evidence to the contrary, into saying "AIDS is no longer a gay disease." We desperately want to believe that the gathering storm clouds will break elsewhere this time. Inherent in our ability to ignore the continuing influence of AIDS on gay life in American is our systemic effort to strip gay life of all associations with the radical sexuality of the past. If there is no sex, no memory of sex, and no current sign of sexuality, then we can hope that AIDS will pass by our doorway this time.

No less true when I write now than when Moore wrote it ten years ago.

I live a half generation past Moore, carrying with me that double bitterness, but tinged with hope. Gay identity may be accepted, but queer sex is still shameful. Yes, the sexual experiment might have faded under the onslaught of respectability politics, but it has not died a complete death from AIDS. Even as the cold water of assimilation and homonormativity have attempted to douse the flames, embers have lived on, occasionally flickering to life.

Moore sees the sexual experiment as over, the times have passed.[14] I've documented in this book the fact that it hasn't died completely and may be coming back to life, sparks of radical queer sexuality rejecting the respectability of the charmed circle, even if just for moments or in certain spaces.

Yet those flickers exist within an overall environment of assimilation, a neighborhood with institutions serving "the good gays." The connection between AIDS and radical sexuality led to a backlash, a turn toward respectability politics. The "safe sex" movement produced a newfound insistence on condoms as the only way to stem the tide of infections but also an insistence on limiting the number of sexual partners. Places thought to be vectors for disease shut down. For instance, San Francisco has no bathhouses because they were closed as locations where HIV was spreading.

Sexual conservatism found new purchase in this environment. The gay and lesbian rights movement became a movement about identity, rather than one about sex. The mainstream LGBT movement started insisting, "We're just like you. We're normal."

Warner asks, "What could be a better way of legitimating oneself than to insist on being seen as normal? The problem, always is that embracing this standard merely throws shame on those who stand farther down the ladder of respectability. It does not seem to be possible to think of oneself as normal without thinking that some other kind of person is pathological."[15] That is, if I may interject, it's not possible to think of some as being normal without insisting on a divide between the inside and outside of the charmed circle. To claim the dignity of the inner circle is to insist on the deviance of the outside.

> The embrace of the normal is also a prime example of antipolitical politics. The point of being normal is to blend, to have no visible difference and no conflict. Sullivan's *Virtually Normal* claimed that gay politics reduce to only two issues: military service and marriage. Everything else is mere private difference. If you are queer and don't want to enlist or get a marriage license, then politics is not for you. The message, which Sullivan later took to gay audiences in promoting his *Same-Sex Marriage: Pro and Con*, is that the lesbian and gay movement is essentially over, or will be when gay couples can marry.

Now, we have military service and marriage. Should we, in Sullivan's words, "have a party and close down the gay rights movement for good"?

No, because we should question how much assimilation has necessarily occurred and at what cost.

Same-sex marriage is a way for queers to seek safety in straight society. Safety from HIV. Safety from stigma. Safety in being normal.

It is the belief that if we act like straight people, if we get married like them, if we have children like them, and most importantly if we judge sex like they do, "then we can hope that AIDS will pass by our doorway this time."

Alexander's shaming of Joel makes sense within this environment. His straight sexual attitudes—his assimilation—conflate "dirty" sex outside the charmed circle with HIV and death. Nothing he did with Joel gave him have a chance of transmission, but his fear and his shaming of Joel is intimately connected to Joel being "a slut" that could give him HIV.

Ultimately, though, I am not writing to lambast same-sex marriage as good or bad, or as a tool of hegemony or a pathway to equality, or even to question whether marriage is straightening up queers or whether we are queering the institution.

Instead, my focus is on how the desire for same-sex marriage arose from the terror of HIV/AIDS to seek safety in the bastions of straight society. Today's desire to be one of the good gays is rooted in this history, this fear of death. To be a good gay is to tell the world: I don't want to be different; I deserve life.

That's OK.

But who is left behind? Who do we throw shame on when we clean up and act nice?

Warner suggests that "this message goes over well with a key constituency: middle-class white gay men, many of whom were never happy to be political, anyway."[16]

For many, assimilation isn't possible, because the values expressed by the inner circle are middle-class white values. Values requiring money. Values built around punishing those that deviate from the white middle-class norm.

People will be left behind when gays assimilate. Who are those people going to be?

■ ■ ■

Writing this chapter, I was reminded of how piecemeal assimilation has been.

Sitting in Everybody's Coffee, just north of Boystown in Uptown at Wilson Avenue and Sheridan Road, I was enjoying an Americano, when a man walked by the front window. I turned to look at him pass by, as I did with most people that pass by the front window. Part of the appeal of writing by the window is having a parade of images from which to draw in my daily writing. He didn't disappoint.

Slam! The window rattled from the side of his fist banging against the glass. He stared at me mouthing, "You faggot bitch."

Those words transported me to only two days before, when Austin and I were walking from our apartment north along Sheridan to Crew, a gay sports bar in Uptown. "Oh my god!" Austin exclaimed, showing me that I had a patch of gray hair hidden among the blond along my right temple.

"No!" I wailed. I was growing older. We laughed together. I threw my arm around his shoulder. "Guess you'll find me more attractive now?" I joked.

"Fucking faggots," a man in a goatee with two bags walking south from the Jewel-Osco grocery store spat at us as he passed by going the opposite direction.

Back at Everybody's Coffee, it was as if that the man who slammed the window had said, "How assimilated are you, you faggot bitch?"

Despite the narrative of progress—"We can live anywhere now!"—how fully assimilated are gay and queer peoples in American society? Much has been made of the fantastic strides in legal equality and inclusion within our families of origin. We are married! The movement is over!

Tolerance often feels more like an "I love you anyway" kind of inclusion.

Being one of the good gays then takes on additional meaning. It means that we are worthy of love. Straight culture doesn't accept queer people if they act queer, with all the sexually deviant, genderfucking, weird relationships we invented.

It seems even other gay men now don't find you worthy of love, as Alexander did to Joel, when you exist outside the charmed circle. This is assimilation not as acceptance, or a folding in, or blending between two groups, but assimilation as lack of exclusion. Assimilation as the unchanging blind acceptance of the morality handed down from our parents. Assimilation as staying straight.

For some.

The narrative of progress, of "it gets better," should always add "for some."[17]

Queer people are expected to relish the fact that it is no longer assumed that we are deviants. No longer being kicked out of our homes. No longer denied housing, health care, or jobs. No longer excluded from society to the point of being driven to suicide, drugs, or drink.

For some. For some. For some.

Many still attempt suicide, abuse drugs, become drunks to deal with the pain.

These facts drive queer separatism, the desire to have our own space, to have a Boystown.

Reflecting on what had just happened to me, after the shock of the jarring slam had finished reverberating through me, it also seemed he was saying, "Go back to your neighborhood, you faggot bitch."

Uptown is gentrifying. I have no idea whether this man lived in the neighborhood, but these interactions strike me also as a reaction against gentrification by young professionals sitting in newly opened coffee shops in our leather jackets, skinny jeans, and flannel shirts.

Perhaps, he thought I was staring at him for other reasons, a young white man looking down on a middle-aged Black man in one of the Blackest neighborhoods of the north side. The choice of words reads heterosexist, but the context is subtext. It is almost immaterial that I am a faggot. I read as an outsider, a newcomer. I should get my faggot bitch ass back to Boystown where I belong.

These are the contexts in which gentrification happen. It is hard for me to believe the triumphant progress narrative when it doesn't matter if we are one of the good gays.

We can live anywhere we want, officially. Our relationships are recognized, officially. Yet, how much of that matters? Who does it matter to? This tension is behind the gayborhood impulse, the animating drive of Boystown.

Boystown remains as a destination for gay men, a gay Disneyland of wonder, even amid the assimilationist trend, the desire to blend, because even the good gays are unwelcome outside. No matter how much someone insists they are normal because they will have kids, they will have sex in the home, they will get married, they will be monogamous, and they will be HIV negative, they will still be different.

Assimilation changes Boystown. The good gays may not need to go to Boystown. They might be postgay, but faggot bitches can't go anywhere they want. They go to Boystown. Does Boystown still want them?

10

Straight to Halsted

Boystown's tourists are intentional.

There is nothing gayer than Sunday Funday: afternoon brunch mimosas followed by cheap drinks into the evening.

I fucking love brunch. I don't care if it makes me a basic bitch, but I don't think I can state it any more clearly how much I enjoy going to Boystown on Sunday. As I began to wind my fieldwork down, I largely stopped going out on Fridays, because I enjoyed Sunday's activities so much more.

After a night out, I will roll out of bed between ten and noon, because it is criminal to go to brunch before 1 P.M. Two glasses of water and a cup of coffee later, Austin and I are ready to head out for a relaxing Sunday Funday.

Sun shining, we will walk slowly from our apartment at Sheridan and Buena Avenue in Uptown south into Boystown to our favorite brunch spot, Angelina Ristorante, or Angelina's.

Several of these brunch spots dot Boystown. Kit Kat. Taverna 750. Angelina's.

Others offer more classic breakfast, minus the mimosas for those nursing hangovers. Nookies. Melrose. Stella's.

Others later got in on the Sunday Funday brunch game, offering unlimited mimosas and an entree at a slightly lower price point: D.S. Tequila. El Mariachi. mEAT.

Walking into Angelina's, I'll often spot a friend at another table, or a former trick. It can seem like all of Boystown is out on a Sunday.

Two, five, or eight mimosas later—they are unlimited after all—the server will hand us a coupon for a free bottle of sparkling wine at Progress. Several of the restaurants have these arrangements with bars, although usually with other bars managed by the same people, or owned by the same company, like Taverna 750 and Scarlet.

By this time, it's usually three in the afternoon, but Progress is already packed. Formerly Cocktail, the half-naked go-go boys have been replaced with tasteful seating, a green herb garden, and an arty lightbulb ceiling installation. Austin and I will stand at the window, drinking our free bottle of bubbly, so bad it has to be diluted with orange juice to make it palatable, and people watch.

Inevitably, someone we know will walk by—Matt, Caleb, Brandon, and so on—and we'll pull them inside for a drink.

Everyone has work the next day, but the afternoon has barely begun. After Progress, it is time to walk across the street to Roscoe's for dollar beers, perhaps the only time I can convince people to go into Roscoe's. A few beers later at 7 P.M., it'll be off to Scarlet to get some dancing in before wandering home at 9 or 10 to get ready for the work week.

Sunday Funday.

In this way although reflecting an earlier cultural activity of the Sunday tea dance, Sunday Funday, today, is a manufactured outing in gay Disneyland. You are on rails, escorted from one venue to another by deals worked out between bar owners. Boystown wants to keep you in it, spending money.

But it doesn't just want gay money. It wants bigger profits. The Northalsted Business Alliance wants to bring people "Straight to Halsted."

■ ■ ■

The Northalsted Business Alliance are hard people to get ahold of. Like the Center on Halsted and other elite organizations, they are insulated and worried about their image. They want to control the message. Confidentiality, combined with persistence verging on annoyance, can get them to talk.

I cold-contacted Tom after reading an article about his business in one of the local publications.[1] He ignored my first several e-mails, but then replied with vague agreement but no commitment for a time to interview. After seeing him at a community event, I pressed again. Finally, the e-mail stuck, and we agreed to meet at his place of business.

The evening was rainy. I wore a purple oxford shirt and a gray blazer with a faint houndstooth pattern because I wanted to look professional. Between the humidity, the slick of the rain blown sideways under my umbrella, and the speed at which I was walking to get there on time, I arrived breathless and sweaty, the very picture of someone overplaying the degree of his professionalism.

I shouldn't have worried. Tom wasn't ready for me. One of his employees directed me to sit nearby and wait for him. Ten minutes later, he arrived, turned down the music, and directed me toward the back where we could talk.

He talked and talked and talked. Fast. My typical interviews last an hour and fifteen minutes to two hours. He covered the same material in forty-five minutes. He talked in a manner both nervous and authoritative, like he was used to commanding a room with long speeches of his opinions, but as though he was uncertain who I was, unclear about the purpose of the interview, nervous that I might have some hidden agenda other than the one listed on the consent form he signed.

Like most business owners in Boystown, he was a member of the Northalsted Business Alliance. I was attempting to tempt him into letting me present to the alliance a proposal to do establishment surveys—they ultimately turned me down—when he segued to another way the alliance was attempting to shape the clientele of the neighborhood.

"Actually, we are starting a marketing campaign called 'Straight to Halsted' and we're advertising for Sunday Funday. It says 'Sunday Funday Straight to Halsted' with a rainbow separating the two slogans. We know that on trains and buses we're marketing to a straight customer. We want everyone to know that we're a place where we can go to have a lot of fun. It's not to shy away from being gay in Boystown—that's what the rainbow is there for—but it's opening up people's mind to say, 'We're here too. We have amazing establishments. Come visit them.'"

Another tactic to increase neighborhood visibility had been in the news lately: a hotel. I asked him about it.

He responded, "Neighbors with kids. Gay neighbors. Straight neighbors. Having a thirty million dollar project with jobs, I feel like would be a positive thing for everyone. It gives the neighborhood a face-lift. It gives an energy to the neighborhood. It gives publicity to the neighborhood. Makes it international."

He briefly then discussed the architecture of the proposed building, his likes and dislikes about it, a discussion not relevant here.

He continued, "As for Boystown and the gay community itself, I think it is great. Gay men, especially, travel, and gay women but I can't speak as much to them, but gay men travel for gay destinations and cities that are marketing themselves as open and accepting of gay culture. This will put Chicago on the map as one of those cities. Chicago is number five in terms of gay tourism as a destination. It's actually tied with two other cities. *So* we're top eight. We should be number two or number one, if that is possible. This will help get us there. It will allow us to have a place, a place to gather [for people] that are like-minded. It's exciting to have that option. I can stay downtown as well and have that kind of environment, but the OUT Hotel will give you that option. I would want to give that business my money."

"'It would give the neighborhood a face-lift,'" I echoed his sentiment back to him. "Turning to Boystown right now, rather than what it could be after the hotel, because I'm not really that interested in the hotel as much as, what do you mean by—does Boystown need a face-lift? What are your thoughts on that?"

He responded by listing more of the programs the alliance was engaging in to increase street traffic, though only from a particular kind of customer. "The street itself definitely needs a face-lift. There definitely needs to be space on the sidewalk to sit and eat and drink. Roscoe's had the first windows that faced Halsted, Sidetrack was just that itty-bitty sign that faced the outside. No one really wanted to be seen inside these bars. The bars landed on streets where people didn't want to sit outside. They didn't want to have cars drive by and yell at them. Nowadays, we need that. We want to sit outside. We want to be part of the community, but our streets don't really allow for that. [The alliance] has a twenty-year plan that's evolving. The idea of widening our sidewalks or providing park spaces. The face of Halsted should be uplifted that way."

Breathlessly, he continued his litany of projects: "The look of all the buildings. We have a facade program. We refund people that put money and effort to improving their facade, but it's not always done. The security of the street. We have a lot of problems. We have a cultural problem that arises after midnight. Where some people come from other cultures of the city and they just want to stand in one place, they are used to sitting down on front doorsteps and, you know, not really doing much and just standing and socializing which doesn't really work on this street."

His words were tentative, choosing them very carefully, given the racial overtones of his statements on these "other people."

"And it causes problems because the more people that stand in one place, it spills over into the street. Cars can't get by. They start pushing each other, and fights develop. And all that. With this hotel and with a more modern approach to this street we can alleviate these issues with twenty-four-hour security."

He started to run out of steam, but kept going. "Um, and lighting, and uh, and down the neighborhood needs more lighting. This hotel might bring the revenue to invest in those types of progress. Every street in Chicago needs a face-lift. I think it was the nineties that the pillars got erected, and that was the last big time the street—maybe the planters but those planters don't do us much good especially with our culture problem. People are sitting on them, putting drugs into the planters for other people to pick up, rather than using them for beautification. We need to reanalyze how the street works and feels. We want a more twenty-four-hour destination thing where you could walk during the day, sit down and have a cup of coffee and get a haircut, grab a donut, and feel like it's a walkable stretch of territory. Where in the past you'd want the cab to drop you off and then speed away, run inside."

■ ■ ■

The tourists are intentional, but not just the straight ones. The business owners want to bring the straights to Halsted, but also they also want to bring the gays back.

They are threatened by the fact that people don't need to spend time in the neighborhood because gays have become more accepted in society. The combination of acceptance outside of the gayborhood and internalization of straight norms means that the old concept of the gayborhood as exclusive community isn't economically viable.

New opportunities to find men online and acceptance in the more traditional settings of family and work leads some people to avoid the gay bar. Or rather, they are no longer forced to go there to meet people.

As Alexander, the good gay, said, he doesn't need to go out to the bars. He can find men through work events, through casual interactions in the straight world. He can find people the way his straight friends find people.

These changes scare the business owners who are afraid their livelihoods will disappear should the gayborhood empty out. Without men needing to come to the bars to meet others, or feel they have a safe space, then their businesses, the work many of them have poured their entire lives into, will disappear.

Their reaction has been to market the neighborhood as a destination of style. The gayborhood doesn't disappear. It reacts. It engages in "heritage commodification."[2]

■ ■ ■

In early 2013, a property group announced it would hold public meetings with neighborhood condo associations to discuss building a hotel in the heart of Boystown called the OUT Hotel, modeled after the OUT Hotel in New York City's Chelsea neighborhood. A journalist leaked the time for the meeting called by Triangle Properties, which represents condo owners living in buildings west of the proposed build site at Halsted and Buckingham Street. The room overflowed. Thirty-three neighborhood residents, fourteen business owners or employee representatives, and many more unaffiliated queer people, political staffers, and journalists filled the tiny room at the Addison Street Police Station. When I arrived only fifteen minutes early, I already had to take a seat at the front of the room facing everyone. Awkward for the everyday observer, but a perfect seat for an ethnographer taking notes.

Figure 10.1. Women waiting at Scarlet bar

The OUT Hotel's developer, Ian, began his presentation with telling words: "Boystown needs to be cemented as the gay epicenter of Chicago. I've noticed a migration trend away, but I want to revitalize it." The developer explained that he had the full support of Minibar and Sidetrack's owners, although neither was there at the time. Apparently, Minibar's owners were headed back from a political fundraiser, while Sidetrack had sent a representative, since they were away in Cuba for their humanitarian work.

The proposed building would be twelve stories, facing a center courtyard, with Minibar moving to the roof as a lounge, and a ground-floor door that opens directly into Sidetrack.

"There is no hotel for the LGBT consumer." Ian explained. "At best you have homo-friendly hotels."

Similar to the OUT Hotel in New York, there would be no closets. "Out of principle," he laughed.

He finished his pitch with an appeal to Boystown's future vitality.

"This will bring business to the neighborhood. Thirty million dollars and a hundred jobs to your community… the publicity will be good for nearby businesses."

The question-and-answer period began largely negatively. The building brought out many of the concerns every community meeting in the neighborhood revisits. Straight families were concerned the hotel would bring more noisy traffic to the neighborhood.

"My husband and I raise a family here. This is a residential neighborhood!" one white woman practically screamed.

Another resident expressed, in a much quieter tone, similar sentiments: the neighborhood was becoming a magnet for people from 'other' parts of Chicago—the implication always is the south side—that would bring their crime to the neighborhood. She was in her late fifties, and with a level, serious tone emphasizing each word she started by saying, "I raised children here."

Having fewer people at the bars during the week was a positive development in her opinion, she explained. She wanted more overall quietness.

"Lately, we've had such not so good traffic, too, which you might have heard about."

This is the specter of Black youth and crime that Tom had evoked earlier, which I will return to in chapter 12, "Take Back Boystown."

"You are going to bring more of that drama here."

Continuing the litany of complaints by mothers, a board member of the Triangle Neighborhoods challenged Ian by saying: "You're missing the families that live here."

Her main concern was that she saw that New York's OUT Hotel had a shared room that young people could rent.

"I'm not sure that's the right kind of clientele [for the neighborhood]," she explained.

Ian responded, "This is nothing like Steamworks!"

Everyone in the room laughed.

Except the owner of Steamworks.

"Hey!" he exclaimed with a jovial tone, causing Ian to profusely apologize.

Ian reiterated there would not be any "hanky-panky" going on in these rooms. He said they were only shared rooms for people of all sexual orientations and genders that did not have the full fare, but wanted to stay in the area. "I can take it out if there is community resistance." He assured her.

Only rich good gays allowed apparently.

However, then, when it seemed as though everyone in the room was against the building, Stuart, an owner of Minibar, gave an impassioned speech in support of the project. While he obviously stood to gain substantially from the proposed building personally, his reasons for supporting the project were more community oriented.

After living in the area for twenty-seven years, he said the neighborhood needed a gay project like this to revitalize it in the face of young people moving north.

"We can't just let the LGBT part die." He stressed. "We're dying here! Young gays go elsewhere—It's not like it used to be. It is changing. We need to bring change to bring this back to what it used to be."

What it used to be.

To recapture the vivid gayness of the neighborhood's early days, there was only one proposed solution: make Boystown a tourist destination for style.

Even straight people would want to stay at this hotel, Ian said, because "the place is funner, better decor, trendier, better food, better music."

In short, it would have all of the cultural objects one could buy to support a gay habitus. Straight people would desire a gay sensibility and could acquire it by consuming appropriately in gay spaces.

The proposal that they needed to bring a gay sensibility of style—and that the OUT Hotel would secure straight visitors wanting to stay at that kind of hotel—led one white-haired resident to wonder aloud: "So, is taste only for gay people? I'm concerned about the LGBT versus straight [dynamic here.] Life will never be like it was. The more we get our rights, the less relevant our businesses will be."

Building a hotel would save the neighborhood by bringing outsiders in to keep the lights on, to keep the business afloat. The only way to save the neighborhood was to engage in heritage commodification. A concept from tourist studies, heritage commodification refers to the process by which a culture becomes sold to outsiders.[3] For example, a luxury African safari, in which companies, and sometimes the state, collude to create an "authentic experience" that may or may not be recognizable as authentic to insiders of the culture, like having a mash of different African tribes' ceremonies and foods under the bill of a single unified Africa.

Business owners in Boystown have a stake in the financial viability of their businesses. More than that, they have concern for the continuing "gayness" of the area. How can it survive in the face of assimilation into the straight mainstream? How can they keep their businesses, and the neighborhood, relevant?

They translate this concern into a concern about Boystown's viability as a destination. How can it attract gay people that have moved out of the neighborhood back to consume a gay lifestyle? How can it attract wealthy gay travelers to have a city experience? How does consuming this gay lifestyle and this destination result in the continuing of a group known as "gay" that will ease this business owner's concerns about "dying"?

These business owners, advocating passionately for the OUT Hotel, reveal that the changes to Boystown are not driven solely by cold profit. They do not just want straight people to come on safari. They see Boystown, a gay neighborhood with gay businesses, as a way that gay culture gets transmitted. Through heritage commodification, they can create a gay Disneyland, one that will instill a gay habitus in visitors, a set of dispositions that transmits gay culture from one generation to the next.

■　■　■

I've felt like a historian the further along I have gotten writing this book. The bars on the strip are changing, sold out from under us as I write this. I continually came back to this section, updating a new bar that has been sold to straight owners, or a new institution lost to the tide of heritage commodification.

The general "there goes the gayborhood" sentiment led business owners to shift their tactics to save the neighborhood. If rents keep rising such that they can't afford their businesses or if the customers who used to come have all moved away to Edgewater, then how they can afford to keep their businesses open? They have to shift with the market realities. They have to change how they are going to stay afloat in the rising tide of gentrification. They have to sell themselves. They have to sell gayness.

Assimilation changed Boystown. As gay people are accepted in society, they no longer have to live in the neighborhood. They can live anywhere that they want. Yet, despite not living there, or never having lived there, as is the case for Black and Latino gay men, gay men still travel from across the city to partake of Boystown's gay Disneyland.

Figure 10.2. Woman with stroller walking by the Kit Kat Lounge and Supper Club

Business owners feel like their investments are threatened by the residential movement north by white gay men out of the neighborhood. Their livelihoods rely on gay dollars. If people don't live in the neighborhood, how can businesses attract that money back to the neighborhood? Again, the answer lies in its transformation into gay Disneyland. They can only save the neighborhood—and gay culture—by selling it. By selling it, they could keep the institutions and space of a neighborhood that could teach a new generation how to be gay.

However, heritage commodification changes an area to make it more palatable to those that have the wallets to buy it: primarily upper-class white gay men and straight white women. It whitewashes. It cleans up. It removes the messiness in favor of a curated experience.

Kit Kat Lounge, for instance, primarily makes its money from the straight women who come to Boystown to have a night out on the town. Kit Kat is designed to make money from bachelorette parties. On their website, you can find a list of their divas and coordinate your bachelorette party with the male revue across the street in Circuit. From its design choices, to its drink choices, to its entertainment and staff, Kit Kat is a *Sex and the City* version of gayness.

Any night I walk by Kit Kat and peer in the windows, the only people I see in this business—ostensibly a gay bar—are tables of straight women.

And I'm not the only one to notice this. Once, when walking to the Whole Foods attached to the Center on Halsted, which is across the street, three white macho straight 'bros' were walking back from the Whole Foods toward the Wrigleyville neighborhood, each carrying a large case of beer.

As they walked by the bar, I overheard one of them say, "Huh. I thought that was a gay bar. It's all chicks!"

One Easter, I went with a group of gay men to get brunch at Kit Kat. I had to see it for myself. The staff who greeted us at the door stepped out of the gay "plastic" stereotype: name-brand designer pants and shirt, twinkish, gelled hair, white. While we weren't the only gay men there for brunch, the one other table of three gay men was sat right beside us at the window, as though we were on display for those walking by, validating this as a gay establishment.

Kit Kat specializes in "martinis." Their four-page menu overflows with over forty types of cocktails served in conical glasses, as though the glass's shape gave it the right to be called a martini. (There's gay habitus! You can hear my condescension at their taste.) This being brunch, mimosas were the best option for us. The whole venue sparkled white with silver and pink details, not exactly the most masculine color palette.

Midway through our meal, we were treated to the main attraction: a drag queen performing in high fashion style.

As she paraded up and down the length of the restaurant, she lingered longer at the two tables of gay men, since we were actually handing her dollar bills. A placard on the table advised:

Do not stand on the tables or chairs to take pictures.

Please tip your performers! It is considered polite to give dollar bills to performers during their songs.

It is inappropriate to touch a performer without their permission.

Evidently, these kinds of guidelines were needed for Kit Kat's regular customers. I can only imagine what happened one night to warrant that last proscription.

But it is this kind of novelty that brings straight women to Boystown.

In my interview with Celeste, a straight white woman in her late twenties, I asked her about the last time that she came to Boystown.

"The last time we went out was probably to D.S. Tequila. Um, we like to do brunch there."

"Uh huh."

"I'm thinking the last time was brunch at D.S. Tequila."

"Sort of like a Sunday Funday kind of thing?"

"Oh yeah! And an evening outing? Was Kit Kat Lounge?" she hesitated, but then shook her head affirmatively.

"Tell me a little bit about Kit Kat Lounge, and then we'll talk about DS," I asked.

"We had a new person start at work and I found out that they live just south of me, south of Diversey actually, and they were new to the area. They just moved from the east coast. And she was, like, 'I haven't been to Boystown yet, where do you suggest?' And I said, 'Let's start at Kit Kat and see where we end up.' It was five of us including me, girls from the office. We had our own little banquette, and we ate and drank and enjoyed the entertainment."

"What do you like about Kit Kat?"

"In the summer, I really like the outdoor area."

"The lounge-y sort of thing?"

I'm clearly articulate in interviews.

"Yeah," she confirmed. "I also like that about Kit Kat,"

She paused, maybe unsure of how to phrase her words properly.

"It's not your run of the mill night out."

"What do you mean by that?" I asked.

"Bars are bars are bars, by the end of the evening. With Kit Kat, it's more of an experience. It's not just cocktails with friends. There are other things the establishment brings to the table—"

I laughed, remembering the establishment needed to literally keep people off the tables.

She continued, "—that you don't find everywhere. Plus I think, it borders on it being a novelty a little bit, but I also think that, but they do get a lot of repeat customers, because it is just fun, it's not for every night, but it is fun and you go back."

"So what is it about the novelty of it that makes it more fun?"

"Because it's different! Because it's different! And it's not the every weekend Friday nightspot. [It is for] maybe someone like me or my group of friends." She paused, mulling it over more. "It's interesting. I never thought about that."

Heritage commodification doesn't have to be flashy like Kit Kat. It doesn't have to be explicit. In fact, heritage commodification works better if the space isn't explicit, because then it is more likely to at least retain some of the gay men that the business is trading on when they attract other customers.

An easy example of this kind of space was the change over a year of Spin Nightclub to several different bars. Spin was a nightclub in the style of Sidetrack farther up the street. It had a nineties vibe, from back when gay bars were megacomplexes meant to contain you for the entire evening, moving

Figure 10.3. The line outside Manhole

from one room to another, a gay Disneyland of spaces within one bar, instead of spread out across the neighborhood. Spin had four different spaces, although most of them weren't used as the club got less busy.

In a surprise announcement in the spring of 2014, the space was sold to three straight men, who broke apart the different bars into two different clubs. The main part of Spin was turned into Whiskey Trust, a craft cocktail bar focusing on making their own house bourbon. The downstairs bar was turned into Chloe's, a dance club.

It is interesting to note as disconfirming evidence, Chloe's was also short lived, it only managed to stay around for about two months before the owners turned it into a different kind of club, a revitalization of Manhole, which also closed after a short time. Chloe's and Whiskey Trust failed because they were geared toward straight people. They traded on Boystown's gayness, they had the right consumption choices to correspond to gay habitus, but they weren't gay enough. They didn't inspire enough gay men to return to make the space feel authentic. Similarly, Manhole was rejected by people in other sexy communities because, while it had the trappings of a sexy space, it didn't encourage actual sexiness in an authentic way. One can't foster sexy communities by merely throwing on a leather harness and calling it a leather night.[4]

Almost every club on Halsted Street has transformed, a new clean upscale establishment replacing a dirty gay dive bar.

Whenever I introduced this topic to people over fifty, often one of their reactions would be, "Like LA Connection?"

LA Connection used to sit where Kit Kat is today. LA Connection was known most of all as a hustler bar, a place for johns to pick up hustlers for the night, and for everyone to score drugs. That it should now be Kit Kat, the pink wonderland of heritage commodification, is perhaps the biggest change of all the bars on Halsted.

Cocktail changed into Progress. Dirty dancer stripper bar to clean, well-groomed, bright Progress bar. Even the name cleaned up.

Buck's Saloon was a classic older dive bar, with an older male crowd, that became Replay, an arcade that serves craft beer.

"Buck's is the neighborhood bar," Adam, a middle-aged Black gay man, stressed to me.

"Buck's," I repeated as I wrote the name down on the map of Halsted Street I would produce during my early interviews with participants, as they explained the different spaces in the neighborhood. Buck's was still open at the time.

"Buck's is the neighborhood bar," he stressed again.

"Interesting," I tried to be noncommittal to get him to go on about the scene there. He obliged me.

"It is the most welcoming, friendly, gender-neutral, low-attitude place on the strip or anywhere you'll ever find. It is great. And Cocktail used to be like that, too, but everybody forgets about Buck's."

"Only one person has mentioned Buck's to me and they were, like, 'Uhh, I'm never going to Buck's again,' but it's different from that?" I asked.

"Yeah, if you want to have a nice, regular time and you don't care if anybody notices your Armani and, you know you didn't blow your entire income on Prada," he said to my laughter. "And you just want to have a beer and you wanna have a conversation—"

"So, it's not Minibar?" I joked.

"No, God," he said.

Even Hydrate, that dark late-night hookup bar, attempted to change its image.

"Hydrate aims for 'totally different feel' after major renovation," proclaimed the headline of a *Chicago Phoenix* article on the subject.

The owner, Mark Liberson, is quoted as saying:

> "The amount of money is significant," said Liberson, who declined to disclose the actual dollar amount. "From the initial plan to now, we doubled our budget. We kept extending to it more and more, and ultimately we ended up ripped out the bars in both rooms. We're rebuilding it. It's time. We've served a lot of cocktails over the years, but it's time to breathe new

life into Hydrate and to bring something closer to where the block is heading. We want to grow in the community, and we want the street to be that great piece of gay nightlife."[5]

"Where the block is heading." Dark late-night hookup bars are out. Sleek modern design, cleaner, is in: "'We're adding a lot of upscale finishes to the space, and a whole new feel from the exterior to the interior,' Liberson said. 'We're redoing the bathrooms, redoing the bars, changing all the materials, and even changing the exterior of the bar. We're changing everything. It's about as completely new as you can get..... We decided that it was time to create something that has a totally different feel.'"

Do all of these changes to Boystown—all of these bars and spaces that have been warped by heritage commodification—mean that sexy community has been lost in Boystown? Do they only want straight women and upper-class gay men to come spend money, and then go home to other areas?

This common refrain is the "ideology of lament."[6] It is the idea that community has been lost and we must return to other, older values.

In her book, *Jim Crow Nostalgia*, Michelle Boyd discusses similar changes and reasoning by Black leaders in the Bronzeville neighborhood in Chicago's south side.[7] To encourage investment, resettlement, and tourism, Black community and political leaders framed community life as being better in the olden days. Black-owned businesses, strong Black neighborhood groups, Black churches. However, by emphasizing these elements, they sanitized, idolized, and in many ways covered up the true workings of oppression during Jim Crow.

In contrast, here, I am not sanitizing or idolizing the olden days of the darkness of stigma that queer people endured. I'm not singing an ideology of lament.

Instead, I want to emphasize that we haven't lost community. It has shifted, moved. But that movement changes the people we become from these spaces. Several communities overlapped in these physical spaces of the gay bar. Now, they diverge, gay and queer. Sexy community spaces may be leaving Boystown, but sexy community isn't being lost. The stage of Boystown is changing because of economic pressures, but also because of different characters coming into the scene. That doesn't mean it's going away, it means that people are finding it in different ways and making it possible through different means. It's not lost, but the gay habitus that Boystown teaches changes.

While it may seem as though this chapter has been building to a castigation of the "evil, ruthless business people" that changed Boystown's nightlife, instead here is a different reveal:

I go to these places more.

That's economics isn't it? If the old bars and clubs—LA Connection, Cocktail, Buck's, Spin, etc.—made as much money as the new bars, then they might still be open.

They didn't make that kind of money though. The old guard that frequented them got, well, older. They didn't keep going out to spend money at bars. Young people want different kind of spaces today: fancy cocktails, brunch specials, different decor.

I am much more likely to go to Replay to play a game of Frogger while drinking a twelve-dollar glass of scotch than I was to go have a three-dollar Bud Light at Buck's. I went to Chloe's more in the first three weeks of it being open—dancing the night away with friends either as a way to end the night or just as a quick jaunt in between bars—than I did in the previous year of Spin being open.

And I'm an ethnographer! I went to those places to get a sense of the neighborhood. If I didn't go there that often, if I felt like it was work to go there, imagine what the rest of people who frequent Boystown felt about them.

That doesn't mean there wasn't a profit motive involved. The bar owners and the Northalsted Business Alliance could make more from young white men, and the middle-aged white men with money who chased them, than they could from poor kids on the street.

However, these reimagined bars stay open. That is a form of resistance to assimilation. This may seem contradictory at first. Gay Disneyland's goal, the goal of heritage commodification, is to sell the experiences, the objects of consumption, people believe will lead them to a gay habitus.

It is the goal of a culture to perpetuate itself. Cultures can die. Boystown and those who run it fear the postgay era. If Boystown could be saved without heritage commodification, it would be doing so. Gay Disneyland is a transformation of Boystown, but also the gay habitus of the gay people that frequent it. It resists complete disappearance into straight culture, complete assimilation, by retaining an identity as a separate culture that can survive by being sold to outsiders.

Yet the outsiders to whom it is being sold are transformed into insiders through those acts of continual consumption. It is that transformation, the slow internalization of gay habitus, that gay Disneyland is built for.

Assimilation in the context of gay people is not about gay people taking on the values of straight culture, as though there is something essential to being gay that means that you want to have multiple partners and listen to divas.

Assimilation is a matter of not acculturating newcomers to gay society. We've already grown up in straight society. One doesn't need to learn how to be straight as we are accepted into straight society. We already know how to act like straight people.

Heritage commodification is less a matter of selling out and more a matter of survival. For all of the problems I discuss throughout this book—sexism, racism, queer repression, that tangled intersectional knot—we should keep this in mind. Gay Disneyland has no malicious intent.

No one is born gay. We must become gay anew with each generation. If we don't learn it in Boystown, through gay cultural outlets, through the Internet, then we don't learn it at all. Gay culture dies.

Who is surviving though, when I say that gay culture dies? Which voices are privileged in the process of survival?

The voices of the young men, women, and trans people that populate the street at night are not present in these new clubs. The voices of queers, of sexy community, and those that are on the outside of the charmed circle are not present in these new clubs.

Full assimilation would be people not acculturating to gay habitus. But assimilation can also be piecemeal. Gay habitus is not static; it is changing.

Moreover, heritage commodification answers some of the questions raised by Ghaziani's *There Goes the Gayborhood* and other scholars about the future viability of gay neighborhoods. In many ways, those that run these spaces— whether explicitly, like the Northalsted Business Alliance, or disembodied in the economist sense of the collective decisions of business owners—saw the pressures of people moving away and they responded. They responded in a way allowing them to remain open. They responded in a way that makes the gayborhood live on, even if it's a rebirth in a different form.

Has or will the gayborhood disappear? Perhaps it depends on our definition. Whom is a gayborhood for? The obvious answer—gay people—might be less relevant in today's context.

Boystown has become a gay Disneyland, a tourist destination for people around the city, and across the country, to consume gay culture. Assimilation changed the profitable bars, the acceptable bars, in ways that may be irreversible. The sexy community that these bars used to contain may not be attainable anymore, without the mediating technologies of augmented reality hookup apps. Gay men's newfound acceptance changed the bars, as new people started to come enjoy them. However, it attracted them for a reason. Who are these new patrons, these social tourists? Why is Boystown so attractive to them?

11

Girlstown

When straight women come to a gay club, they go on safari. When I go to a straight club, like those across the Red Line train tracks in Wrigleyville, it feels like visiting the aquarium.

I'm not the one on display. I don't feel somehow more gay in comparison to the hypermasculine "no homo" antics of the bros around. Sure, I feel my sexuality heightened. I notice the difference in my display of masculinity. I feel tenser. I'm on guard. I can sense the presence of power.

But I'm watching the scene through glass, not fully one of the people that are milling about in the tanks. There is something separating me from the predators inside. My maleness, the privilege of my gender, keeps me safe in these situations. The same is not true for women.

Even in a friendly space, like Holiday Club on the corner of Irving Park Road and Sheridan Avenue, just on the border between Boystown, Wrigleyville, and Uptown, I feel uncomfortable, not at ease. Austin and I stopped in for a bite to eat after a movie one night, desiring some bar food with salt and grease. The Holiday Club is a welcoming, safe space. It hosts open-mic reading nights. It has nerdy trivia nights. I didn't feel out of place as a gay man, but it certainly was not the kind of bar space I usually attended.

Straight spaces have their own sexual fields, their own political economy dictating the rules, their own consumption-creating straight habitus. When the sexy waitress sidled up to our table, she leaned toward us slightly, pushing her rack in Austin's direction. She wore a tight, low-cut white T-shirt over blue jeans. She had her own economic incentives. She might make better tips from a table of two men if she gives off the allure of sexuality.

After ordering, while Austin read the show notes from the indie theater, I took my own show notes about the scene of straight spaces, these nightclub places I don't normally go. A few feet away from us a table of three straight guys stood near the center pole holding up the ceiling. While I ate my fries, I watched the hunt.

One of the men approached two women near the bar having a beer. One tall, the other my height. The man, in his business suit pants that said he was stopping in for a beer with friends on the way home from work, likely having gotten off the Sheridan Red Line stop just a half block away, asked them if they wanted to play pool. I watched the five of them walk over to the pool table.

Laughing, joking, a good time. It seemed friendly enough. After all, in the popular imagination, isn't this the heterosexual equivalent of the bar sexual space I've described? Straight men and women—or presumed to be straight—coming together to flirt, share a few drinks, a game of pool, and maybe exchange phone numbers at the end of the night. This is their sexual field. This is where straight people feel the spirit of the night.

I watched from afar, not only distanced physically, but mentally. I don't quite understand their dance, a ritual that to my eyes looks wholly imbalanced.

The women who were asked to play pool could have said no, I suppose. But even that would cut into their night, a reminder they are in a space for male sexual attention. They said yes, though. They looked to be enjoying themselves. Yet I felt uncomfortable because I was watching the predators feed. Sharks circling, separating out some of the fish from the school before diving in to bite.

I can only imagine what it would feel like to be the prey.

Celeste doesn't have to imagine.

"It's funny, because I was talking to a friend about this interview," Celeste, a white straight woman in her late twenties, told me a table at Caribou Coffee in Boystown, only a few blocks from her apartment.

"I was, like, 'We're going to be talking about Boystown,'" she said. "She was, like, 'Are you going to bring up the fact that it's one street away from the bro-y-est frat street in the city? How juxtaposed those attitudes can sometimes be? How close they are? Things like that?' A lot of people want to live in Wrigleyville because they graduate from college, they are young, they are white, they are professionals, they want to be in a fun area so they can get hammered every weekend and spend all their money. It's just funny how literally you feel it crossing over the street [to Wrigleyville]."

Wrigleyville is straight Boystown. The area around Wrigley Field, the baseball stadium where the Chicago Cubs play and often lose, is a playground for the largely white, young professionals that hit the many bars that line Clark Street. Wrigleyville is an entertainment district bringing in young straight people to drink, flirt, occasionally hook up. It also entertains hordes of older Cubs fans from the suburbs, who take the train or drive down and fill the neighborhood on game days, which being baseball, seems like every damn day in the spring and summer.

Boystown is not drawing people "Straight to Halsted" from just anywhere. Straight women come as an alternative to Wrigleyville. And Wrigleyville pushes them out as well.

"Yeah, tell me, how does it feel to be out in Wrigleyville. If you were going to go have a drink over there with your friends?" I asked.

"It feels loud," she laughed. "It feels loud. It feels like—if you're a single person in Wrigleyville, you're out to find people to hook up with. That's what I feel. You're out with your group of friends, you're out with that college group of friends that maybe you met when you were all twenty-two because when you're younger that's where you hung out. I think there's a college mentality there. But coming to Boystown? Here, I just think that, for a straight woman like myself, it doesn't feel as pretentious as Wrigleyville. It feels more relaxed, accepting. No one is putting on a front about how big a bro they are."

She deepened her voice, caricaturing a bro, much in the same way that Sam, the gay man mentioned in chapter 2, "On Safari," had caricatured women like her with a high-pitched squeal. "Like they are some big bro," she growled.

For Celeste, Boystown draws her in, not just for the fun novelty of a place like Kit Kat, but also because it is so opposite the straight male space of Wrigleyville. Her sexual field is across the tracks in the most "frat street in the city." That's the place she goes out if she wants to have a night as a single woman looking to enjoy the hunt, the sexual game of hooking up.

Boystown, however, is more relaxed. Without bros around, she can be more at ease. Boystown isn't just a space selling her a fun gay night out, it's also a space that by virtue of its gayness lets her have that kind of night. She can experience a night without men, at least ones hitting on her.

"So I know what you mean when you say bro-y, but explain it to people that may not know, to those eventually listening to this stuff on the recorder. How would you explain it to someone who wouldn't be in that culture, what is bro-y like?" I said.

"OK, OK, so I would describe it as, um," she tried to pick her words carefully. Too carefully.

I laughed. "Yeah it would be like describing red without the word."

"It's like describing water," she said.

"Yeah, it's, well, wet? I mean, they play Xbox?" I said with a twinkle.

"They drink Bud Light?" she laughed. "Like *all the time.*"

Her voice turned more somber. "I would describe it like a selfish—irresponsible sort of outlook, very all about me. OK, maybe not selfish, but just more focused on yourself, egocentric. A disregard for human connection. Almost robotic, a sort of template response to things."

"OK," I said. She evidently had some strong negative reactions to the bros she'd had to deal with in the past.

"You know, everything is a joke," she continued. "I mean there are some good qualities to this attitude because for some it builds confidence. If they can perform certain activities—" She gave the words a tone that said sex, but also inappropriate behavior.

"And build up their self-esteem to a level where they feel comfortable being themselves. Women can find that confidence sexy. I guess it, um, god, it's really hard to describe!" she said.

"So what's it like—you've talked about this a bit. What is it like being out with your girlfriends? What it's like having bros around?"

I laughed despite myself because she wrinkled her face in disgust.

"Oh. I think you just sort of have to manage your reactions a little bit. You have to be more mindful. Are you playing into it? Are you giving them that inch that they will take a mile with? You have to be really mindful about what you say. I think it's a bit challenging to feel totally comfortable."

How is Celeste supposed to have a fun night out on the town when she has to deal with this? How is she supposed to enjoy herself when she has to constantly be on guard?

Instead of being swept up by the spirit of the night, feeling a moment of collective effervescence on the dance floor or in flirtation with a man over drinks, she brings protection in the form of the other women of her group. She puts her guard up, watching her words to make sure she doesn't imply sexual attention that might put her safety at risk.

Straight women are inundated with stories from all parts of our society about the sexual violence that awaits them if they let their guards down. In many ways, the erotic sexuality of queer male spaces like the Hole or Hydrate's dance floor can happen only because the threat of sexual violence doesn't linger over the space. As men, they feel invulnerable to sexual assault, feeling as though they can protect themselves or say no should it happen, although gay men do rape and get raped.

For straight women, Boystown can be a refuge from Wrigleyville. As NBC-News Chicago reported in the summer of 2014, "Police are searching for an attacker after a woman reported being sexually assaulted inside Wrigleyville's The Irish Oak bar over the weekend. The 27-year-old woman told police she was pushed into a bathroom stall and assaulted in the lower level of the bar, located in the 3500 block of North Clark Street, just before 12:30 a.m. Sunday."[1]

According to the same new report, "Kevin Feldman, who manages a nearby bar on Clark Street said such crimes affect all the local bars. 'I think all the bars work as a team together, and pass the word along to each other. We try to make it a safe, fun environment, and we also we work hands-on with the police department,' Feldman said."

However, the sentiment that Wrigleyville bars are spaces where women must be on guard was shared by the women residents quoted in the article: "Neighborhood residents said they weren't surprised to hear of the news of the crime, though. 'It can happen anywhere, unfortunately, but especially here, because there's a lot of drinking involved,' Kara Johnson said. 'These incidents are increasing, so whenever I hear something, especially close to home, of course I'm going to be looking out around to see what's going on around me.'"

Similarly, "Resident Jaime Gandolni pointed to the rowdy reputation the neighborhood has earned. 'It's obnoxious, but I mean that's part of the lure of it, what people want it to be,' Jaime Gandolni said."

However, it's more than just these bouts of extreme violence, which are easy to overlook as aberrations—to say, "Well, I wouldn't do that" or "That wouldn't happen to me." Rather, we should look at the situations straight women are regularly in within these spaces: the collective rituals of objectification, sexism, heterosexuality, the policing and production of gender roles that sociologist David Grazian calls, "the girl hunt."

In his book, *On the Make*, Grazian examines the production of straight nightclub spaces, and the people who go to them, through the essays and observations of his undergraduate students at the University of Pennsylvania.[2] These young adults are younger, somewhat, than the men and women who frequent Wrigleyville, but the atmosphere of these clubs is similar.

The "girl hunt" refers to the collective game that men play when out in groups to "score" with anonymous women and thereby prove their masculinity. It is a scene so stereotypically played out in mass media I barely need to describe it. A group of men spies a group of women across the dance floor. They discuss the women's attributes and beauty, divvying them up. One man approaches his target with a pick-up line or some other "in" to start conversation. They talk, dance, flirt, and attempt to hook up. If he's following the tactics of so-called pickup artists, then he'll subtly insult her a little, a practice called "negging."

However, as Grazian points out, the girl hunt might be more myth than reality, at least in terms of its success. Research points out that, despite cultural images to the contrary, one-night stands are not incredibly common among straight men and women. Although their numbers differ—men reporting more and women reporting fewer because of social desirability bias—the percentage of people having one-night stands is likely lower than 20 percent.

Furthermore, Grazian documents the resistance women have to being hunted. Rather than submissive acquiescence to the hunt, women put off unwanted advances, resulting in the push-and-pull game of straight men advancing, and straight women rebuffing their advances.

I did not do significant fieldwork in Wrigleyville. Documenting the sexism of these straight spaces was not a goal of my fieldwork, as it would have diverted attention away from the queer spaces I mean to argue are important, directing attention, instead, to heterosexual spaces. In the same way, researchers whose primary focus is women or racial minorities, for example, are often obliged to evaluate their findings in relation to comparable work regarding men or white communities, respectively.

What I want do, though, is argue that the dynamic of the girl hunt—that sharky feeling of being hunted I've observed and that the straight and queer women I've talked with have experienced within straight spaces—divide the experience of women in these spaces. It isn't possible to just go out for fun. It isn't possible to find a place to "just dance" like Celeste wants to. A woman is always going to feel on guard in these spaces, unable to experience a moment of collective effervescence because she is worried about the violence, or even rebuffing a come-on.

To find places less fraught with sexual anxiety, straight women go to Boystown. In Boystown, they can find the good time that eludes them in the company of straight men. While Boystown's heritage commodification provides the structural context allowing tourists, Boystown pulls and Wrigleyville pushes in more ways than one.

■   ■   ■

What do women get out of it? Why come to Boystown? What is bringing them straight to Halsted?

There are three reasons behind coming to Boystown. The first of which, as already discussed, is that hetero spaces can be sites of sexual violence, fear, and, at the very least, a constant on-guard feeling that prevents fun. The gay men within Boystown are seen as safe.

The latter view, while aligning with offensive heterosexist ideas of gay men as less violent because they aren't "real men," is still frankly true. Straight women are not going to experience the same kind of harassment in Boystown they would elsewhere.

Second, gay habitus—what it has become and represents—is desirable. Heritage commodification shapes the neighborhood to become what is economically desirable, such that it becomes a gay Disneyland. It is this gayness that certain straight women want to learn, to be a part of, because it represents fun, fashion, and an aspirational lifestyle.

Let's revisit the concept of habitus, which I will now argue does not adequately consider our agency and our ability, our desire, for change. Habitus, as Bourdieu considered it, is our social psychological structure that reflects

Figure 11.1. The bachelorette party store, Batteries Not Included

the outer structure of society. Wacquant argues habitus is learned and taught through physical action. I argue we should go further: people seek out a habitus through changing their habits of consumption.

Bourdieu says of the relationship between habitus and lifestyles: "Through taste, an agent has what he likes because he likes what he has, that is, the properties actually given to him in the distributions and legitimately assigned to him in the classifications."[3]

In a footnote, he then elaborates: "An ethic, which seeks to impose the principles of an ethos (i.e., the forced choices of a social condition) as a universal norm, is another, more subtle way of succumbing to *amor fati*, of being content with what one is and has."

Bourdieu theorized within a European class condition that perhaps is not easily translated into the American context. While we may not have the kind of class mobility we think we have, we consume as though we do. As Tocqueville documented early in our history, Americans have an optimism that we can become better-positioned people.

We consume and we make choices to become those better people. We know that some tastes are better than others. Habitus isn't simply an invisible set of rules we unconsciously absorb—we also attempt to shape our own. We try to become different kinds of people, with a different, better set of tastes, through conscious choices of consumption.

In Boystown, bars sell an experience, a chance to get a better set of tastes by consuming appropriately. Boystown gives women a *Sex and the City* experience on *Girls* prices. *Sex and the City* shows four fabulous white women living a totalizing lifestyle of brunches, late-night martinis, and beautiful houses. Three of the four are rich, whether from family money, their careers, or divorce. The main character though, Carrie Bradshaw, is portrayed as a sex columnist and, in the style of television of those years, somehow "middle class," struggling yet living in her own Manhattan apartment.

As Emily Nussbaum, wrote in her *New Yorker* essay, "Difficult Women: How 'Sex and the City' Lost Its Good Name":

> "Sex and the City"... was pigeonholed as a sitcom. In fact, it was a bold riff on the romantic comedy: the show wrestled with the limits of that pink-tinted genre for almost its entire run. In the end, it gave in. Yet until that last-minute stumble it was sharp, iconoclastic television. High-feminine instead of fetishistically masculine, glittery rather than gritty, and daring in its conception of character, "Sex and the City" was a brilliant and, in certain ways, radical show.
>
> [...]
>
> So why is the show so often portrayed as a set of empty, static cartoons, an embarrassment to womankind? It's a classic misunderstanding, I think, stemming from an unexamined hierarchy: the assumption that anything stylized (or formulaic, or pleasurable, or funny, or feminine, or explicit about sex rather than about violence, or made collaboratively) must be inferior.[4]

The women on *Sex and the City* navigate a glittering, stylish Manhattan, one that Nussbaum reminds us is "not even especially dated: though the show has gained a reputation for over-the-top absurdity, I can tell you that these night clubs and fashion shows do exist—maybe even more so now that Manhattan has become a gated island for the wealthy."

Carrie Bradshaw and her cohorts, despite their flaws, are to be admired: "I'm a Carrie!" "I'm a Charlotte!"

Compare that to *Girls*, *Sex and the City* for millennials. These women struggle to get by, sometimes barely working, mostly living off their parents, always only one step from moving back home to Michigan.

I'm not a media analyst, but the economic insecurity portrayed by the *Girls'* girls is the reality today, even as they aspire to a *Sex and the City* fabulousness. Consuming gayness allows straight women to cheaply partake in particular kind of lifestyle even as the rest of their lives are plagued by douche-bag guys and limited job prospects.

Because, for all of the ways in which Boystown has become an expensive gay Disneyland, it is still cheaper than Lincoln Park or the Loop. For many of the women who come to Boystown, it's about a one-off night, not being a regular. Straight women splurge on a night out at Kit Kat for a special event or a brunch. Martinis at Kit Kat are still cheaper than those downtown. Boystown is expensive compared with what it was historically. For those traveling to consume it, it's much cheaper than what they'll find elsewhere.

Third, Boystown's changes may represent a lessening of queer sexuality within them for the gay men who attend, but they are still vastly more queer, sexual, and erotic than straight clubs for straight people attending them. These spaces allow straight women to display kinds of sexuality, and take pleasure in sexuality, that would otherwise be denied them in straight spaces. They want to learn a mode of perception allowing them to seize a sexuality denied to them.

Celeste told me that's one of the main reasons bachelorette parties come to Boystown.

"One thing that I've—a topic for me has been these bachelorette parties. Why Boystown for a bachelorette party over someplace else?" I asked her.

"Here's what I think! I think that there's—especially for people in their twenties—there's going to be a mix of girls in the group that's going to be married, single, divorced. I think that an environment where no one has to worry about getting hit on or calling attention away from the bride or getting separated because people are talking to whatever. The potential to stick together is greater," she said.

Boystown is a morally safe space for women in relationships. Their boyfriends and husbands are still watching over them even when they are not nearby. To go to Wrigleyville, where straight people hook up, would be to invite accusations of allowing men to hit on them. For women in straight relationships—which are presumed to be monogamous because of the charmed circle—going to a straight club is wrong. A gay club is a place where she can have fun, be safe, and have a sexual atmosphere without accusation of immorality.

Furthermore, she can—like the straight women who come into gay male strip clubs like Lucky Horseshoe or give money to go-go boys at Cocktail— express her desire for men, sexualize their bodies alongside the gay men, without being "sluts."

In this sense, while heritage commodification changes Boystown to be less queerly sexual, and thus more respectable for gay men, it is still more sexual than straight spaces for straight women. Boystown can sell not only a gay night of fashion but also the sexuality of queerness.

If it seems as though I want to push the buck onto someone like straight guys making straight bars uninhabitable for straight women, as though they are ruining queer spaces for queer men, then that is a misread.

The reasons I've given for heterosexual women coming to Boystown are meant to be explanatory, but not exonerating. Straight women, perhaps because of limited social power and lack of money, would rather flee to gay clubs to have a "novelty" time than to create their own spaces. Straight women don't actually have the social power though to transform their own spaces, to rid them of sexism. As a consequence, they go to another space, a gay space, that doesn't, won't, or can't keep them out.

Sexism feeds heterosexism.

■ ■ ■

Heterosexism feeds sexism.

Cyon Flare looked fabulous on the stage, a makeshift raised platform that Northstar Healthcare Medical Center brought into Jackhammer for the annual CD4 event. The night was to celebrate the poz community, people living with HIV/AIDS, and their allies.

It should be no surprise the event was at Jackhammer, a space of sexy community that has both more HIV-positive people and more people of color, who more often contract HIV. The event was also diverse in another way.

"We're so glad to have women here tonight," Cyon said in the middle of the speech welcoming people to the event, praising everyone for coming out to "not only be positive, but to be *positive!*"

"We're so glad to have women here tonight," Cyon repeated. "Because those are the girls that were taking care of our asses when we were down."

Many in the crowded bar nodded, some men standing next to the lesbian, queer, bi, and straight women that were their sisters, supporters, or best friends.

Women were taking care of gay, bi, and queer men when we were dying of AIDS. Queer women and straight women, whose communities were less devastated by the illness, came through for us when we needed them.

That's not the only time we needed them, though. We still need them, and when we do, they take us to our first gay bar, support us through our break-ups, and drink and dance with us when we are celebrating.

Women are an important part of queer male life.

Yet, when women come to Boystown, they are often met with derision and sneers. Bartenders ignore them. Some people tell them to leave.

Queer men brought women out to bars first, often as a way to get into those bars, as a safety net when we didn't know any gay men.

Moreover, most of the time, when I hang out in a queer space, I want to bring my friends with me. Some of those friends, some of my very best friends, are straight women. Why shouldn't they get to come along? Why should I have to abandon queer space to hang out with straight women?

In June 2014, a few weeks before my wedding, I had a bachelor party. One of my best friends, Elizabeth, arranged it as my best lady, in consultation with my friend Eric, who acted as gay consultant on the places in Boystown that we should go. Elizabeth had been out with me in Boystown several times before but didn't know the best places or the best times to go to each.

I sat down a few months later and talked with Elizabeth about that night to get her sense of what it was like moving through these spaces as a straight woman not on safari.

"It started out as—the group dynamic was me, Margaret, and Alex [her husband], and then all your gay friends that I had never met before were coming in. There was this sense that—moving around in the space is precarious sometimes for me, because there is a sense of friendship and love and ownership of our friends, and it is hard sometimes to navigate that with your gay friends because I don't want to come across as presumptuous with your affection or something. I don't know how to describe it. There is this sense of like—they know you in a way that I will never know you. They have shared connections with you in a way that I never want to infringe on," she said.

"Right." I said.

"So I'm always nervous that they aren't going to like me or hate me and just be like, go away," she said. "Or! They will perceive me as being a fag hag and that I only want to hang out with you because you are gay."

The specter of the "fag hag" hangs over the interactions between straight women and gay men. We have an easy script to fall into, but the cultural trope of the fag hag—an ugly woman that falls in love with her gay best friend because she can't get a boyfriend—can be insidious, damaging the relationship. Similarly, there is a suspicion that a gay man may be friends with a woman merely to use her as a beard—a disguise to throw people off about his sexuality—or as a substitute for the boyfriend he doesn't have in his life. The fag hag trope implies that they are using each other as a crutch and not enjoying real friendship.

The fag hag hangs over the interactions of queer men's female friends when they are brought to queer spaces, putting them on guard that they will be perceived as being on safari.

"So the first place we went to was the Horseshoe," Elizabeth said, referring to the Lucky Horseshoe gay male strip club at the corner of Belmont and Halsted. "I remember when we walked in, we had some bachelor party gear, and I had the notepads for people to write on, and the glow sticks."

"And I had my whistle," I said.

As best lady, Elizabeth organized the party as she understood the trope of pre-wedding parties to be fun, with games to play that would make it a bachelor party, and not just a regular night of drinking. She wanted to give it that something extra Celeste discussed earlier, by using the template of a bachelorette party. In this case, we played a couple of games for points. Working in groups that combined my straight friends with gay friends, my friends got people to buy me shots, give me advice on my upcoming nuptials, well wishes, and phone numbers. For my part, I had a whistle I was supposed to blow whenever I saw someone on safari, her having read that chapter before. The first person to point out who it was would get points.

I blew that whistle a lot, even in the Lucky Horseshoe.

Elizabeth continued, "And I remember feeling nervous about the fact that we tricked out people. Because the game involved us walking separately and talking to people in teams, but I never wanted to be unaccompanied by one you guys because I didn't want people to think that I was there as part of a bachelorette party."

She said, "But there were two other bachelorette parties there that night. There was a group of middle-aged Black women that were in the mainstage bar area. There was actually this weird moment where there were two lap dances going on both for two different female bachelorette parties. The other group were these white girls, younger, and clearly very wealthy, and they were both getting lap dances. And I remember as part of the game. There was a point in the game I could have gotten from them, but they wouldn't give me the time of day or look me in the eyes, which was interesting because I tried."

Frankly, there were probably more straight women getting lap dances than there were gay men getting them that night. That economic reality did not go unnoticed by the bar owners and staff, because now there were straight men working as go-go boys dancing and mingling through the crowd. A gay bar, but only a few steps away from a straight strip club.

"There was this one part, where you and me and Eric were standing there admiring the guys and I pointed to the one that I liked, you told me 'of course, you picked the straight guy out there,'" she said.

"Yes, I do remember that. Yes, I do remember that!" I laughed.

"And I thought that was pretty funny," she said. "And then he came over and we got you a lap dance from him. The one that was kind of bro-y?"

"Yeah and while he was cute, it was the most uncomfortable lap dance ever because he was gay for pay," I said.

"Yeah."

"And he had such a better time getting money off of the women coming through," I said.

"Yeah, and I took a picture with him for the game, and we went to take a picture with him and he put his hands around both of us, and he put his hand under my dress into my thong," she shuddered at the memory of it.

"I did not know that," I gasped a little.

Elizabeth laughed. "You were drunk," she said. "I told you at that time, and I was not happy with that."

Even in Boystown, she can't escape the sexual objectification and inappropriate, unrequested touching that she would find in a straight club.

Eventually though, we left to wander farther up the street. We danced for a while at Chloe's, where other queer men, queer women, and straight women all mingled on the dance floor, feeling a bit of the spirit of the night settle into us as we gyrated, light-headed from drink.

"And then we went to Jackhammer and then, OK, so here's the interaction. So all week long we had been talking and we knew we wanted to end the night at Jackhammer because it was your special day and that would be fun. We got all dressed up so you could go down in the basement and I wasn't planning on going down there, but I wanted to at least, like, come down and say good-bye because the rest of us were going to be leaving," she said.

"Yeah, and it's not uncommon for women to come down there," I said.

"Yeah, and I wanted to see what was down there because you write about it a lot."

"I feel like people might feel it's more of a constant circus orgy than it really was."

"Yeah, I was surprised at how small it was! But yeah, I wanted to know what was down there, and so, god, I can't remember all of what happened," she said.

"First, you went down there, and the doorman was like, you can't take your top off, and I was like, *Whaat*? that is not true," I said.

"Yeah! You said I couldn't get down there unless I took my top off, and then when I got down there he said I had to put my bra back on but not my shirt."

"Yeah, and that didn't seem true."

"Right, but I didn't want to make waves, but I was drunk so we hung out for like two or three minutes."

"Yeah we were already drunk and Margaret and Bruce were left upstairs," I said.

"Yeah, I was like 'I'm gonna go back up' and as I left, the guy working the door was like, "Did you see what you wanted to see sweetie?' in this very condescending way. I was like, 'I wanted to say good-bye and end the night with my friend because it's his bachelor party and I'm the best lady.' And he was like, 'uh huh.' I went upstairs and remember feeling bad. I really did wanted to see what was in there, I'm not gonna lie, but I also felt like, I just wanted to hang out with you and this guy made me feel like a creeper and I kind of felt like a creeper because of it," she said.

"Even though you were doing all of the things that—If I could create a list of how not to be on safari, like you were doing all of them. You were with someone. You knew the space. You weren't giggling and pointing at people. You were just enjoying being there and you were following all of the same rules."

She said, "He wasn't mean. He just had a knowing judgment. 'Alright princess: back up the stairs.' So then I went back upstairs, and there were two women there who were with their guy friend who was gay. They came over as I was finishing my drink. I wasn't the only other woman in the room. There was that woman …."

"Yes, Charlotte."

"And she was really nice to me. But then these two women came over to talk to me and they were like 'you can go down there if you want, you know. You just have to take off your shirt.' And then they started telling me—they were white women, midtwenties, suburban middle class, they kind of had that look you have when you just get out of college and are just figuring out your style, and they were telling me how they were from the suburbs and were visiting their gay best friend from high school. He was hanging back and looking mortified that he was being seen with them. I was just like, 'Oh my god.' I felt bad for these girls because they looked like they didn't belong. They looked like tourists. They were elated to be here. This was the most exciting thing that's happened for them."

I said, "Yeah, they are getting to have a new—"

Elizabeth jumped in: "A new adventure."

"That's what's great about being a tourist on safari. It's really fun."

"But he [their gay friend] was really like—" she struggled to find words.

"Sure we're putting things on them, but this is where he wanted to go. That's where they ended up at least," I said.

"Yeah, I don't know. Yeah." Elizabeth struggled to explain her feelings in that moment. "I felt simultaneously bad for these girls, but then really hoping that I wasn't being taken for being like these girls as this completely unknowledgeable person moving around this social space. They were like, 'You need to go down there. Take your shirt off and go down there.' Asserting that I had a right to go down there, and I was just like, 'Ok, did you go down there?' They were like, 'Yeah we went down there and took off our shirts and went down there.'"

She paused, building up to the revelation. "So that guy that was working the door. He had that experience."

I broke in, "Yeah, he had had that experience ten minutes before. Those experiences drive him to be rude to you and continue the cycle of sexism and heterosexism feeding each other. Because then he's rude to you as someone who's trying not to be rude to this space when you want to be with your friend."

"There was this time when we were down there and I was reeling on my heels, but I was acutely conscious of time. Like if I go up right now I'm just going to seem like I came down here to see what it's like. There was constant intentional impression management to look like I was not on safari and it did not work."

Elizabeth, like Celeste in the straight clubs being hit on by men, was made hyperaware of her presence, making sure that she was not fulfilling stereotypes of tourists on safari. She wasn't able to have any of the experiences of naked intimacy that make that space great. She didn't get any of the benefits.

After describing that theory to Elizabeth, she responded, "Right, not in that space. I did have that experience when we were dancing at Chloe's because there was also more women there and it was a less—" She trailed off.

"But," I said, "that was also a space purposefully built for those kinds of interactions. That ties in, there are reasons why women come. You don't feel naked intimacy in queer spaces, in the spaces the queer men feel it because you're so worried about being on safari and people are pushing back saying you're not supposed to be there. But you do feel it in places of heritage commodification that are purposefully for women to go and dance there."

Heritage commodification is successful at saving Boystown, keeping it alive, because it creates these kinds of middle-ground spaces. Just queer enough. Just sexy enough.

As the neighborhood becomes assimilated, there is also backlash to women being in these spaces by gay and queer men looking for the kind of space that they feel that they have lost. The "get off me bitch I'm trying to suck this guy's dick" attitude of men like Sam reflects this sentiment. Women are the good consumers, the good friends, but ambivalently so, because they are survival consumers. They are accepted because they have to be, not necessarily because they are wanted.

One of the concerns of intersectionality has been how forms of oppression are mutually reinforcing.[5] In the gay bar, it's possible to see the intersectional knot: the sexism on the part of straight men pushes straight women to go to gay bars because, due to their heterosexism, they assume these spaces are safer and they are going to be more fun. In turn, their heterosexism reinforces the sexism of gay men who respond to this with being sexist.

That sexism is perhaps most evident in the experience of queer women and trans people of all genders.

Queer women and trans people have long been a part of queer male spaces. Moore discusses that some integrated spaces began during the seventies before AIDS.

Charlotte is one of these queer women, a bisexual woman involved in the leather community who frequents queer male spaces like the Hole. Kade is one of these trans people, a queer person who is sometimes feminine presenting, sometimes masculine presenting.

Most men that I talked to would say that it was only the straight women that they had problem with in the space. However, when asked about it, queer women and trans women reported they had experienced problems too.

For instance, Kade told me during our interview, "You know, we used to go to Boystown. I thought it was the place to be."

I laughed. "Does that imply it's no longer the place to be?"

"It's the place to be for some people."

"So what type of people, then?"

"I don't know. People who like to party? People who get drunk? The thing about Boystown was always, from my experience—Boystown is mostly gay male owned. The clubs, the bars. I just remember when I used to go out in Boystown, it would be hard to get a drink. As someone who people read as female," she said.

"Is there a particular story about that? That you have, like, at a particular bar?" I asked.

"I don't think so. It was just something we used to complain about. All my friends used to complain about or you would go to—I remember a lot of times my friends were getting frustrated. They would go to Spin or Side-track and they would be like, 'we are going to meet girls.' And then they be like, 'All the girls there are straight and are with their gay male friends.' So overwhelmingly the women in those clubs are straight women who come with gay friends. I used to be really frustrated by Boystown in that sense, cause all the straight people."

Unlike with sexual racism, this situation doesn't change in the sexy communities of places like Jackhammer. I specifically interviewed women involved in those spaces—as rare as they were—to get their perspectives on being involved with spaces that still remained largely hostile to women's involvement. Because even while men insisted they only rejected women's involvement when they were on safari, queer women would report hostility as well.

Charlotte, a queer leather woman and a member of Marcus's leather family, involved in the sexy community spaces of Jackhammer and Touché, spent much of her interview discussing the difficulty of swimming upstream. Charlotte has a dominant personality—in more ways than one—and isn't someone who is going to let others dictate her involvement.

"So, that's my question. I've been to these things before. It hasn't changed. Women being there hasn't changed anything. They are *leather* women after all," I asked.

Figure 11.2. A bachelorette and her bride outside Kit Kat Lounge and Supper Club

Charlotte clinked her glass of red wine with her nails.

"Changing these events and bitching about IML. It is not *us*," she sounded exasperated. "The leather women at IML are not weakening IML. The circuit boys are weakening IML. IML is not as much a leather event as it used to be not because of people like me and [other women]. We are not the ones that are making that shit less leather. It's the boys showing up in their flip-flops and cocktails that think it's sooooo interesting."

Her tone reminded me of Sam's caricature of women on safari.

"They are making it less leather, so why are they turning the ugly on us? Ugh. Back in the sixties? No, there weren't any women around. But there were women in the catacombs in San Francisco in the seventies. [Name] was elbow deep in someone in the seventies. If seventies San Francisco fisting boys can deal with women in their space, what is your problem?"

She took a sip of red wine, finishing, "You know what, when men started dying, women that they dealt with were the only ones that kept that knowledge and passed it on."

Maybe we have girls to thank for having a Boystown at all.

12

Take Back Boystown

The summer of 2011 was hot. Some say the heat brought people out on the streets. The heat made people drink too much. The heat made people violent.

For others, the explanation is more essential.

"Make sure that when you are writing this book, you write about both the good and the bad changes to the neighborhood," an older, affluent white gay man said to me after I told him about my project at Buck's, a gay bar in Boystown that has since shut down.

We stood in the front near the door, to the right of the bar, in a group of four discussing the neighborhood. Ron and John, an older retired couple who lived in the area that I had met at Spin, sat behind me at the bar, surrounded by many of their friends. Buck's had an older crowd, filled largely with white men who still lived in the neighborhood, many of whom bought their condos years earlier before severe gentrification. If someone disagreed with the characterization this man offered, they didn't speak up.

The good changes? "How nice everything is nowadays."

The bad? "The ghetto trannies and gay kids on the street."

These were the people "from the south side" or "from other neighborhoods" who came here and committed violence.

These were the people from whom "we"—he included both of us as white men—needed to "take back Boystown."

The Take Back Boystown movement brought me to the neighborhood. I watched the events of 2011 from a computer screen, following the news from Madison, Wisconsin. I was down in Boystown several times that summer, but never close enough to capture these flashpoints firsthand.

Needless to say, I talked with many of my first interviewees about Take Back Boystown. I have to be vague about many of the people I quote for this chapter, because their knowledge about the events implicates them, exposes them. I try to be as specific as I can, so that you may place them and

Figure 12.1. 7-Eleven, by day and night

can weigh their information, but I am aiming for plausible deniability. Some quotes have been edited to remove identifying details that might reveal clues about their positions, organizations, or roles.

I sat down with Robert at the Caribou Coffee on the corner of Halsted and Cornelia, across from Hydrate and Little Jim's. Robert is a journalist, affiliated with one of the several publications and blogs that followed the ongoing Take Back Boystown story from the beginning.

Throughout our conversation, the door next to us kept opening and closing, people walking by constantly crossing next to our discussion and the recorder.

"Basically, what happened is there was a stabbing by the 7-Eleven. Are you interested in the story or…?" he asked.

"Yeah," I said. "I read a whole bunch about it, but I'm very interested in hearing you relate what the story was, and stuff like that."

"Basically there was a stabbing by the 7-Eleven and it was a white, out gay, more affluent, I would say. Not super rich, but had money and was into bars et cetera. And he was stabbed by a nineteen- or twenty-year-old Black man who was visiting here from either the south side or Indiana. I've covered a couple stabbings. Some were south side. Some were Indiana."

It's easy to see why Robert mixes up the details here. Which stabbing was it? It is hard to keep the stabbings straight in the wave of hysteria that gripped the neighborhood after the three stabbings that summer.

This particular stabbing was on June 18, 2011. A twenty-year-old Black man residing on the south side of Chicago—this detail is specifically mentioned in all reports—stabbed a thirty-four-year old white gay man after they argued outside the 7-Eleven. The white man's residency was unmentioned, but presumed in retellings to be in Boystown. Black south side; white Boystown.

"A lot people in the community freaked out and were like, 'Oh my god, a Black hoodlum is, like, stabbing our men,'" Robert said. "Part of it was that it was stabbing and violent, which was kind of rare. Part of it is that one of the stabbings was caught on YouTube, incidentally by the people who created the Take Back Boystown [Facebook] page."

I don't think it was incidental. Two white gay condo owners, whose home overlooked Halsted Street, started taping when another fight broke out on the night of July 3.

In the video, a twenty-four-year-old Black man from Indiana—this detail often omitted in the later oral retellings of the episode, the south side substituted—stabbed a twenty-five-year-old Black man.

Two groups of young Black men came together. There was short argument, and then a burst of violence as one group piled on one of the other men.

The condo owners leaked the video to the mainstream Chicago media, prompting articles, ten o'clock local news coverage, tweets, blog posts, and a Facebook page asking about the "sudden crime wave" in Boystown.

"Around the first two stabbings," Robert said, "people created the Take Back Boystown Facebook page. And started posting all this really racist, hateful, vitriolic stuff that was just terrifying."

"Absolutely terrifying," he repeated. "And it was about all these Black kids and these hoodlums from the south side terrorizing their neighborhood and all this stuff."

"It's the blacks tearing the neighborhood apart."

"They're a bunch of monsters."

"Most of the drama is caused by black a-holes who live in other neighborhoods who come here and don't respect the area."

"I've lived in Chicago for 46 years. These comments aren't racist. They are true."

"Go back to your hoods!!!"[1]

He took a sip of his black tea, looking over his shoulder to see if someone was listening, before continuing. "And this guy, the first guy, he went on the Facebook page and posted from the hospital. He was like, 'I'm in the hospital. I got stabbed. I'm okay. Please stop writing such hateful stuff on my behalf.' He was like, 'I was drunk and I picked a fight with this kid. Did I deserve to be stabbed? No, but I wasn't innocent. I brought this on myself. I was being an asshole in 7-Eleven.'

"So the guy said that, so then his friends posted stuff like that on Facebook and people still kept freaking out. They wouldn't listen. It had taken off on its own by that point."

Take Back Boystown picked up the ambient energies about crime in the neighborhood. In addition to the Take Back Boystown page, an event was held in the neighborhood, at the 7-Eleven parking lot kitty-corner to Roscoe's. Ostensibly, the call was for "positive loitering" to show a presence of residents in the neighborhood, to show that they wouldn't let the neighborhood be taken over by violence from outsiders.

The Chicago edition of the *Huffington Post* reported on each stabbing. After the third stabbing, they wrote:

> The perception of a trend prompted some residents to create a Facebook page titled Take Back Boystown and call for a 'positive loitering' walk, which was held Saturday, July 2 in the same parking lot where the June 18 stabbing victim was injured. Their stated goal was to raise awareness about safety and noise concerns in the area.
>
> The Facebook group has now attracted nearly 2,000 followers, and the 'positive loitering' event attracted some 50 walkers, according to the 23rd

District's police commander Kathleen Boehmer. But some are concerned about the tone of the conversation surrounding violence in the area. During the Take Back Boystown event, a counter-demonstration was held. About 30 protesters, many affiliated with the group Gender JUST, said queer youth of color in the neighborhood have been targeted following the recent reports of violence.[2]

These two groups—Take Back Boystown, together with local residents, versus Gender JUST, together with other nonprofits and area youth—clashed at the Community Alternative Policing Strategy (CAPS) meeting held shortly after the events.

Kate Sosin, of the *Windy City Times*, the Chicago gay paper of record, reported:

> In the midst of a community uproar over violent crime in Lakeview, the much-anticipated July 6 CAPS 2324 and 2331 meeting, drew nearly 800 people and a debate so heated that it often turned into a screaming match across auditorium aisles.
>
> Nearly everyone who attended the meeting seemed to leave the Inter-American Magnet School, 851 W. Waveland, bleary-eyed and exhausted hours later.
>
> The CAPS (Community Alternative Policing Strategy) meeting, which is held regularly, was widely attended due to a string of recent violent attacks that have increasingly concerned residents who say that the neighborhood is unsafe.
>
> [...]
>
> Also in attendance were several queer youth who claimed that the organized response to crime in the neighborhood was unfairly scapegoating them for the attacks. The "Take Back Boystown" Facebook page, which has drawn attention to community fear about crime, has also served as a space where people aired frustrations about LGBT youth who come to the neighborhood for social services. Some on that page blamed queer youth for noise and violence in the neighborhood, setting off a community discussion about race.
>
> One man who spoke at the meeting said that some youth who come to the neighborhood are perpetrating violence. "Sometimes people just need to be told how to act in this neighborhood," he said.[3]

The proposed solution of many residents—and people outside the area who think of themselves as belonging to the neighborhood, what Theo Greene calls "vicarious citizens"—was a typically conservative one: more cops, private security for the Halsted entertainment strip, and closing social services.[4]

For Pauline, having lived through a similar episode in her own neighborhood, the response in Boystown had racist and classist roots. I sat down with her in the break room of the Center on Halsted, a multimillion dollar LGBT community center. I'm not sure that we should have been there. Pauline works at the center, and, although she chose the space, I don't think that she felt very free to talk about her role combating Take Back Boystown. She was tight-lipped, unsure about what I was using the information for, despite the consent form. I had to assure her several times I wasn't interviewing her as a center employee, but as someone who knew about, and was involved in protesting against, the Take Back Boystown movement.

We were discussing racism in Boystown, when she commented, "Although discrimination happens on the other side of town, they do it in such a way— like I said, it's racism and it's classism. And I think, in this neighborhood, they feel as though 'I spent all this money for this condo so this and this better happen.'"

"Okay," I said.

"So, they started putting pressure on the police officers and the business associations and they were trying to shut down nonprofits. They just operate differently than other parts of town. Very differently. I can even give you an example."

"Sure."

"So, there were these random stabbings here in Boystown. I live in [a south side neighborhood]. There was a random stabbing and the community came together and they said, 'Well, what can we do to prevent violence?' Never once did they say, 'Let's shut this down, let's shut this down.'"

She waved her finger in the air, as though she was back at the CAPS meeting for a moment.

"It was nothing like that," she said, again becoming more reserved, sinking in her chair, arms crossed.

"Like, 'let's get rid of social services.' Yeah," I said.

"They gave a description of the perpetrators. And they never used coded language. Take Back Boystown, they'll say, 'roving mobs of Blacks.' You know? [In that south side neighborhood,] you just got the description. The person was Black, they were five foot eleven, a hundred thirty pounds. They just left it at that. With Take Back Boystown, it's always something extra. They were calling for the police to arrest people if they were in groups," Pauline said.

"Yeah, I remember reading something about that. In which someone was, like, the police should just stop people and grab them if they 'clearly aren't from this neighborhood,'" I said.

"And that's kind of problematic because a lot of people here hang out in groups. Who comes here alone? They were trying to implement a gang ordinance. So if there's three or more people out there, I don't know what the police will do, but they're supposed to maybe arrest them."

"If three or more people are hanging out?"

"Mob action. Mob. Action."

While residents and vicarious citizens called on the police to crack down on outsiders, they also railed against the community groups they saw as bringing people in from other areas to use social services. The largest and most often attacked of these were the Center on Halsted and the Broadway Youth Center, a social services organization for LGBTQ youth run by the nonprofit LGBT health clinic Howard Brown.

I spoke with a Center on Halsted senior official about these issues as well, whose details I am leaving obscured, as though behind a panel and voice changer on a television exposé, because of the potential ease in identifying them. I heard a similar story from a senior official with Howard Brown, organizers at Broadway Youth Center, and other nonprofit workers in the area.

They said, "I also believe that Halsted Street has now become more of an entertainment district. So it's drawing not only LGBT youth but everyone that's kind of hanging out on the street. So when we move to the topic of violence in our community and the response of our community's blaming LGBT people."

"Perfect. Going there for me," I said, given I had come to discuss precisely this issue with them.

"I know," they smiled with the trained candor of someone who had media training. "I really challenge that. That the center is the cause of this. Obviously these people don't know the history of Lakeview. That Lakeview has always been a destination for young people. Young people coming out. Young people wanting to know where the activity is. Young people who are homeless surviving."

They sighed and continued: "But now you add in the whole entertainment district that you have straight people coming to check out what's going on who are not of age, who are not allowed in the bars. But they can come out and hang out in the street and watch things. So that happens when the violence happened last summer, I can tell you that our young people were very sad that they were targeted by the individuals creating this. Because they felt that that was an injustice. Because young people come here wanting a safe, welcoming environment. Because they don't have that in their communities. And then the door being shut in their face is really sad. The one ugly violent fight that took place on Halsted Street that triggered the massive town hall meeting and a lot of the calling for the center to close, the stabbing—"

"This is the one that was on YouTube?"

"Yes. The stabbing. It was later determined that the person that created the stabbing was from Indiana, and he was straight. And the person that was stabbed was a DePaul student and [had] nothing to do with the Center on Halsted. But that story never came out. It may have come out, but it never was like, 'Look, they had nothing to do with the center.'"

"So why did people immediately jump to that it must be the center?"

"Right. So we go back to: what's community? That lacks in our community. That doesn't exist. So instead of blaming, why not look for solutions? Why not say, oh, there are homeless youth there, how do we take care of our homeless youth? Are there enough beds? Are there enough resources? People should be outraged by that. Instead, they look for a reason to blame."

They sighed again, and said, "And I think also that for some individuals, there is that discomfort. It's Black trans youth. And for them, that makes them uncomfortable. They will say that they're not racist but when you really drill down and ask questions of who is 'those people'? And if these young men were Caucasian white men hanging out on the corner who look like you, would that be okay? Or is it because they're African American and they're homeless, that's what makes you uncomfortable? And now we're dealing with racism, classism, sexism, socioeconomic injustice, trans issues. And that's to me a real complicated landscape of issues that we all have to come to grips and respond to. Because the center is not going away. We are a force on this street. Just like the bars are."

They were getting heated, some of their personal anger at Take Back Boystown cracking the surface of their media relations experience. They said, "The center was out there trying to find solutions! But where are the bars that are making millions of dollars on this tourism? Where is their response? How do they help build community and how do they help be part of the solution?"

As I've discussed, it's not that the bars are incapable of building community, perhaps even more capable than the Center on Halsted has been, because a wider range of people are brought together. Sexy community used to live in those bars. Sometimes it still does.

Rather, the bars are no longer building that kind of community anymore. The spaces have changed. Heritage commodification changed the perception of who belongs in the neighborhood. Gay Disneyland created Take Back Boystown.

Who is Boystown being taken back from? It's not the straight white women, the actual new outsiders, but the queer Black youth, who have always been on the street.

Yet, when confronted, Take Back Boystown supporters denied that their issues were with a specific kind of person.

On the Take Back Boystown Facebook page, one Black man commented,

Why are you focusing your attention on the black gay youth? Boystown is the only place where black gay youth can come and feel comfortable. I would say that there are a few bad apples but there are also hard working black people such as myself. This past Saturday I was profiled by an old white man and was told to 'go back to where I belong you Nigger Thug.' I work full-time in the Lakeview neighborhood as a gay black man that happens to look young, i'm 31, and i'm profiled. It feels like that this page is only for angry gay white men that doesn't like black people. It's sad but I will continue to do the work that I do to change lives so to all of you racist assholes kiss my black skinny ass.

The first two responses are illustrative.

First, someone with a generic John Doe name and a fake cartoon picture, responded: "No, we're focusing on the violence—it just happens to be that the perps of the majority of the troubles are black. Were u dressed a certain way that might have brought this on? Maybe you should talk to your fellow black 'youth' that are walking the streets, shuffling, pulling up their pants why they are being stupid and ruining it for all the blacks in the neighborhood. I think we're done trying to justify ourselves."

Another person commented: "'Boystown is the only place where black gay youth can come and feel comfortable.' Then why not focus on the black community, and the reasons as to why the black youth can't feel comfortable in their own area??? Does this give them the right to come into the most liberal area of the city, and cause all this drama? I'm so sick of the race baiting. Get over it already."

Go back to your own community. Stop violating the segregation of Chicago.

I talked to George, a white gay man in his midthirties, about his experience with the CAPS meeting. He felt that any discussion of race was shut down by others arguing they were only against "crime."

He said, "They were shut down quickly and vociferously by folks who said, 'No, it's not about race.' And, and it definitely is. Listen to the audio and you'll hear people at the CAPS meeting shutting it down. Go to—have you been to the Take Back Boystown Facebook page?"

"Oh yeah, trust me, I've been capturing screen shots. Some of the comments have been—uh—quite explicit."

"Yeah, like I remember reading one that said, 'Ship those animals back to the south side.' Now how can someone make that statement and then say this conversation is not about race? Because it is and there's no denying it. When you're referring to African American youth as animals and assuming they are from the south side because of the color of their skin or assuming that the youth that come to the center are the same youth that perpetrated the stabbing on the street because they are both Black, or both wear baggy clothes, or they're both trans. That's an issue."

They were "only talking about crime," but talking about crime is the same as talking about race. Take Back Boystown is a reflection of perceptions of crime. Supporters feel crime has risen. However, perceptions of crime are not a reflection of actual crime. It is a perception of the racial composition of an area. It is a perception of disorder, of something out of place with an area that has become a gay Disneyland.

Robert, the journalist back at Caribou Coffee, said, "So, then, they hooked up WBEZ local news with that video and they did a lot of really irresponsible reporting, I think. All the stations did."

"What are some—?" I asked.

"So they put the video out there and they were like: 'Crime is up! Residents are mad! Blah blah blah.' They never looked at numbers to see if crime was actually up. And crime was down, numbers wise. It wasn't that crime was up. It was a couple of high-profile cases and people were freaking out about them. Because people who made the Take Back Boystown page, they made that clip, they posted that clip, and they sent it to the news stations, if I remember correctly. I know they made it and posted it. But I'm pretty sure that also sent it to everyone because they sent it to us."

"That would make sense based on the report in which they do—they're talking about taking the clip on the news station. 'And this is where I saw it out of my window.'" I said.

"And when they did the clip," Robert continued, "if you watch it—maybe they did it beforehand but something that bothered me about it is you just hear them in the background over it like, 'Are you getting it? Do you see this? Do you see that?' I don't think anyone ever called 911. At least in the clip. My first thought is, 'Oh, fight on the street? Let me call the cops.' Their reaction is holding out a camera."

"Why do you think there was such a higher perception of crime? What was the spark of all this?" I asked.

"Part of it was that it was high-profile violence. Stabbings. Talk to CPD [the Chicago Police Department] about it and they will be like, 'It's kind of rare for this area but in other parts of the city, there's a stabbing a day.' I think part of it is that this area normally never has anything [in terms of violence]. So for it to have that type of crime at all, people were freaking out," he said. "The official stance was always like, it's an entertainment district, it's summer. Come on, guys."

"And people are regularly out on the streets at all hours of the night, drunk," I said.

"Exactly. All the time and drunk. And it's summer and hot. It's just standard. And it's unfortunate that the crime that happened happened, but the numbers were steady or dropping. It was really perception."

That perception persists beyond that summer. A crime blog catalogs every incident in the neighborhood. Additionally, even people who do not live in the neighborhood believe Boystown is crime ridden, full of people that come to the area to commit violence.

After the Pride Parade in 2013, a gay bartender of color who lived in one of the northern neighborhoods that now have many gay people—Andersonville, Edgewater, Rogers Park, Uptown—posted the following, representative of the comments from even non–Take Back Boystown participants about Boystown's climate: "I had an amazing time yesterday. Great friends and company. That being said after living in boystown/lakeview for 8 years, making the move up north was a smart decision. Lakeview is going down the drain. It's really sad. It was such a prime location. Given the fact that it was pride fest weekend.... I know the crime and nastiness was elevated. But it is a nightly occurrence in boystown with all the muggings, loitering, crime. Make the move up north boys and girls."

One of his friends responded: "Sounds like the general consensus of this past weekend just solidifies how happy I am that I moved away when I did. Every neighborhood has its issues but the crime log for Lakeview this weekend alone was scary. Glad you had a good weekend though!"

To which the bartender replied: "Isn't it sad? I mean you lived a few blocks away from me (I think we made the move about the same time). There was yellow police tape and blood on what seemed to be every corner. I'm glad I moved. I wasn't going to continue paying $1,300 for a one bedroom and have my safety compromised."

Yet this perception is just perception. *Windy City Times*'s Erica Demarest put together a report showing that crime in the neighborhood was not rising.[5] The data show citywide crime was down by 7 percent. The Lakeview area had a lower crime drop than the citywide data, but still showed a 2 percent drop from the previous year, indicating perhaps that the majority of the crime drop happened in higher-crime neighborhoods than Lakeview.

While the summer of 2011 did have a slight uptick in crime compared to the proceeding spring, that is typical of all summers. Plus, there were other months as well that had just as high or higher violent crime, such as October, in which sixty violent crimes were reported. Overall, almost two hundred fewer crimes were reported in 2011 than in 2010.

These numbers, though, covered the entire area of the twenty-third district, an area that covered much of Lakeview and small parts of Uptown. Take Back Boystown supporters responded that while these trends might be true for all of Lakeview, Boystown itself was seeing more crime. Their argument was that crime in the rest of the neighborhood had dropped so much that it hid the crime spike within Boystown.

If crime was down, what was behind this persistent perception of the neighborhood as newly crime ridden? What makes these crimes so visible?

Lincoln Quillian and Devah Pager found that perceptions of crime in an area do not reflect actual crime rates of a neighborhood. Using survey data from Chicago, Seattle, and Baltimore, they looked at neighborhood residents' perceptions of the crime in their area, rather than their personal fear or risk of being the victim of a crime. They controlled for a variety of factors believed to be associated with the perception of crime, including, of course, the actual crime rate. However, there could be other variables that could be confounding the results. Some people don't report crimes.[6] Women perceive more crime than men.[7] People also stereotype the poor.

Even controlling for these factors, they found that crime was perceived to be higher when an area had a higher percentage of young Black men.

Who is it that Take Back Boystown is most against? Who do they feel is "coming to the neighborhood?" Who is it that they are taking it back from?

Boystown is not merely a reflection of wider American racism. It also perpetuates this perception because we learn to "see disorder." Sampson, in reviewing his earlier research in his book *Great American City*, discusses his theoretical perspective for these perceptions of crime: we have frames, stereotypes, and clues we look for when evaluating crime within neighborhoods. Using systematic observations from neighborhoods around Chicago, interviews, census data, and other quantitative data about crime, neighborhood condition, and poverty, Sampson and colleagues found poverty and racial composition mattered most in perceptions of neighborhood disorder. That isn't to say that these aren't grounded in real-life observations of disorder. They still found a connection between, say, seeing trash on the street and graffiti on the walls, and the actual crime rate.

However, conditions of poverty and a Black racial composition amplify the perception of disorder. People see actual signs of disorder as more meaningful, more disordered, when they are in conditions that are already stereotyped as crime ridden in our consciousness. We learn to make guesses about "bad neighborhoods" not from experience or data but from stereotypes. This makes crime in a good neighborhood a blip, an aberration, while crime in a bad neighborhood is evidence of the prejudices we already harbored, a confirmation bias.

Therefore, I am not arguing that residents shouldn't be angry about violence in their neighborhood. Rather, I argue these perceptions were amplified, made meaningful, by a perception that it was outsiders, racial others, who were poor and in need of social services, or gender deviant and trans, homeless, or otherwise "not respectable" people who, "don't know how to behave," attacking an upper-class white neighborhood.

Yet Black people have always been in the neighborhood. Just as when we examined assimilation and gentrification, we must look at how and why people go places, not just where they live. We must pay attention to pleasure. People of color have never lived in Boystown in any great numbers; they've always traveled.

When the neighborhood began, just as today, people came from all over Chicago to partake of the entertainment. Today, since young, poor, white people can't afford to live in the neighborhood, they, too, travel to Boystown from other neighborhoods, such as Logan Square or Edgewater. People of color, however, always mostly lived in racial-majority neighborhoods, given the context of Chicago's extreme segregation. That's not to say that some people of color, especially those that have money, don't live in Boystown. The 2012 American Community Survey lists the neighborhood as 82 percent white. The perception of rising crime isn't related to a new influx of people of color coming to places like the Broadway Youth Center or the Center on Halsted. There is, in fact, a long history of people of color traveling to the gayborhood; many older participants discussed this very fact.

When I interviewed Michelle, a middle-aged Black woman, I asked her an agonistic question, challenging her on the perception that Boystown was more racist than other spaces to get her to defend herself. "A lot of the things you're describing," I said, "the ways in which people are made to feel unwelcome, are those necessarily different from the ways in which, outside of the gay neighborhood, there's discrimination? Or anything that's unique to Boystown?"

Her response, though, not only highlighted some of the persistent racism of the neighborhood and the reasons why people travel to it from other neighborhoods in Chicago but also the history of such traveling.

It was telling that she answered the question with laughter.

I tried to cover by saying, "There's a lot of discrimination, there is."

"There is. There is," she said. "And I'm trying to think if it's unique or not. I have not been carded twice anywhere else. When we were younger, we used to hang out at the Belmont Rocks. It was all Black. They shut that down. It's—our communities are not really open to homosexuality. I would say that it's a bit unique to Boystown and the reason why I say that is because I just think some cultures aren't welcome at these clubs. Trying to think."

She paused for a long while.

"It's different because I'm a woman. The Black male experience is what you should hear about. I've heard them complain a lot but I don't have their experience. I'm sorry."

"That's fine. But people, particularly the youth, they still—we've been talk-ing about all this negative—and yet, they still come. Are less people coming to the area?" I asked.

"No, no." She laughed. "It doesn't matter. They still come here. This is just a popular area. Despite what's happening. They still feel free compared to the south side. They can wear different clothes, like made for opposite sex, and they don't feel that they will be threatened. It's a sense of community. I mean everyone's gay right? So you feel good. You don't have that on the south side. You don't have that nightlife. It's a huge difference."

"Okay. Okay," I said.

"It didn't stop them last year. It didn't. It didn't stop us either. It wasn't until I got older that I really withdrew and I was like, 'They don't like me why should I come?' But I still came because I just want to make it better for the people that come after me. I'm just reflecting on how hard it is for them. It's really hard."

If Boystown has always had queer people of color traveling to the area, why were they newly visible such that these acts of violence would be perceived as part of a larger problem with demographic change and social services?

As Michelle asked, do they just not want Black people? Is Boystown just racist?

That's the wrong question. Asking, "is this racist?" devolves into discus-sions like the one I had with Aspen, a Black gay man that I sat down with in the lobby of a hotel near the Roosevelt station of the Red Line. As Aspen points out, you end up debating individual wrongs, rather than considering wider questions of racial privilege.

Aspen is a long-time resident of Chicago. He was born here. He went to private school here. He occasionally goes to Boystown, but more often he prefers to go to other neighborhoods as well because, as he said, "Boystown is like college. It's one strip and everyone knows everyone. I get—I can't—I'm trying to look for the word. I feel smothered. If I was to only hang out in Boystown. Or even just Gold Coast. If I was only hanging around just any one neighborhood all the time, I would feel smothered and I would feel suffocated."

When he does go to Boystown or gay-identified spaces, he goes to those places most associated with his income, background, and habitus: Minibar, boat parties, private events, and other spaces associated with the plastics. He is one of "those people that live on the south side" but he is hardly the same demographic as the homeless Black trans youth who walk Boystown.

We agreed to meet in the South Loop. Riding the Red Line train down from Belmont to Roosevelt, I was struck at the demographic change. After Jackson, the last stop in the loop, the racial composition of the train com-pletely reversed.

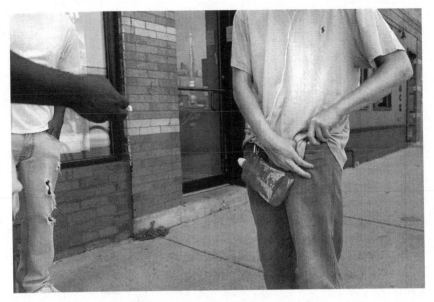

Figure 12.2. An exchange, on the streets of Boystown

I met him at the Starbucks next to the Roosevelt train station, but we decided it would be impossible to talk there, since it was cramped. The person sitting next to us would be able to overhear every aspect of our conversation.

Instead, we walked a few blocks north and ducked into the lobby of the Hilton Hotel, sitting down in their cafe. Aspen was wearing blue boat shoes, a pink polo shirt that his enormous biceps threatened to rip at any slight movement, and checkered board shorts. So preppy.

We had been talking about Take Back Boystown, when Aspen remarked, "Yeah, the CAPS meeting. It didn't help. Are they doing something now? They sort of had this, I guess, two- to three-week stint. Are they still trying to take Boystown back? I don't agree with people who loiter—I hate loitering on the streets. Like, have some place to go. I don't care who's loitering on the streets. I can't stand it when people just hang out on corners. That has nothing to do with me. I have some place to go. My problem is when people take that and extrapolate it to an entire community. Like there's no difference from me hearing a few racist comments from a few white people and being like, all white people are racist. That's stupid. That's crazy."

"Well, a lot of them are," I said to his laugher.

"I was just talking about my own personal experience. I'm not saying I've experienced it every single weekend. I'm not saying it happens every other weekend even. But the mere fact that it happens more than once—"

"Do you have a story that you could tell me?"

"I'll never forget this. Minibar was having a party for Gay Black Pride. I know the owner [though Minibar is owned by two people] and I was like, 'I think this is great that you're doing this. I've never seen anyone on Halsted have a party for Gay Black Pride ever.' He was like, 'Yeah, I think it's cool, to me it's just another party.' He was very whatever about it. And I'm like, this is great! My friend and I go to Sidetrack later that night and we overhear these two white guys saying, 'Oh my god. Minibar was having a party for Black Gay Pride, I'm so happy we left.'"

"I find it interesting that Minibar hosted it," I said.

"It's funny. A lot of people think Minibar is racist. I've never had a problem with Minibar specifically," he said.

"Okay, so you say—I didn't even finish my sentence!" I laughed.

"I know. I know. I knew you were going to—" He laughed as well.

"You say that a lot of people think Minibar is racist. Why do you think that is?" I said.

"I think so. And it's funny because at [this fundraiser], I got approached by him [one of Minibar's owners]. *In Our Words*, which has actually become a really popular blog on LGBT stuff, I guess one of the editors flat out said that Minibar is a racist bar and how his friends couldn't get in because they were Black."

Aspen and I got sidetracked for several minutes discussing this blog, identifying key writers there for me to read about queer Chicago.

He returned to his story after I prompted him with: "So anyways."

"He just came and talked to me. He was like 'I was kind of bummed because no one came to Minibar's defense. This is how a place gets a reputation by someone saying it's racist.' I told him, 'I never thought Minibar was racist. I've had other issues at Minibar but racism wasn't one of them. Maybe something did happen and it just went over my head, but I don't think so.' The co-owner asked me to write a piece about Minibar not being racist. I was like, 'Like, that's douche-y. No.'"

"Yeah, here's a list of the following bars that are and are not racist in Boystown," I said. "Although if you could provide me that list, that would be great." We both laughed, though I was only half kidding.

"Keep track of that list, so I know where to stay away from," Aspen said. "I told him, keep doing what you're doing. I'm like, 'I don't think Minibar is racist. You were the only owner that threw something for Gay Black Pride and that speaks volumes.' But just because I don't think it's racist doesn't mean every Black person shouldn't think it's racist."

"I'm not asking you to speak for the entire African American community," I said.

"Exactly. People are like, 'Well, I have a Black friend and he thinks its racist.' Just because I'm not offended by something, doesn't mean other people aren't going to be offended."

Aspen is right on that point. That's a terrible way to define racism, as I've tried to point out several other times throughout this book.

The question isn't whether Boystown offends people in incidents, whether people have had individual moments of discrimination, even if these add up to systemic problems of access, which I believe they do.

Rather, I want to ask, why is race newly salient in the neighborhood? How has race changed in the neighborhood as an axis of oppression and privilege? Why are people of color—present from the neighborhood's genesis— newly seen as outsiders such that acts of violence would be connected with their newly perceived presence and seen as indicators of a crime wave gripping the neighborhood?

Why was Boystown suddenly seeing the Black queer youth who were always there? Like ghosts unseen haunting the streets, but then, with a flash, they are all around us. What changed?

I propose the answer lies in the intersectional knot, that tangled intertwining of assimilation, gentrification, movement of sexy community, the rise of gay Disneyland, and the tourism of white straight women.

Raazia, an activist with dark wild hair who sat down with me to drink black tea the next summer in 2012 cautioned me, though, to not see Take Back Boystown as an isolated or gay-only event but as evocative of wider issues in Chicago.

"To me, that is the height of neoliberal Chicago, really. And the way in which the city—I don't think this is just about Boystown. I actually think this is about Chicago. Boystown is all about Chicago's racism sort of displaying itself. And I think people are making a mistake by isolating it. And seeing it only as a Boystown issue. It's not. It's a big Chicago issue. I don't think it's going to get much better very soon because I think the city has a serious race problem. The city has a serious inequality problem. The city has a serious neoliberalism problem. And Boystown, I think, is kind of the epicenter of that."

"In what ways do you see it as emblematic? What are some features of that?" I asked.

"I think one of the important features is the question of what happens when white liberals are made to confront the reality of the economic inequality that's prevalent in this city. I think Boystown is exactly what happens. Because what happened at the Center on Halsted is, when they founded it five years ago, they actually had no idea."

"Okay."

"I asked a board member friend of mine who was, at the time, a board member of the Center on Halsted. I said, 'What the fuck?' and she said, 'You know, I don't think they actually even realized that there were Black and Latino queer youth.'"

I must have looked confused. How could they not know?

"I think they kind of knew," she said. "But didn't know or didn't want to know is more like it. I think what essentially happened is you got a lot of—"

She switched gears. "You know that the founding of the Center on Halsted was pretty controversial right? Because of all the private money that was sunk into it. I don't know how many millions, right?"

"I mean, the building alone is like seven million dollars," I said.

"And it's not pretty. I don't now I have mixed feeling about the building."

"Yeah."

"I can also tell you about the disappearing furniture at the center. The furniture has disappeared because they don't want the kids to use it. There are no electrical outlets anymore in places," she said.

"You're right. Last summer, I came down several times and I remember the whole top area used to have a lot of couches and people were always hanging out at them. I was, like, 'What a lovely space to hang out.' Now it's, like, barren," I said.

"They removed the furniture. Because they don't want those kids even sitting down."

"I find it hard to believe they didn't know queer people of color were hanging out on the street, considering I have interviews with people talking about how ten, fifteen, twenty years ago, as queer youth of color, they were hanging out on the street. To me, it doesn't seem like a new thing. What's your perception?"

More agonistic interviewing.

Raazia replied, "I think they probably thought—white liberals in Chicago are a clueless lot. They are clueless because they are so protected by the city's racist and classist structure. They can actually live in those bubbles, right? So they can see queer kids on a summer day in Chicago in, let's say, 2007, right? And they see them as visitors. They come and they go. They come and they go."

She was on a roll, talking faster and faster. "What happened at Center on Halsted is it gave them a place to actually come and stay," she said. "And then—well, if you're supposed to be a Center on Halsted, where are our services? So there was then this push for more services. They saw it as a kind of holding place. So instead of just being a place [Boystown] where queer kids would sort of come in, but then you could figure out ways to get them out. You could be really rude to them when they entered your store, you could ask them for three IDs, you could ask them for their bags. You could make it really uncomfortable for them, you could call the cops on them. But the kids would finally return."

She continued: "But then the Center on Halsted. Now there was a physical location they could actually go to. They could use the bathrooms. They could wander around the Whole Foods and so on. And that, I think—the other thing you have to remember about Take Back Boystown, and people are forgetting, is that most of those people on that page are fucking liberals. They are not racist Republicans. They are Obama-voting liberals. And I think it is a great mistake to assume that these people are the same as racist, quote-unquote 'redneck.' People from somewhere else. They're not. They're the epitome of the white liberals who control City Hall. If you want to ask probing questions about politics, you'd find out I'm sure that most of them voted for Obama, are pro-choice, green homes, go to yoga in the morning carrying their sustainable energy yoga mats, their bamboo rush whatever the hell. They recycle. They bike to work."

She took a breath, the rant seemingly coming to a close. But then it continued: "The big mistake a lot of people are making is to assume that these are some sort of retrograde Paleolithic human beings who are just aberrant. They're not aberrant. They are typical Chicago white liberal. The difference is when a white liberal moves into his or her own sort of white liberal ghetto and is comfortable knowing that the cops will keep sweeping the POCs, will keep sweeping the poor people out. They're comfortable with that. But when a physical structure enters the neighborhood like Center on Halsted and becomes a place that people can actually go in, that becomes troubling for them."

I see that at the Center on Halsted nearly every time I go there. Several times, I have sat in the Center on Halsted for long periods of time— reading, waiting for someone shopping at Whole Food's, or working on my computer—and received no attention whatsoever. Yet staff would tell nearby people of color, doing the same thing, to leave.

"I want to remind everyone in the lobby about the Center on Halsted lobby policy," a staff person announced once. "If you are eating food you bought at Whole Foods or attending an event at the center, welcome. Otherwise, you cannot linger."

I thought at first he was talking to me, since I had been sitting for ten minutes, waiting for Austin, who was shopping in Whole Foods. However, I'm white. I should have known better. Four young Black and Latino men and women were sitting a few tables away talking.

"You talking to us?" one asked confused. "I think he's talking to us."

What happened in Boystown is emblematic of other processes going on in our society.

It's not about the stabbings, or the protests, or the counterprotests, it's what they represent and what came after. A change in who Boystown is meant for.

Gay Disneyland is a white space, whitening the gay habitus sold through heritage commodification.

By stripping out the queer, by removing sexy community, Boystown was sanitized. Sanitized, respectable spaces are associated with whiteness.

People thought that crime was rising in the neighborhood because suddenly they saw the queer youth of color that were hanging out on the streets and thought, "Those ghetto kids don't belong here. They don't know how to behave." That is, their racial identity, being unrespectable, didn't belong in a respectable space.

Near the end of my project, I sat down with Samir in the Dollop Coffee in Uptown. I asked him where he liked to go to have fun. He was just telling me about how much he hated the pretense at Minibar in Boystown.

"The place I would rather be at on any night in general is Big Chicks," he said.

Big Chicks is a bar in Uptown, known for bear nights, queer trans nights, lesbian nights.

"Why Big Chicks?" I asked.

"Because precisely that. There's less pretense on the part of the staff. The space is beautiful in art deco and famous art, but also—but it's not sort of shiny and white walls or fancy lighting and stuff. It's not glamorous. I don't think I'm looking for that when I go out and I think the crowd there sort of replicates that."

That is, any given space encourages people to act in particular ways. It teaches them a particular habitus.

He continued: "It's not that I want some gritty dirty place and I want to get robbed on the way to the bar. But it's still like, I don't feel like I'm entering a really sort of sanitized space either."

"Does that mean that going into a place like Boystown, you do feel like you're entering a very sanitized space?" I asked.

"Especially after two, three years ago. All the stuff that happened with the Black kids on the streets. They were being sort of protested out with this, like, what is it called? Positive loitering," he said.

"Positive loitering. The Take Back Boystown stuff?"

"Yeah, I mean I was really grossed out by that and that it was by whatever merchants association."

"The Northalsted Business Alliance."

"Yeah I was just really grossed out by that. I make broad assumptions about who's going. I know that a lot of people who are going to the bars there are from suburbs or other neighborhoods. I understand that, but the businesses have something to do with the way I perceive this space as well."

Figure 12.3. Security on Halsted Street

Samir is responding to the Take Back Boystown events by reading the neighborhood differently. If Take Back Boystown proponents wanted to defend their community from people of color, I suppose they have been successful and unsuccessful.

They've failed because people of color still come to Boystown. JJ and his friends come to Boystown several times a week after a long day of work, dancing their asses off into the night. I met Jon and Darren at Roscoe's, one of the most diverse places in Boystown. Circuit, although it opens and closes frequently, is a club almost exclusively for Black and Latino queer people.

They haven't taken Boystown back from anyone. It wasn't theirs to take.

However, they've succeeded in changing the image of Boystown. Rather than a place where people of many different racial backgrounds come to drink and be gay, Boystown is a space for white gays. A place to celebrate an identity they feel has little impact on their everyday lives, except for giving them license to have a parade and drink excessively, much like many white people's illusory experience with Irish identity in the United States.[8]

Gay Disneyland is respectable, even in its entertainment, and respectability is white.

Samir, and many of the other queers of color I've talked to, see Boystown as a white area. It's not that they experience more prejudice today than they used to. Boystown still and always had discrimination, just like the rest of our society. After all, Boystown didn't have a single Black bartender until 1994, almost ten years after it started forming.[9]

In this way, assimilation, especially the kind of sexual sanitation and movement of sexy community out of these spaces that gay Disneyland creates, codes them as white.

Take Back Boystown used this coded language in describing what they saw as problems. Problems that were new because of the sudden new perception of the people of color in their midst. Problems because gay Disneyland is at the center of the charmed circle now, no longer on the queer outside. Respectability that is upper class and white and male.

Black feminists have discussed respectability before, the conservative sexual politics of Black communities trace back to protecting Black communities from racist attacks. They were a defense against attack. One has to be even more respectable than white people, be even more conservative, have families that are even stronger, be more sexually repressive, so as to not invite perception they are unrespectable.[10]

Of course, as queer-of-color critique highlights, being already unrespectable from one's race also makes it easier to transcend these respectable boundaries of sexuality and gender, disidentifying popular culture to transform into queer possibilities.[11] The inner circle/outer circle stereotypes don't just describe sexual acts. They also describe the stereotypes thrown at people of color. The inner circle is white. Then, to be black makes queerness easier to achieve. As gay men become respectable, more conservative, and homonormative, the category of gay becomes connected with whiteness.

Take Back Boystown shows us the racial consequences of gay Disneyland and the heritage commodification of gay habitus. The transformation of these spaces to respectable inner circle morality encourages us to think about gayness as a kind of white ethnicity.

There is some truth to this perception of gay ethnicity because people perceive kinship similarly, developing non–blood ties that feel like blood. After all, isn't that the kind of tie that naked intimacy inspires? A family beyond family, a connection beyond blood? Sexual kinship that extends beyond our family of origin to encompass people different from us?

Habitus is internalized and feels natural. It feels essential to us. This naturalness gives it a quasi-ethnic aspect, a sense of kinship based on descent.[12]

Racial groups, for instance, are bound together by the perceptions on both sides of the racial hierarchy that they are biologically related or culturally distinct in a way based on descent. These categories are fake in the sense they are social fiction, but they are real pragmatically, in terms of their consequences.

However, other less biologically associated groups also feel connection based on descent. Farmers have a perception of descent based on a connection to the land, that similar people in similar situations are connected to them through being born to the land, to this land, to this occupation.

Similarly, gay people have an imagined community based on descent. The LGBT social movement has done hard work to essentialize gayness, to make sexual orientation a biological fact, passed down between generations, rather than a cultural group teaching each new generation how to be gay anew. Heritage commodification of the gay habitus furthers this goal, making the gayborhood a tourist destination similar to other ethnic neighborhoods in Chicago. In that way, this habitus is white. People treat gayness as a kind of white ethnicity.

After all, why did the city of Chicago give Boystown a beautification project?

Mayor Daley gave four different Chicago neighborhoods improvement money to build iconic art pieces that would distinguish the neighborhoods as destinations for their respective groups. Each area represented a major cultural group in Chicago, and perhaps in the unconscious of the planners, the different ethnic groups of Chicago.

Bronzeville, the iconic Black neighborhood in south Chicago, and Chinatown, the Chinese neighborhood that's come to represent the Asian American neighborhood, received beautification projects. Humboldt Park, a Latino area, received a giant wrought-iron Puerto Rican flag that hangs over one of the main thoroughfare entrances to the neighborhood. Boystown received its iconic rainbow pylons, the "golden phalluses" that line Halsted Street from Belmont to Grace.

These beautification projects marked these neighborhoods as tourist destinations, iconic designations that represented the far-flung vicarious citizens of that group throughout the city. Three major ethnic groups of Chicago, the top three racial groups besides white people, received a project. Gay people received one because they were seen as being in the same category, a white ethnic group, a natural cultural group based on descent.

When I first proposed this concept to a colleague, he responded, "What is their food? Most ethnicities have a cuisine that is associated with their nationality and culture. Soul food, Chinese, Midwestern casserole dishes. Is there a gay food?"

Alcohol, partying, and the spirit of the night. The consumption associated with gay habitus.

Habitus is the method of transmission of this gay ethnicity. It becomes natural, assumed. By extension, I propose that habitus is the method of all cultural group transmission. Assimilation happens when the habitus instilled within people adjusts because of structural and cultural changes to the habits of consumption embedded within community spaces consumed for pleasure.

For gay people, the essentializing political work of the LGBT social movement congealed our group into an imagined community of descent. As gayborhoods experienced existential threats from assimilation, heritage commodification sold gay habitus to outsiders, but a habitus stripped of the queer radical sexuality that once permeated these spaces. Without sexy community and its penchant for connecting people across racial boundaries, gay Disneyland became more strongly associated with whiteness. As Boystown became a place for "good gays," it became respectable in a way that excludes people of color. To be a good gay is to be white.

13

Queer Is Community

With a snap and a crash, shards of glass flew as the front window of Spin nightclub shattered in front of me from the weight of the horde of people pressing against it. The woman standing next to me inside the relative oasis of calm within the club rushed to sop up the blood welling on top of her foot, people grabbing white cocktail napkins in a panic to help her. The crowd in front of the window struggled to stay out of the glass, but the hundreds of people trying to occupy the same sidewalk between Spin and the police barriers on Belmont kept throwing people into the mess. Eventually, three police officers managed to hold the group at bay while a Spin employee swept up the danger.

For my part, I went to the backroom, where JJ and his friends were swept up in the music, to tell them what happened. "Boystown Pride is fucking crazy," I say.

JJ, high on E, just looked at me and smiled as we watch the Pride Parade floats from the television nearby. Boystown's reputation as a white, racist space seemed more reflected in the white marchers than in the room that was in front of me. Tamera and Maria ground their brown bodies against each other as JJ pressed "Loca Blanca" (that's me) to go buy another round, palming a twenty into my hand. The demographics of this room didn't vary much from those of the queer pride, the "antiracist," the "antisexist" pride I had attended the previous day.

■　■　■

The day before at Dyke March, I was marching alone. Others I knew—participants, friends—were ahead. A reporter from *Windy City Times* darted among the crowd, taking photos for the next paper. We were on the streets to let others know queer people were everywhere. Our pride wasn't contained to one neighborhood.

"On the streets" might be stretching the truth. Ten minutes before, we had been neatly marching on the sidewalks as a police car slowly followed us along the streets of the Uptown and Argyle neighborhoods. After all, a permit to march on the streets costs money to pay for police presence. There were too many of us, though, our line snaking as far back as I could see. So the police notified the organizers that they had closed off the remaining stretch of Dyke March, along Argyle Street from Broadway to Margate Park, so that we could go faster. They wanted us to get it over with.

Dyke March, and the small festival following, wasn't about taking Boystown's Gay Pride out into other neighborhoods of Chicago. It was a counterpoint. Boystown was corporate. Dyke March was grassroots. Boystown was white. Dyke March was in a community of color. Boystown was an expensive party. Dyke March was a free celebration. Boystown was . . . for boys. Dyke March, well.

Boystown was gay pride. Dyke March was queer pride.

The women from Amigas Latinas walked about four feet behind me with their banner, and four young white queers chanted ahead of me.

"Who's streets?"

"Our streets!" they answered themselves.

Our streets? Argyle is a Vietnamese American neighborhood. People were coming out of the stores and leaning out of their windows to watch us. Our streets? These seemed like their streets.

Recounting this story to Kade a few weeks later at an Edgewater cafe, she told me, "That's always like an interesting—"

She seemed hesitant, her voice bobbing like Lake Michigan's boats on a windy day.

"Actually I don't really know much about Dyke March," she backtracked.

And yet, she did. She had quite a bit to say about it, as she leaned over the tiny table we shared next to the window and whispered to me. Thankfully so, as her voice came through on the recorder sitting between us louder than the halting breathy speech I wrote about in my field notes. Perhaps she was afraid of being misinterpreted, choosing her words carefully to express her support for Dyke March even while criticizing an aspect of it.

"I had the same thought. People who were looking through the window like, 'What is happening?'" she said, before again qualifying: "Yeah, but there were fewer complaints that [white racial claiming of an ethnic neighborhood] was a problem from what I heard though."

There were fewer complaints comparatively.

Kade explained: "One of the complaints that people had about Dyke March in South Shore was that it didn't interact with the community enough. Like, you know, one of the reasons why we decided to start moving it around was so that it would be present in all communities and break down the idea of a gay neighborhood or area. And also provide visibility and interaction with other communities. But when we were in South Shore it sort of felt like people were excited and shouting out their windows but people were saying the interaction in the South Shore community could have been stronger and so they moved it to Uptown. One of the arguments made was that—I don't remember the acronym—they do like Asian LGBT advocacy work and have strong connections in that part of town, that they would be a good sort of bridge between their community and ours. So seeing that, fewer people complained."

Dyke March exists as an alternative Pride, a political pride.

Z explained it better than me. Z is genderqueer and uses gender neutral pronouns. After being connected by another participant, we met in the back of Dollop, the coffee shop where I regularly interviewed participants and wrote most of this book.

I asked hir why ze went to Dyke March.

Z responded, "Why do I go? I think that a lot of the LGBT Prides that occur have been very corporatized and very mainstream and everyone is just, like, getting drunk. They're not politicized. There's just a party and there's no real dialogue around issues."

Ze stared at me, perhaps wondering if ze should continue, or if I was going to ask hir another question. Instead, I waited, hoping to draw out additional information through my silence.

Finally, the seconds stretching out, ze continued: "I think that's part of the purpose of dyke march and trans marches. I think there's also—again, because this subgroup or because this LGBT culture is part of a larger culture, which is, you know, full of patriarchy and racism and blah blah, and within this culture there's still, like, racism and sexism that occurs and classism, whatever. Once you start getting to those with more privilege, [they] end up being the ones with control and I think that's what has happened. I think what Dyke March is about is challenging that and recognizing there needs to be different spaces for people who don't have those privileges but experience oppression differently. To have a queer space."

This kind of queer space was definitely in evidence at the festival that greeted us at the end of the march, after we finally got to the park at the end of Argyle Street, sped along by the police who had kindly allowed us to use the streets.

At the festival grounds, a mild gathering started. Kids ran around in the field, picking wild flowers and weeds out of the high grasses before running back to their parents. I sat eating a free hotdog from one of the community groups with Ryan and a few of other of his white queer friends. Off in the distance, near the stage where artists were about to perform, I saw Raazia, another participant, swirling her hippy skirt on the edge of the crowd that was sitting patiently for the performance. Activists wandered among the crowd passing out Chelsea "Bradley" Manning literature.[1]

There was actually no more dialogue around issues at Dyke March than there was at Boystown Pride. People were just having fun, although without the sexiness or radical rejection of respectability embodied in the people at Boystown's Pride. Instead, it was an alternative respectability. Neatly marching on the streets, a quiet gathering. Calling it queer, declaring the space political, had it queered in anyway the dynamics?

■ ■ ■

"It gets better," cries the popular refrain. This is the promise of assimilation. The promise of a world of tolerance. Now, we don't have to live in the gayborhood, we can live anywhere we want. We can love whomever we want. We can be whoever we want.

For many queers, though, it hasn't get better. Throughout this book, I've discussed those groups. It hasn't gotten better for Black trans queer kids in Boystown. It hasn't gotten better for queer people of color. It hasn't gotten better for the poor.

It didn't get better for Mark.

On a Monday night, Mark and I watched *RuPaul's Drag Race* at Spin before heading off to Berlin, that decadent genderqueer art scene of outsiders. Mark inhabited their—they used third person pronouns—own sense of beauty. I knew Mark in college, but we hadn't hung out much until I moved to Chicago, two Texans in the north. Mark had moved to Chicago to attend the University of Illinois at Chicago's master of fine arts program. They first pointed me toward "the monthlies," the various parties in "the queer diaspora outside of the gay ghetto," as they put it. They wore their pentagram harness, shirtless, dancing along to the music, as Carlos, their friend, in his oversized platform heels loomed over us, smoking his e-cigarette.

The following Friday, I went to Madison, Wisconsin, to attend a birthday party. By ten that night, I had gotten the call bringing the frivolity to an end. Had I heard? Mark was dead.

The art community at Mark's campus put together a memorial in their honor, where I saw many of the members of the queer art community— many of whom I had seen before at Berlin—come together. The giant, white gallery space filled with people, many sitting in tiny plastic chairs in small circles, talking about Mark.

I discuss Mark here not to pull on heartstrings, throwing the memory of my dead friend in readers' faces. Assimilation didn't kill Mark. Gentrification didn't cause them to commit suicide.

Figure 13.1. Berlin Nightclub

I mention Mark because queers are the ones still most likely to have bad shit happen to them. With a rate of suicide and violence much higher than cisgendered straight people, queers have a lot of better to get to before they even get to OK.

Queer communities are the spaces, the refuges, where people shut out by gay Disneyland can turn. The land of misfit toys and the space of resistance. Queers can provide the only space left when you can't go to any of the other clubs. Queers can form the only community who will accept you, when you have a gender identity that doesn't fit into Minibar. You might feel you don't belong at Sidetrack, and there might be sneering men telling you to get the hell out at Wang's, but Berlin's art queers will welcome you with open arms.

Queers are great. Queer is community. Sometimes, queers can be the only community left.

What kind of community is it?

■　■　■

The three spaces mentioned most prominently in this chapter—Berlin's queer art scene, Boystown's Pride, and Dyke March—embody different, but sometimes overlapping, meanings of "queer." While the mainstream Pride Parade is assimilationist, with its corporate floats, marriage banners, and rows upon rows of elected officials lobbying for gay votes, the festival surrounding it also embodies a kind of queerness: queers rejecting respectability, queers who like getting drunk and high and fucking.

I have called this kind of queer space, the kind rejecting straight respectability in favor of erotic sensuality, sexy community, arguing that it can erode intergroup discrimination on the basis of race by bridging divides through intimate contact, rooted in the body; through ritual moments of collective effervescence; and by leveraging what the philosopher Bakhtin calls "uncrowning." While those attending Boystown's Pride might not be politically discussing issues, the bodily connections made—grinding against each other or drunkenly talking with each other—accomplishes a queer goal.

What the queer Dyke March embodies is different. Rather than rejecting respectability, queer leftism is an ideology of alternative respectability, which creates an alternative path to being a good person, by destabilizing one's identity toward an essential humanity, by questioning racism, but not dismantling white control over space or queer colonization. The parade itself sports banners, like from Amigas Latinas who marched behind me, arguing against racist conceptions of queers as only white. Yet the white queers in front of me still enacted possession of a neighborhood of color in the name of "bringing the neighborhood out across the rest of Chicago."

Sociologist Jane Ward, in her book *Respectably Queer*, compared two similar groups: queer leftists and Pride Parade planners.[2] She described the queerness of the Pride planners, arguing they fit a definition of "queer" even though they might not define their identities as queer. They might even find the term offensive. Yet they reject family politics and "talking about issues." They reject the political and embrace the queer fun.

In this chapter, I want to talk specifically about queer leftist spaces because they are often given as the alternative—or even the "answer"—to Boystown. I argue that these queer ideological spaces lack sexy community and alienate those that might share their goals of antiracism and antisexism. Other people, also queer, still might not feel safe in these spaces. They are alienated from the queer project because of, what I call queernormativity. They reproduce similar dynamics of race because of a focus on rhetoric, individualist self-definition, and identity deconstruction. As opposed to the homonormativity of assimilationist groups associated with Boystown, queernormativity focuses their spaces on perpetuating queer ideology, and alternative respectability, rather than sexy community. Queernormativity's relentless politicalness stifles dialogue, making queer ideology a hard sell for some people, even as it seeks to help marginalized communities.

■ ■ ■

In the summer of 2012, a new Tumblr came on the scene. For posterity, since the Internet is ephemeral, and you can never be sure what will disappear only a few years later, Tumblr is a microblogging platform, with short posts, but no character limit like Twitter. Like most Tumblr blogs, someone anonymously posted GIFs and memes.[3] They called it When in Boystown.

Like the Center on Halsted, When in Boystown's reception was polarized. The blog posted mostly about Boystown's party atmosphere. Often, the title set up the gag, which the GIF completed. For instance, the title might be "The Boys at Minibar," followed by pictures of the plastics from *Mean Girls* talking about their clothes and cuticles.

Most jokes were similar, such as the title "Big Chicks," the name of the bear bar, followed by a picture of a bear mauling someone, riffing on the double meaning within gay spaces of the word "bear," or the title "Pride," followed by a time-lapse animation of someone fucking and drinking in a room all day.

Other jokes though, referenced the youth on the street, sometimes using racial stereotypes, reminding people of the Take Back Boystown events of the previous summer.[4] "The Center on Halsted" title, for instance, is followed by a GIF of three Black women twerking upside down against a wall. "Belmont Station" shows an animation of a Black woman, approaching a car and placing her large boobs inside the window, with subtitles indicating she was a prostitute. As I've written elsewhere, these jokes were crass, calling into question the humanity of the butts of the jokes and access to Boystown, rather than participating in the shared "uncrowning" the philosopher Bakhtin says is the key to a good joke. When in Boystown, much like Take Back Boystown, claimed through these jokes that Boystown was a white space.[5]

Queer leftists responded with an event called Queer Is Community.

I found out about the event from several sources. I had been living in Boystown for five months, focusing on nightlife ethnography, when Jon, my weekly *RuPaul's Drag Race* watch partner, texted me: "Have you heard about this thing at The Center?"

He had been invited to a planning meeting for a response event to the When in Boystown Tumblr and had been surprised that I wasn't there already.

"What's the group putting it together?" I texted him.

He responded: "Not one specific group, right now it's a collective and trying to encompass any group that wants to help or participate."

I shouldn't have been surprised. Queer leftists are often grassroots collaboratives.

Concurrently, one of my contacts at the center told me of the event. They knew I would be interested. Jon invited me to the event's announcement on Facebook where I saw the organizers looking for volunteers. I was in.[6]

Figure 13.2. The Center on Halsted

I was given two mundane jobs that were perfect for an ethnographer. First, I was in charge of directing people who came into the center to the third-floor theater where the event was being held. I didn't take a tally, but three kinds of people generally were coming in that hot afternoon. People of color and young white people would walk upstairs when I told them where the event was being held. White people over the age of thirty-five weren't interested. They were bound for Whole Foods. Straights and gays to the right. Queers to the left.

As the time of the event approached, one of the organizers came down to tell me I could come up to watch the pre-event community mic. "Just put up a sign."

I went to the front desk to ask them if they had a sheet of paper and a pen I could use to put up a sign for our event. The receptionist was friendly, but panic-stricken. "I will print one out for you. If Tico [the CEO] saw that, he would tear it down." The Center on Halsted, a corporate nonprofit, is yet another example of the difference in professional image-management disconnect between largely grassroots queer leftist groups and the LGBT nongovernment organizations.

Upstairs at the event, they were not letting people into the theater yet. The foyer was filled with people, a huge space overlooking Halsted Street and opening out into a rooftop garden. At the front, a white woman in her early-twenties—who later told me, with a smirk, that she identified as a "Trannysaurus Rex"—encouraged the group to step up to voice their thoughts.

The event's description said it was about responding to the transphobia and racism in Boystown that When In Boystown made salient. The speakout, though, made it clear that queer spaces, while identifying as "antiracist," have significant problems with structural racism.

It's not that only white people spoke—which Jane Ward identifies as a white queer definition of diversity, "diversity by numbers."[7] An older Latina woman, for instance, gave a lovely speech about her experience transitioning and telling her children from her previous marriage about her gender identity.

Rather, the room was divided spatially by race, and the speak-out's topics became predominantly about transphobia, the topic that white queer activists wanted to talk about. Discussions of racism were never picked up as topics by white speakers after raised by people of color. With the speak-out happening at the northern wall of the room, near the stairs and opposite the elevators, it was closest to the area where young white queer people were standing. On the opposite side of the room were standing nearly all of the people of color in the room, and all of the Black people. No one from that side of the room ever approached the northern wall to speak.

The speak-out did not intentionally exclude people of color's voices, but the room's segregation eased the inclusion of white voices, and made the barrier to entry to the conversation—walking across the whole room through the large crowd—much higher for the people of color in the room. As a result of the racial imbalance between speakers, the topics revolved around issues salient for those doing the talking: experiences they had with discrimination in Boystown because of gender or gender presentation. For most people of color to enter the conversation, they had to shout or speak in response to the person who just spoke at the official front of the room. One Black woman, for instance, when the front of the room was debating such questions as "Who is queer?" and "What does queer mean?" had to talk over someone else to be recognized as a speaker. She said that queerness, for her, "can't be summed up." Queerness was "a living vision of beauty." Queer was complex. She was boundless and not able to be easily defined.

"Gay is definite. Lesbian is definite," she said. "Queer is not defined."

So undefined, apparently, it took endless rehashing and took over any discussion of When in Boystown and solutions to the problems proposed for consideration.

I saw this focus on rhetoric, self-definition, and identity destabilization again once the doors opened and the presentations began. My second job was controlling the stage curtains, giving me a backstage view to the presenters. The event was organized with nine speakers presenting, using mediums from dance to polemic, followed by a panel on which each of the presenters sat. Each presentation attempted to shift the conversation away from the personal and accusatory toward the systems level and the dialogic. Yet when the question-and-answer period began, when dialogue should have occurred, queernormativity took hold. In the interests of space, I want to focus on one particular incident.

One speaker, during her presentation, brought up the then-recent murder of Paige Clay, which lead another presenter to chastise: "People know more about gay marriage than they know about her murder." This comment sparked a conversation during the question-and-answer period about the reporting of her murder, including incidents of misgendering (using the incorrect pronoun, thus reinforcing her trans-ness not her murder). The consensus was that the community needed to respond.

Not to the systemic violence. Not by asking trans women of color, many of whom were in the room, what could be done materially to make them safer. Not to the relentless reporting of trans people only when their deaths force a media blip.

Instead, the response was: this woman died—let's make a press packet about using proper pronouns.

This is the effect of queernormativity, an ideology that constrains dialogue because of the relentless focus on the individual and the naming of things.

I want to draw a difference between an oppression Olympics and a hierarchy of impact.[8] Which is to say that all oppression is equally bad, but given the choice between addressing whether someone will be killed or whether someone will be referred to by the correct term, I believe we should take a beginner's mind to those that are willing to be wrong.[9]

For all of the promise of the rhetoric of leftist queer movements—of which I have been a part of and still consider myself to be—the reality of these queer spaces has not been communal. Queer leftist community spaces—those that deliberately call themselves "queer" rather than "LGBT" or "gay"—attempt to have diversity, but often only with words. And while these verbal nods to diversity can create an increase in the attendance of different kinds of people, they remain primarily controlled by white people to address white queer issues.

They are diverse, but not inclusive. Such organizations are alienating to outsiders and beginners. A divisive diversity that springs from word policing, privilege checking, and "no platforming."[10]

Queer leftist spaces exist to counter a Boystown environment they see as racist, classist, and sexist. Given the problems I have discussed throughout this book, I'm glad they do so. They are the refuge of those that no longer belong, can't belong, and don't feel safe within Boystown's Disneyland. But are these spaces as safe as they purport to be? Does their reaction to Boystown's Disneyland produce the sexy community that erodes sexual racism?

I argue they do not. Maybe not all spaces need to have sexy communities though. Still, there is something missing, something alienating, in these spaces.

Queer leftism, with its roots in academic queer theory, encourages the destabilization of identity. While their spaces are politically opposed to Boystown's assimilation, their spaces are similarly desexualized. These spaces have developed an alternative respectability, a safe queer, based on saying the right things and identifying the correct ways. Beginners are unwelcome, alienated by intolerance for mistakes. Instead of the homonormativity of Boystown, queer leftist spaces have "queernormativity."[11]

Queer is community. It's just not a community you'd want to live in.

To state it more explicitly, there were three elements of queernormativity on display at the Queer Is Community event, elements that I argue are part of the moral fabric of queer ideological spaces, chilling their possibility for sexy community.

The first is identity destabilization. Queer ideology has its roots in queer theory, which argues for the destabilization of identity, a project of unanchoring gender boundaries and sexuality (and other aspects of identity) by showing their historical production. They are produced only in context. As Green reports, queer theory's "deconstructionist mandate, by definition, moves queer theory away from the analysis of self and subject position including those accruing from race, class, and gender and toward a conception of the self radically disarticulated from the social. This 'anti-identitarian' position has been a source of criticism among some sociologists, who find in queer theory an indefensible 'refusal to name a subject.'" In the words of someone at the Queer Is Community event, "Queer is undefined."

And yet, the very lack of definition for "queer" enables a radical individualist self-definition. The focus turns away from the self in society, to a "be true to yourself" philosophy in which one defines oneself as unique or essentially human, not confined to a named group.

Combined with queer theory's roots in literary criticism, this creates a powerful focus on the rhetorical and the power of language. The dialogue becomes stuck at the level of defining discourse, forever creating new "awareness" of issues, without discussing issues of marginality and pragmatic ways to fix them.

These facets of queer ideology constitute an alternative respectability, built on identifications beyond identity and using the proper language to articulate your and others identity-less states.

Austin and I are standing in the kitchen of Frank's friend Hart. We're here for his birthday, drinking Trader Joe's two-buck-chuck Merlot out of plastic cups and waiting for the pizza to arrive. Most guests are in the living room; all four roommates' furniture has been pushed against the walls to make space. People are sitting down on the floor on a variety of pillows strewn around the room with purposeful randomness and constructed whimsy.

Austin and I are talking to the only two Black people at the party. They've retreated to the kitchen for reasons similar to our own: they didn't feel that comfortable with the rest of the group, while Austin and I are too queer in the pleasurable fun sense compared to the political queers. Austin is also not leftist enough, and, frankly, I don't trust him not to get in a political argument. I don't trust a libertarian at a leftist party.

Words and actions sometimes diverge. It's an ethnographer's job to discern why. Which do we believe? I often believe both.

Monica, the Black woman we had been talking to, and her gay male friend were the first people to leave the party. They said they had to leave because they had other plans. They had decided to stay only a moment.

But last in, first out is a dynamic I can spot. It says you weren't having fun. It says you were uncomfortable.

They might have been uncomfortable for any number of reasons. But based on what I've seen happen at a variety of queer events, my guess is that their discomfort arose from being the only person of color in a room, which can be exhausting and alienating. No one wants to sit segregated on the outskirts, in the kitchen, the whole time.

Queer leftist spaces declare themselves as a check against Boystown's racism, transphobia, sexism, and classism. Why do actions in these spaces diverge from that idea?

Queer leftist spaces end up re-creating many of the same dynamics they say they are against because these issues are addressed from an individualist stance. Each person is responsible for saying the right thing. Everyone will "check" each other if they don't say the right things. Instead of racism as a systemic problem, it is a character flaw. These spaces are just as white as Boystown, but don't acknowledge it.

I'm not any better. If you took a census of the people I hang out with on a regular basis, you'd find mostly white people. My social networks are produced by our society's segregation, too. Racism isn't about whether you have Black friends. "Oh, but some of my best friends are Black..." is one of the most popular phrases of racism deflection. "If you hang out with Black people, then you can't be a racist" makes racism into a personal character flaw just as much as "but I have sex with Black people" did in chapter 5, "Sexual Racism." My point here is that calling a space queer doesn't make anything magically better. Calling yourself antiracist doesn't change the segregation of our cities or social networks. Antiracism doesn't change our cultural frames for stereotyping.

I suspect the two Black guests left because they were exhausted with feeling "in the line of fire," a sense shared with me by other participants. I described this sense in other research that I've conducted on situations in which people are in "intergroup dialogue" moments, when two people who differ in some way are forced to contend with their difference. In majority/minority interactions, the person in the minority is often called to account for their identity, for their very being, to explain themselves.[12]

In the example I described in this earlier research—coming out—it could involve someone asking invasive personal questions afterward, but it could also be just being in an environment with others who you know don't fully accept you. When in the line of fire, you have to spend energy, doing the "emotional labor" of managing your actions, your words, and your very presence in the space to not provoke conflict with the person(s) in power.[13]

Queernormative spaces, because they are built as an oppositional identity to the majority politically, don't want to acknowledge that within their own spaces, they are the people in power.

Therefore, people who haven't properly learned the rules of the space, who haven't absorbed the queernormative culture of identity destabilization and learned the correct rhetoric, feel exposed in these situations.

However, I want to go further to propose that perhaps being in the line of fire, forever managing your words and presence, is part of queernormativity. Even the people who identify as queer and frequent queer leftist spaces are constantly vulnerable.

The consequences of being in the line of fire are important. If the only consequence of my critique of queernormativity was that it's hard work always being on guard, then that would be fairly useless. A lot of important activities are hard work. We shouldn't shy away from doing the emotional labor of making sure what we say and do doesn't harm others.

Rather, the problem with queernormativity is that, just like other forms of respectability politics, such as those embodied by the inside of the charmed circle, it makes sexy community difficult because it makes intimacy hard to achieve, alienates outsiders, and can make interpersonal discrimination worse.

One of the most common ways of dealing with moments of feeling in the firing line is to run. If someone makes you constantly uncomfortable, or a space seems unwelcoming, then what incentive is there to continuing to frequent that space or talk to that person? In my previous research, people regularly told me they would disengage with people that took aim at them. Or, they said, they wouldn't let these people get close to them, cutting them off from certain parts of their life, limiting the amount of information they had, or otherwise minimizing their interactions.[14]

These forms of intimacy management have been shown to actually make intergroup situations worse. One innovative study used chair distance to measure how uncomfortable people were with each other in a group.[15]

Say that you walked into a room where there were two other people, both men, and a researcher. You are a white man. Of the other men, one is white and one is Black. The middle of the room is empty, but there is a stack of folding chairs off to one side. "Grab one and form a circle so we can all talk," the researcher tells you. While you think the purpose of the study is to talk about your perception of current events, the researchers really want to measure how far your chairs are from each other and the perceptions you have of the other members of the group. While other groups read an innocuous story to discuss as a group, you read a news item about racial discrimination.

The study made a counterintuitive discovery. Those who are white and extremely concerned about racism in America placed their chairs farther away from the Black participants when reading the story about racial discrimination. The Black participants perceived that distance as evidence of prejudice against them. Those who were not concerned about racism had no difference in chair placement. Concern about being perceived as racist led to worse intergroup outcomes. A fear of accidentally offending a Black man sitting next to them closed that person off to intimacy. Not only were such people psychologically distant, but they placed their chairs at a physical distance as well.[16]

If queernormative spaces keep people constantly on guard, fearful others will attack them for a wrong move, then those spaces will be alienating, even for those who stay within them. Intimacy—the kind that breaks barriers—will be hard to come by, aggravating tensions already present. What's worse, this effect happens when people are actually concerned about their prejudice.

■ ■ ■

What is the source of this guardedness in queernormative spaces?

There are two promises of "queer": the pursuit of separateness based on the idea we can be equal yet different, and the quest to destabilize identity to the point of universality among differences. These are different dreams, different visions. Within academic queer theory, Green calls these "radical subversion" and "radical deconstructionism."[17]

Queer leftism, as opposed to the queer embodied literally in sexy communities, espouses the latter. It seeks to undo our attachments, supplant our differences with a universal appreciation for difference. Yet, more often, queer leftism has become its own form of tribalism, with its own rituals of purification and rites of flagellation. Like many ideologies, it shares features of a religion, marked by a propensity to be "more queer than thou." It has become its own end, becoming an identity, and "identity excludes."[18]

In Jonathan Sacks's *The Dignity of Difference*, he argues that Western civilizations' answer to tribalism has been universalism: the search for a truth beyond the particulars.[19] The root of universalism,[20] he says, is what he calls Plato's ghost.

First, a note: Sacks is a Jewish scholar. He is writing about the ability of civilization to handle religious differences in the context of globalization. True to his message, he is arguing from his own particular standpoint as a Jewish scholar, steeped in his own traditions. It is easy to get sidetracked by the religious tone of his voice, to argue about whether there is a god, rather than consider the role of his philosophy. I've chosen to do the latter.

Plato's ghost is the quest for universality. Western philosophy argues that while there is diversity here on earth, there is unity in heaven. There is something essential to be shared by all humankind. Plato's famous allegory of the cave, for instance, argues that while we see the imperfect shadows of reality, there are perfect forms—ideal types—casting these shadows from the blinding light behind us.

Sacks argues that Western philosophy has been haunted by Plato's ghost ever since. After all, is not the goal of science to sweep away the differences between situations to discover the commonalities, the shared causes hidden behind the biased messiness of reality? Modern positivistic science, indeed much of sociology, attempts to do just that. Sample enough people and we can discover "the truth" behind their differences.

Of course, the opposite is just as dangerous. If we only sought after the particulars, we succumb to relativism, a different kind of tribalism, or to a postmodern belief that we cannot know anything outside of ourselves, a "radical deconstructionism." Rather than Plato's ghost, we become haunted by Foucault's—not, however, the Foucault of his writings.

Queer theory departs from Foucault in its radical deconstructionism. As Green says, "If Foucault had captured a form of human subjectification crystallized in the creation of the modern sexual subject, queer theory would take this analysis as the cornerstone of a politicotheoretical enterprise, and then work decisively against the insight."[21]

In other words, while Foucault saw the creation of the modern subject, an actor with essential identities, queer theorists saw within Foucault's writings the destabilization of the subject, and then sought this out in the modern context. In doing so, they allowed Plato's ghost to settle within Foucault's body of work, creating a revenant that today terrorizes queer spaces.

This revenant is queernormativity: the relentless political focus on the destabilized self through the policing of discourse. Rather than queer separatism (as embodied in sexy communities) with the goal of "the dignity of difference," in Sacks's words, it seeks the universal essential self behind these destabilized selves. It uses intersectionality as a way of canceling out privilege rather than an intersectionality that recognizes our embeddedness within multiple particular groups. By focusing on the individual and their sins, we forget the group. Identity alone cannot change a space. Instead, it hides the power working in these spaces through structural categories.

We must seek a middle way, between positivism and postmodernism, between the Fou-cultists and Plato's ghost. Elsewhere, Michael Bell and I have called this approach multilogical.[22] As in essentialist and social constructionist debates within LGBT studies, sociologist Michael M. Bell and I see such approaches not as *either/or* but *also/and*. We must go beyond the kind of dualistic thinking in science, politics, and other debates that constructs one side as wrong if the other is at all right.

Sacks, as a religious scholar, finds this *also/and* for him in Judaism. He argues that we can only understand each other, and make peace with our differences, if we recognize that our shared humanity is given form through our differences—that we should search for our wondrous particularity, and what it has to teach others, rather than our commonality.

"We are particular and universal," Sacks writes, "the same and different, human beings as such, but also members of his family, that community, this history, that heritage. Our particularity is our window on to universality."

For Sacks, religious dialogue is only possible through recognition between Christians, Jews, Muslims, and others that they share a common humanity, but that humanity is expressed through different traditions. Each group has obligations to themselves that do not necessarily apply to others.

For instance, Sacks identifies within Jewish philosophy the "problem of the stranger" which, of course, relates for me as a sociologist back to the philosophy of Georg Simmel in his essay "The Stranger." Sacks discusses Jewish philosophy's command to "love the stranger." But why? "Not from reason or emotion alone.... Instead it speaks of history: 'you know what it is like to be different, because there was a time when you, too, were persecuted for being different.' Indeed, that is what Israelites are commanded never to forget about their shared experience of exile and slavery. They have to learn from the inside and always remember what it feels like to be an outsider, an alien, a stranger."

For Simmel, the stranger is someone who is outside of the group, but who, because of their social position, "often receives the most surprising openness—confidences which sometimes have the character of a confessional and which would be carefully withheld from a more closely related person." The stranger is someone both near and far, outside of the petty strife of our in-group dynamics, but privy to some of our closest secrets because of their distance. People implicitly recognize the value of the stranger when they talk to a therapist, spill their guts to a fellow traveler on an airplane, or, as I've discussed, have candid conversations about their lives with people they've never met during a quiet moment of a sex party.

The stranger's distance and difference means it would be easy for the group to stigmatize this person, and the group of strangers they represent. Yet, the intimacy of the stranger bonds us to them. Somehow, we must take Sacks's insight to love the stranger—to grant dignity to their difference. We can only accomplish this love by taking our intimacy for the stranger's distance to our troubles out into our everyday interactions.

This is the multilogical approach.

To apply it to a common problem, consider the queernormative and multilogical responses to the issue of being offended by something someone else has said. One such instance is the furor surrounding use of the word "tranny." It's an offensive word that hateful people throw at transgender people. It's also a word with a history of reclamation by drag queens, who also often get called "tranny." It's offensive to some people. Others use it to refer to themselves. "Queer" is another such word, which I have used extensively in this book.

The queernormative approach would be to shut the speaker down, an action called no platforming. Their speech harmed. It doesn't matter their intentions, since that is often the excuse used to justify such behavior: "Oh, well, I didn't intend for it to be offensive" or "I didn't know it was offensive." What they are really saying is: "Because I didn't think it was offensive, you don't have a right to be offended."

A multilogical approach asks us to consider the situation nondualistically. Can their actions have caused harm they didn't intend? Whether or not the person is genuine in their ignorance of the word's power is perhaps immaterial. Weighing a situation multilogically, one might ask: How can we honor the intention of people while also acknowledging their mistake? If we focus only on the intention, we let people off the hook. The consequences of their actions, as is often the case of microaggressions, were marginalization and otherness. Overlooking their intentions, though, doesn't allow any forgiveness for mistakes. It allows no margin of error. It alienates people who would otherwise act differently the next time.

Put another way, whether something was done intentionally doesn't change the consequences for the person affected, but it should change how we react to the actor. It changes our relational understanding of what happened. This allows us to have a dialogue with the person who perhaps shares our goals but didn't use the "correct" language to express it.

However, I would also argue that the focus on the word, and the consequences it has, is itself queernormative when it crowds out all other discussion. If we only engage in the politics of being offended, then we continuously put others in the line of fire about whether they can use certain words.

I am heartened by the pushback against queernormativity that I see in many of these spaces, such as the Queer Is Community event. An older woman, a transgender Latina, spoke at the speak-out—again, not from the white space of the front floor, but from the western windows where she was standing—in response to the discussion about referring to people as "queer."

"It's a process, but you gotta take the power of a word and make it your own. We have to see prejudice when it's real," she said, seemingly to the people of color in the room, given the direction she was facing. Then, turning toward the front, where other white queers had spoken, she said: "You still are part of the solution."

Nondualistic. Multilogical. We honor the intentions of others by allowing them to make mistakes and fix them. We focus on pragmatic issues of oppression, inviting individuals who might otherwise think that, because of their demographics, they are closed off from the discussion to listen and then join in the dialogue about how to fix things. These changes would prevent the space from being pulled into a chilled censoring that prevents people from letting their guards down. Such changes are essential for having fun and creating a sexy community, allowing people to combine across intergroup boundaries through pleasure.

Queer can be a lovely community. It can be a place for outsiders, stigmatized in other communities, to find space. However, it can also be alienating when a leftist queernormativity leads everyone to feel on guard because they have a majority identity , as do all of us in some way.

Yet, queer is also a community that could learn something from those other queers, those alienated by queer politics who instead embrace the queer fun. Our politics, embracing the stranger, cannot be pushed into opposition with fun, with literally embracing the stranger. Otherwise, we will be forever debating, discussing breaking boundaries and neatly marching along the sidewalks, instead of smashing the glass, smashing our bodies against each other, and worrying about the blood later.

14

Dawn

The promise and terror of the night break at dawn. The darkness of exclusion produces a freedom within queer radical sex. Pressed together for lack of any other place to expand, people make friends with those they have to, clutching at each other for security.

Dawn is breaking. Exclusion turns to tolerance. Today, I am married, an unthinkable prospect for the queer kid of a decade ago. I live an open life. I bring my husband home for the holidays to my parents, in Texas of all places. I can be one of the good gays. I can have everything that my parents have wanted for me.

But I don't have to have it. I don't have to if I don't want to. I can have that and more. I can live outside the charmed circle. I can live in sexy community.

This is the promise, the majestic, wonderful, scary promise of being queer.

On the verge of being kicked out of the house because of her sexuality, British lesbian writer Jeannette Winterson is asked by her mother, the last time Winterson saw her mother alive, "Why be happy when you can be normal?"

Why be normal when you could be happy?

Winterson, retelling a story from Gertrude Stein's *The Autobiography of Alice B. Toklas*, explains why this way:

> Gertrude and Alice are living in Paris. They are helping the Red Cross during the war. They are driving along in a two-seater Ford shipped from the States. Gertrude likes driving but she refuses to reverse. She will only go forward because she says that the whole point of the twentieth century is progress.
>
> The other thing that Gertrude won't do is read the map. Alice Toklas reads the map and Gertrude sometimes takes notice and sometimes not.
>
> It is going dark. There are bombs exploding. Alice is losing patience. She throws down the map and shouts at Gertrude: "THIS IS THE WRONG ROAD."

Gertrude drives on. She says, "Right or wrong, this is the road and we are on it.[1]

It's important and magical and wonderful and scary to be queer. What happens—to community, to ourselves—if you do not have the road map handed to you? You see the landmarks that other people go to, visit some of them, and pass others by. You are able to say, "This is the road I'm traveling; it may not be the way for everyone, but I'm on it."

But then, to be allowed back on the road, to visit landmarks otherwise held out from you, that's new. This is what it is like to be queer today. How can we preserve the lessons that our experience in the night taught us?

There is something to be learned from queers. Something that everyone, whether gay or straight, can use. There is a lot to learn from those on the margins.

Everyone can learn the queer lessons of the night. Sex has a power to connect people across boundaries into sexy communities. Through naked intimacy, we embrace the body, the erotic. However, we can only see this intimacy if we examine sexuality as sex, not sexual orientation, a carnal sociology focused on the body, on pleasure, on our choices of consumption.

Sexy communities, bound together by naked intimacy, break down some kinds of boundaries endemic to our society. I discussed those of sexual racism. Stripped of the presence of everyday life, or at least the pretenses, queers forge erotic connection in the Hole, leather spaces, hookup joints, online sex apps, late-night dance clubs, sleazy strip clubs, smoke-filled backrooms, bareback orgies, steam rooms, saunas, bathhouses, drunken drugged binges, and floating barges.

That freedom of sexy connection requires segregation from the strictures of everyday life. It breaks down some boundaries by reinforcing others. This is the intersectional knot. Oppression is tangled, strands interwoven, producing social structures, cultures, and interactional scripts. Loosen one string, and the others tighten. The queer project is not uniformly good. Racial diversity in some spaces blossoms while women are turned away at the door. The boats of the plastics, protected by class, are not some queer utopia. But neither are the house parties of the political queers.

Heritage commodification, the process of selling an experience to outsiders as authentic, changes the spaces we move through, which change us in turn. By understanding pleasure and consumption as important and driven by a desire to change ourselves, "neighborhood effects" become more agentic and less bound to our residence. Assimilation, the problem of cultural transmission, involves a change to our space and our patterns of consumption, such that our habitus changes. In some cases, that habitus can become essentialized and transform an identity into a quasi-ethnicity.

Figure 14.1. Bartender at Cell Block bar

Because we seek our tastes, we become gay, it isn't merely a sexual orientation. We learn to be gay or to be queer. Given the choice, we should learn to be queer. Gay and straight alike, we can choose to be queer, by fostering queer spaces, by taking hold of the spirit of the night and using its lessons during the day, by embracing our sexuality.

Sex is something that has been taken from us. Sex is a kind of connection we deserve. The lies of abstinence-only sex education, the false moral choices of some religious doctrines, the patriarchal racist and classist code of ethics that dictates that only some kinds of families, some kinds of bodies, are worthy of sex, of love, of the naked intimacy of the erotic. Sex is something we—you—deserve.

Sex is something we deserve, but it is a chaotic good. There are plenty of reasons why society has regulated it so tightly. However, given the lessons of queers, the lessons that we have learned in the night and in this book, I think it is time to question its segregation into a different, secret, stigmatized part of our lives.

The dawn is coming. Boystown is changing, challenging the queer spaces, the erotic sensibility that used to exist alongside the gay. The chief executive officer of Netflix, a company that streams video over the Internet, once said that his goal was to become like the iconic premium television channel HBO faster than they could learn to become like his company. At times I wonder: How can queers change straights—of homosexual, bisexual, and heterosexual orientations—faster than we are assimilated?

Is that our goal as queers? To adjust the charmed circle to be a little friendlier? To pass the buck down the line to those even more sexually stigmatized than us? To be let into the light of rights, legal equality, safety, and family, only by turning our back on the intimacy of the darkness?

No.

I don't want to be on the outside of the charmed circle forever, but I don't want anyone there, because I don't want to continue the bifurcation of ourselves, and the stigma of some people as "other" based on their sex lives, especially because that other is a certain kind of racial other, a gendered other, a classed other. I, as a queer man, must use those lessons for the good of the straight single mom, my sister on the outside of the charmed circle in other ways.

It is time for another kind of dawn, a new sexual revolution.

That sexual revolution is the queer revolution. It began in the backrooms inhabited by queer homosexuals and died with HIV and AIDS, but it now could be reborn with queer heterosexuals. Homosexuals could join forces with those that are on the outside of the charmed circle in respects other than sexual orientation. Queers all.

Sexy communities should embrace the dawn as well. We have to move beyond all-male queer spaces.

Figure 14.2. Daytime discussion outside Roscoe's bar

All spaces are not for all people. I don't advocate a world where every space has a perfect diversity of bodies. However, there are some straight women and men who do not come to Boystown on safari but who come to the queer spaces outside of the charmed circle like the Hole. These people are the future, the spark of queer heterosexuality. These people are the dawn of our next sexy communities.

Many straight people weren't pushed out of their families. These straight people didn't have the pain of HIV or the brokenness of gay stigma. They didn't have to be in a sexy community.

They came anyway.

These are the people that point the way forward to queer heterosexuality.

Significant barriers stand in the way, though. Sexism and violence drive straight women to Boystown, just as much as Boystown pulls them there to learn a gay habitus. Is it possible to have a heterosexual sexy community, one where people do not feel vulnerable but are free to enjoy pleasure without the threat of violence? It has been tried before. App developers, such as Blendr, have tried to replicate Grindr's queer male experience for heterosexuals, but to little avail. Guess what? Most straight women don't want a host of strangers knowing their location. Playing "Spot the Blendr" in a straight space would be creepy, not fun or pleasurable.

However, there are straight spaces that point the way forward to that: queer heterosexuals in BDSM spaces, swingers, nudists, and straight sex clubs. I hope that we see more such places in the future.

For now though, queers do it better. I hope that this book helps people preserve some of the spaces that create sexy communities against the assimilation and heritage commodification of gay male spaces—especially since queers also have a lot of things that they could do better.

We need to welcome queer women into queer spaces, which are often male dominated. We need to do it in a way that doesn't continue to entrench privilege but embraces the fun of desire. Letting pleasure, and the intimacy it can deliver, form a backbone of community.

New technologies and public health strategies are ushering in this new sexual revolution. Although approved in the middle of the period I conducted fieldwork, Pre-Exposure Prophylaxis (PrEP)—a pill that can be taken daily to prevent HIV infection among people who don't have HIV—began to gain wide traction after I finished writing the main text of *Boystown*.

The influence of PrEP remains to be seen. Queers were developing new types of sexuality, new communities, when HIV killed wide swaths of the same-sex male-desiring population. HIV forced assimilation. HIV lead to gay Disneyland. I've shown that the social experience of HIV is changing, strengthening the assimilation of good gays, but having a less meaningful impact on the outer edges of the charmed circle, such as in the poz (HIV positive) community I followed. Will PrEP usher in a world without HIV, where everyone can take hold of the lessons of the night? I don't know.

In sociology, this sexual revolution is the unclaimed birthright of sexuality studies. Arlene Stein and Kenneth Plummer declared back in 1995 that, while queer studies have been infused with sociology, sociology has yet to see the queer revolution.[2] Twenty years later, despite the good work of many sexualities and intersectional scholars, that revolution remains unfulfilled. At the 2013 sexualities preconference to the American Sociological Association, speaker after speaker—Mignon Moore, Mary Bernstein, Janice Irving, Héctor Carrillo—emphasized that, while sexualities scholarship was rapidly improving, it has had a limited impact on wider sociological discourse. It was time, they said, for sexuality studies to demonstrate an intersectional significance of sexuality studies to sociology.

Héctor Carrillo, at that same sexualities conference, presented data showing that the Sociology of Family and the Sociology of Sexualities, two different sections with two different memberships, are studying the same subjects. Sexualities are marginalized families. Mainstream sociology, respectable sociology, looks at the inner charmed circle as though it were normal, calls it "family," without disrupting the paradigm of respectability that supports it. Sexualities studies the outer circle. The stigmatized and the marginalized are put there as though their lives have nothing to say about the center.

As the light breaks, I want us to see that the spirit of the night lives within many different areas, many times in the light of day. Black poverty in the inner city depends on the exclusion and stigmatization of sex. Fertility rates, that classic problem of demography and population studies, one of sociology's main subdisciplines, are a product of sexuality. To understand the birth and growth and decline of populations, you have to understand sexuality. Great love stories, betrayals, affairs, and sexual scandals form the foundation of many popular culture stories. People make labor market choices to support their families, that product and cause of sexuality. Why do we seldom look at sex when considering some of our most troublesome problems?

Patricia Hill Collins, in *Black Feminist Politics*, argued that we need a sociology of empowerment. I want to empower you to reclaim the sexual birthright that has been denied to you. I want to empower sociology, and social science in general, to be unabashedly sexual. I want a carnal sociology not only of the body but of the pleasurable erotic body.

What is the future of gayborhoods? Are they bound for the trash heap? Or, will they become forever gay Disneylands, tourist districts like Little Italies or Chinatowns that have more to do with where a particular flavor of cuisine is found than a space for the people that are in that demographic.

We have to remember that the spaces that we foster are important. Economics—what will be economically viable—shapes the kinds of spaces we are going to see. Those spaces in turn shape us. We must actively foster the kind of spaces that teach the habitus that we want others to have. If we hope to have a queer revolution, it has to come from us.

That means being proactive about building, fostering, and supporting with our dollars, places of fun, of pleasure, of erotic intimacy. Not just in our books, not just in our minds, but with our bodies, with our time, and with our money.

We embrace the dawn in our own lives. Boystown, with all its complications, with all of its fluctuations, is my home. I will no longer live in the darkness, but I will bring its lessons into the day.

ACKNOWLEDGMENTS

———

A book is the product of many authors. Although I wrote the words, many voices are present in this text.

Foremost, I must thank the many people who participated in my research on Boystown and queer Chicago. Some were interviewed for this text. Others casually talked to me over a beer out on the town. Others I eavesdropped on while they talked in a public place. My thanks go out to all of them. Many challenged me on my interpretations. I thank those people most of all.

I also thank my writing group, mentors, and friends, who gave comments on drafts of these chapters: Amanda Ward, Erin Madden, Mya Fisher, John Delamater, Mustafa Emirbayer, Joshua Garoon, Robert Nixon, Cameron Macdonald, Loka Ashwood, and Michael Bell. Without your voices, this project would never have been written.

I gave presentations on this material at many different events. The comments of participants at those events insightfully pushed along the findings, including those at the Interdisciplinary Sexuality Seminar at the University of Wisconsin–Madison and the Center for AIDS Research, the American Sociological Association, the Society for the Scientific Study of Sexuality, and the Sociology of Race and Ethnicity group at the University of Wisconsin–Madison. The Professor John DeLamater Award at UW–Madison contributed funds to the project.

I offer my thanks as well to the three anonymous reviewers whose comments shaped this book from the proposal stage to the final manuscript. The comments led me to welcome changes.

My editor, Doug Mitchell, deserves praise for the steady drumbeat he laid down, pushing this book toward completion but allowing me to experiment in my solos. Thanks also to both Kyle Wagner and Timothy McGovern for their assistance in managing the many tasks that go into producing a book. Yvonne Zipter's skillful editing let it shine.

Finally, my husband Austin supported me throughout this book in many ways. I was already well into my ethnographic research when we met, but the book changed immeasurably because of our long talks, his insightful comments on drafts, his patience with my latest rant, and his bravery spurring me on to be open with myself and readers.

Thank you; I love you.

SUPPLEMENT: PRODUCING ETHNOGRAPHY

I do not usually like methods appendices. An appendix, like its bodily counterpart, often positions methodology as unnecessary, tacked on—as something that could be cut off from the main text without harm, whereas method is an integral part of assessing scientific work. Everyone should be concerned about method, at least enough to be reassured of the veracity of these narratives, to be convinced that I am not withholding key information, and to understand my process of tacking every closer to a true representation of Boystown. Much of this material is in the main body of *Boystown*. However, I gather it together here so that readers can find this information in one place. I present this addendum as a vision of qualitative ethnography.

An ethnography is composed of interlocking data collection methods and an analysis strategy that triangulates between these methods, building a theory through constant comparison and theoretical sampling. I use the multilogical approach, explained in the qualitative fieldwork textbook I cowrote with Michael M. Bell (2015). In this theory of method, the scholar pays attention to the three voices of research: They, You, and We. These voices are the participants, the researcher, and the academic community, respectively. Each voice has a story to tell. The multilogical approach is a middle way between positivist and postmodernist approaches to qualitative methods. Similarly, it is a middle way between deductive (e.g., extended case method) and inductive (e.g., grounded theory) methods, seeing them as two sides of the same coin (Tavory and Timmermans 2009). Before explaining the analytical considerations one must take for each voice, I will discuss each of my data collection strategies at length.

PARTICIPANT-OBSERVATION

My participant-observation consisted of three years of fieldwork starting in June 2011 and focused especially on outings in which I followed six groups of queer people varying by race and class position. I had visited Boystown before June 2011 and knew it by reputation. Those early trips to Chicago for fun—there were so many more gay people and clubs than were available in Madison, Wisconsin—led me to begin preliminary fieldwork in June with observations at Boystown's Pride Fest. The Take Back Boystown events, a subject I discuss in the main text, occurred later that month, solidifying my site choice. A number of trips to Boystown over the next six months gave me background information on the neighborhood, culminating in my move there in January 2012.

Participant-observation fieldwork develops in phases. Those preliminary trips acclimated me to the area, but moving to the neighborhood drowned me in data. Before I found the groups I would eventually follow more intently, I began charting Boystown's clubs and bars, centers, stores, and residential spaces and the kinds of people that moved through them. By day, I did this by working at a location—such as the Center on Halsted—on my freelance work and taking observations while working on these projects, which paid my bills.

By night, I would choose a club to go to and drink by myself at the bar, using my phone as a way to take small notes. These "jottings" (Emerson, Fretz, and Shaw 2011) were covert, given that everyone else in these spaces who was alone—even temporarily—stared at their screens: texting, on Grindr, or reading Facebook. If anything, my practice of setting the phone down, watching the TV, or making small talk with the bartender made my presence more like that of the old-timers who would occasionally be in the bars at night. Eventually, I met others who were alone, in pairs, or, very rarely, groups because of their proximity to me at the bar.

During this period of time, when I had yet to meet regulars, I varied the time I attended spaces to better capture different kinds of crowds. Regular events—like Live Band Karaoke at Roscoe's, Musical Mondays at Sidetrack, or *RuPaul's Drag Race* viewing parties at Spin—provided an opportunity to regularly go to the same space. Although turnover in the service industry is high, I knew many of the bartenders at these spaces due to becoming a regular.

These two methods—varying time and regular events—led me to two of the groups I followed. Group 1 consisted of Darren and Jon—Black and Latino, respectively—who I met after a viewing of *RuPaul's Drag Race* at Roscoe's. They invited me to Spin the next week, and I attended many events with them around Boystown afterward. Group 2 was made up of JJ and his friends, who work very early mornings. Their late nights are our early evenings. So, when I attended Spin one afternoon with the intention to meet old-timers, they were there taking shots. Flo and JJ stood outside the doorway, waiting for the bartender to open up, and asked me why I was there at 4 P.M., too. That conversation led them to invite me to join them for drinks thirty minutes later once we were inside. Eventually, they would take me to many of the queer-of-color nights I attended in Boystown spaces.

I met another two groups through friends who were visiting the city. A friend from Dallas visited me in June 2012 to attend Pride and introduced me to some acquaintances he had met through his travels, group 3, who I lovingly refer to as the plastics. This group, who I also met through a friend of Austin's, shared social ties and the same scene as "the boat people"—men who cruise on boats along Lake Michigan during the summer—such that I consider them together with the plastics as one social group. I met the poz guys, group 4, through another friend, quickly becoming friends with several of them. I am intentionally vague about which of my participants belonged to this group, as I have been throughout the book when describing them, to make it harder to connect their serostatus to specific people.

Finally, I met groups 5 and 6 through being at spaces or attending events to which other participants had invited me. The overlap of these last groups with each other demonstrates the principle of circuits, in which people inhabit the same series of physical spaces but are socially segregated. Jon initially invited me to the Queer Is Community Facebook group (group 5), where I connected with the organizers to attend the event. There, I met Frank and his mostly white queer friends and spent time with them in bars, political groups, and house parties across Chicago. I went to Jackhammer with a variety of people, but mostly several of the poz guys, and eventually got to know Marcus. His leather family (group 6), of which I am now considered a member, forms the final group I had regular interaction with over the three years of my fieldwork.

Don't take the neatness of this post hoc narrative as indicative of preplanning or that I followed each of these groups for the same amount of time or over the whole three years. The truth is always messier. Groups faded. I dropped out of contact with some. Others dropped contact with me. I attempted to make contact with many, many people over the years. Some I didn't connect with. Others ignored me.

There are groups that might have been, and they influence my ethnography as well. Ethnographers are rarely open about the people who influenced us that don't neatly fit into our book's narrative. For instance, I attended Berlin regularly with Mark and several of his queer friends of color from the art community before his suicide in March 2012. While I continued to hang out with Carlos afterward, Mark was the energy that bound me to them, and contact with that group eventually faded as I spent time with other people. In another example, a young Latino man and his white roommate hung out with me several times before they stopped returning my texts for unknown reasons. Just because I don't now count them as a "group I followed" doesn't mean they didn't significantly influence my work, even if our contact was brief.

Other people influenced my ethnography, even though I didn't choose to follow them as a group or they weren't "participants" in the traditional sense. My friend Madeline, for instance, could have given me more information about the lesbian point of view in Boystown. As my analysis increasingly focused on gay male sexual space, and less on how relationships developed within the changing context of gentrification, I chose not to be deliberate about fieldwork with her. I continued to take field notes when we went out, as I did anytime I visited Boystown. But I didn't press for social time in a focused way like I did with other groups.

Similarly, had I formed a relationship with another man instead of Austin, I might have met different groups, or they might have intersected with my life differently. For instance, a Black man in his midthirties who I dated for three weeks had, as one would expect, a group of Black gay friends. Through them, I might have met different people. Boystown is a small town in a big city. People in groups I did follow, and others who were bartenders or acquaintances, were much less than six degrees of separation away. My experience of Boystown if I had kept dating him, or any other person, would have produced a different book. Any relationship—friendship or romantic—influences a project. So does not having a relationship, as I discuss below.

Fieldwork in 2012 was the most intense, as I filled my social calendar with events with various people. For those months, I typically went out four to five nights a week. Mondays I might go to *RuPaul's Drag Race* with Jon. Tuesdays, I might attend a literary reading with Frank's white queers followed by Berlin with Mark's queers of color. I might be too hungover and lacking sleep on Wednesday to go out again, but rested enough to hit the club with JJ on Thursday and then hang out with a one-off connection I was attempting to develop into a longer-term participant on Friday and Saturday. Each of these would involve me staying up until nearly 2, 3, or 6 A.M. When I'd wake up the next morning, I would turn my jottings and audio recordings from the previous night into field notes, write a memo analyzing an aspect that connected to previous outings in the afternoon, and then scramble to complete paid consulting work before it was time to go to the gym and get ready for another night out in Boystown.

This intense period faded as fieldwork progressed—thankfully, for my liver and sanity. Although I continued to take field notes during the next year and a half, more of my time was spent doing analysis, writing memos on emergent themes, and connecting themes together into initial results. Participant-observation in this period consisted less of intense daily fieldwork and more of deliberate weekly participation in scenes that I wished to encounter to further my analysis, contacting groups to see if they were attending a particular event.

Each of these groups provided me with a different experience of Boystown, but I did not hang out with them to chronicle their social scene. Rather, they brought me along their circuits, giving me a more comprehensive picture of Boystown's sexual field than if I had followed one group alone. The specific scenes within this book would likely be different, but I conducted enough analysis, comparison, and triangulation among people, scenes, and data types to know that my theories represent a social process happening in gay male sexual spaces in Chicago.

INTERVIEWING

I conducted twenty-eight hours of formal interviews with twenty-one key participants for an average of eighty minutes per person. During fieldwork, I also conducted countless informal interviews—that is, lopsided conversations—lasting five to fifteen minutes. I recorded and transcribed the formal interviews and included the informal interviews in my field notes. Quotes appearing in the text were transcribed either from interviews or at the time as jottings. These quotes have been at times edited for clarity or to remove identifying details.

As per my agreement with my Institutional Review Board at the University of Wisconsin–Madison, I will not report on the specifics of each person, so as to obfuscate their identity. Indeed, reporting on the statistics of the sample does less to shed light on the nature of my interviewing than it does to orient readers to a positivistic perspective that focuses on whether the sample was representative. I approached participants on the basis of the expert knowledge they would have, institutional or structural perspectives they had, or cultural identities that would influence their involvement in Boystown.

Thus, key participants included nonprofit employees, bartenders, club patrons, journalists, business owners, Boystown residents, and people who haven't regularly visited Boystown in years.

This interview sample is *not* the same as groups I followed ethnographically. Some members of the groups I followed for participant observation agreed to have a formal interview. I did not ask everyone, and several people declined interviews, while agreeing to be followed. Using two separate samples—ethnographic observation and interview—serves the methodological principle of triangulation. By connecting themes between styles, I was able to discern whether something was "truly" happening.

The interviews are not meant to be representative of the people discussed in this book but, rather, they are meant to represent aspects of people's experience that are pertinent to my evolving research questions. Thus, I cannot share with you a single interview guide used to ask questions. Rather, I used the techniques of coconstructed interviewing (Corbin and Morse 2003) to allow interviewees to raise issues, during the course of the interview, that deviated from the questions I would prepare ahead of time. Based on on-going analysis, I would create a list of six to eight topics, with a list of possible follow-up questions for each. These topics were tailored to the person I was interviewing. Why else interview particular people? I considered each an expert in their field, whether a business owner explaining the economic decisions in crafting a marketing plan, a straight woman designing a bachelorette party, or a journalist reporting on an event. These topics typically took the first forty-five minutes of an interview. The remaining time was spent on three questions crucial to any interview: What questions do you have for me? What have we not discussed or missed during our conversation given what we've discussed today? Who else should I talk to or what else should I research to give me a more complete picture? Often, these questions would take another thirty minutes to complete. This section of an interview often gave the richest data.

My first interview took place three months after moving to Boystown, nine months into the project. My last interview took place two weeks before finishing the first draft of the manuscript. Here are a few actual transcribed questions. Early interviews were likely to be informational: "How did you get into the bars before you were eighteen?" Middle interviews were focused on theory building and comparing interviewees' experiences with other data I'd collected: "Why do you think that straight families have moved here? I've been seeing that too and a lot of people have been telling me that during my interviews. So, why move to Boystown? Why move to this part of Lakeview?" Interviews conducted late in the project were more likely to be member-checking interviews (Orne and Bell 2015): "So that's something that I'm writing an article about. How are things the same and different between online hooking up and offline hooking up? How are they similar and how are they different?"

Interviewees chose where I would interview them. Often, when they could not think of a place, I would provide several choices, varying in their intimacy and visibility: a coffee shop, a library, my home, or their home. They almost always chose a coffee shop. One might think people would be unwilling to talk about sex in such a public space. However, that's one of the arguments of this book isn't it? While American society might consider sexuality private, not everyone follows those rules of respectability.

Twenty-eight hours of interviews is over 295,000 words when transcribed. That's three books long if you read the full transcripts and thus impossible to present in their entirety. Some of the topics we discussed did not become pertinent to this book. Sometimes I asked questions already suspecting I knew the answer to see if I was "saturated" on a topic. Some material I left out because it was too identifying. As I will discuss shortly, any project must be selective in the material presented. I hope readers are convinced I've not selectively presented it.

AUTOETHNOGRAPHY

At the core, research—qualitative and quantitative—uses the researcher to translate, analyze, and explain an experience, community, or process for outsiders, often in the form of the academic community. Autoethnography refers to the process of using the researcher's experience about themselves— especially about their memories, emotions, and internal processes to which others would not have access—to elucidate a social process that is hard to grasp or to comment on aspects of an experience that do not fit with re-search conducted through surveys, interviews, and participant-observation (see Ellis 2009).

"Autoethnography" is a term often incorrectly applied to any discussion of the self within research. Autoethnography is not the same as radical reflexivity. Merely discussing the influence of the researcher within a situa-tion, their actions within the situation, or including themselves as a charac-ter within the text does not make a work autoethnographic. Those aspects of Boystown are not autoethnography; they are requirements of all ethnog-raphy properly conducted. As such, I consider them below in my discussion of positionality.

I did use autoethnography, though. Many ethnographers do, though they don't refer to it as such. In particular, I used three autoethnographic tools to enhance my ethnographic data. First, at times I "translated" for participants (Devault 1990, 101). As Devault explains in her research with women: "Since the words available often do not fit, women learn to 'trans-late' when they talk about their experiences." Social structure shapes the language available for the marginalized to use. When the researcher shares structural positions with participants—like being a woman for Devault's research or engaging in sexuality outside the charmed circle for mine—they can use that experience to help participants articulate their understand-ings. At times, I use my own experience and emotions to translate the expe-riences of others, having triangulated with my other data sources, and then member checked these translations with field notes and interviews.

Second, I use "emotional recall" (Ellis 1999): "The process of plumbing the depths of your emotional responses to an event" (Orne and Bell 2015). As a researcher, I only truly have access to my own emotional experience. I can observe others' actions. I can ask others how they are feeling. But the feel-ing of dancing at Hydrate? That can only be partially explained to others. However, with experience, one can learn to express those inner emotions to others through language. When I express the pain of knowing the tragedy of AIDS and having never lived with a time before fear of HIV ruled queer sex lives, I connect that pain to Moore's pain (2004). Through my and Moore's emotional experiences, and by thoroughly examining the context and consequences of those emotions, I enrich the ethnographic scenes I present and add additional layers to the processes I examine.

Third, I consider "enactive ethnography," as advocated by Loïc Wacquant, to be an autoethnographic tool. Enactive ethnography asks: "If we learn through the body, through doing, then how should the ethnographer also learn?" The answer, obviously, is through the body and through action. I am a queer man, who moved through these queer spaces. In some of them, such as in environments shares with the plastics, my own self-consciousness likely led me to be attuned to the role of body consciousness in those spaces. Others—the experience of naked intimacy, for instance—I know to be true because I underwent these experiences as well. I am a sexual being, just like the people I talked with about sexuality. I do not hide this aspect of the text.

Autoethnography's critical pedagogy disrupts traditional research voices, often located in the powerful, by focusing on the lived experience of the oppressed. Autoethnography takes our inner experience and expresses it as a concept others can use. In *An Invitation to Qualitative Fieldwork*, Bell and I point out autoethnography's key position in social science and its usefulness in developing core concepts this way: "Autoethnography is also the main method of one of the most widely acclaimed works ever written by a sociologist, *The Souls of Black Folk*, by W. E. B. Du Bois. He didn't use the term either, writing a century before someone coined it. But you know he was writing about his own experience of race in American when in 1903 he wrote one of the most widely cited passages in the sociological literature: "It is a peculiar sensation, this double-consciousness.'"

I would go so far as to say autoethnography should no longer be classified as such. Autoethnographic tools are crucial to the discipline of sociology. All ethnographers should be using them to make sense of the three voices of research.

PHOTOGRAPHY

The photos for this book were taken by the photographer Dylan Stuckey over two days in September 2015, well after this book was finished. It is telling that even a year after the main research was completed, I was so quickly able to find photographic subjects that fit the themes of this book. All photographs were taken in public spaces, where the subjects did not have an expectation of privacy. That said, to protect the identity of people that attend the Hole I used posed models to mimic the space, with signed releases from all models. The visual ethnography produced through my collaboration with Stuckey elevates the subject matter of the book. I highly recommend that qualitative researchers collaborate with artists in this manner.

THE MULTILOGICAL APPROACH

Data collection is only the start of method in social science research. Three voices are present in all research, though often not all of them are allowed to speak. The participants have voice through the data, resulting in the problems of multiplicity and singularity. The researcher speaks through her choices in data collection, analysis, and writing. Thus, we must contend with positionality and narrativity. The audience—often the academic community, but not always as seen with this book—speaks through the reception of the work, and the choices made by the author to ensure readers find the work useful and well done. Contestability and extendability arise when considering the audience's role. I will discuss each in turn.

THEY

Multiplicity refers to the problem of too much data. Every situation is infinitely complex, with so many different strands of social processes and overlapping contexts. Why follow some strands and not others? Contending with this deluge of data requires a good technique of theory development. Of all the possible questions to ask about Boystown, why the ones that I present here? This is the problem of research topic.

Singularity, though, emphasizes that even though the world is infinitely complex, each situation is also unique, never to occur again with that particular set of contexts and processes. Therefore, while we have infinite points of data, they are all unique from each other in their combination of people, processes, and contexts. A researcher thus must be able to articulate what is unique about the population he or she is studying. Why choose this place over all the others? This is the problem of case selection.

Taking cues from both constructivist grounded theory and extended case method, I worked simultaneously to discover the social processes occurring in Boystown from the ground up as well as asking, "What is this a case of?" This iterative inductive/deductive process works because it shifts the frame of reference and method of analysis. It leverages the "constant comparative method." That is, I am always comparing instances of data, different situations, and different perspectives on the same situation.

Researchers choose a field site for theoretical reasons, to answer particular questions even if those questions are not the ones we end up answering. Given my research specializations in sexuality, social psychology, and race, I chose Boystown as a field site to explore questions relating to interracial relationships in gay communities. Boystown presented a combination of two statistical anomalies: gay men are more likely to be in interracial relationships while Midwestern people are least likely to be in interracial relationships.

However, once in Boystown, while I was attuned to issues of race—obviously, given the subject of much of the book—I inductively followed the lines of inquiry appearing in my data, including issues brought up by participants, those that I noticed in my fieldwork, or those that presented contradictions with existing theory. This inductive process of discovery inevitably leads to a deductive process of testing the emerging theory in new settings, with new participants or with new questions. This process then leads back to inductively exploring new issues to fully understand the process. This process of choosing new data sources to collect and analyze, new questions to ask, new places to go, or new ways of looking at old places is called theoretical sampling.

YOU

The researcher is the conduit through which the audience learns anything about participants and their context. I collected all of the data. I am the instrument through which the analysis of those data was conducted. I chose the research questions. I chose the field site. Everything you know from this book, you learned through me. It is important to understand who I am and how that influences those choices. This is positionality, the problem of reflexivity or "bias."

I am also the author of this book. A book cannot be about everything. Earlier, I mentioned that the hours of interviews I conducted would be over three books of material. Combined with the field notes, essays, screenshots, and other material, I have far more material than I could ever present to readers. *Boystown* presents a limited set of data about a particular set of questions arranged to include a fraction of that material. This is narrativity, the inevitable problem of selection because of the need to present a coherent story, an argument, a thesis.

As I discussed above, I take a position of radical reflexivity, not common among sociologists. I include myself with the text, along with my thoughts, my actions, and my mistakes not only because it makes for a more compelling story but also because it makes for stronger science.

Everything we do is biased. Nothing is purely objective. Because I am a person that makes decisions, collects data, talks to some people and not others, has reactions to what people say to me, and lives within the world I communicated to you what I present is necessarily subjective. To trust my decisions, you have to know information about me. I present that information in the main text of *Boystown*, rather than here in an addendum, because you have to know that information in the moment. Including myself within the text—my identities, my opinions, my fears, my hopes—does not make this study less scientific; it makes it more so because it is acknowledged. Those traits are present in all work. I make them visible.

I present these parts of myself also to make my narrativity visible, rather than engage in the invisible narrativity of positivism. This book could have been about innumerable other subjects, but it is about the ones that I presented here because those were the lines of inquiry that I followed, that I heard the loudest, because they spoke to me the clearest. Other people have researched Boystown and come away with different but intersecting questions and theories, such as Amin Ghazani's (2014) *There Goes the Gayborhood* or Edward O. Laumann et al.'s (2004) *Sexual Organization of the City*, both of which use Boystown as a case. We found different things because we are different people, researchers attuned to different questions. We are also aware of different aspects of these situations because of our research specializations and our own lives. My positionality outside of the charmed circle of respectability—although I didn't articulate it in that way when I began the book—lead me to make choices, to present material about that issue.

I also made decisions about how to present this book in a novelistic creative nonfiction style because of narrativity. Not only can a book not be about everything, but it can't be presented in every way. I wanted to reach an academic audience with my theories, while also presenting those theories in a way that was interesting to read, and understandable enough, that it would be read by nonacademic readers. I wrote this book as much for sociologists as I did for queer people themselves. Some authors try to accomplish this by shifting between presentation styles within a piece of work, including some information for one audience and some for another. I combined all of that information through one narrative.

WE

Knowledge hidden; knowledge wasted. For research to be worth something, it must be consumed, presented, read. "A word is a territory shared," as Bakhtin writes. The audience of research is vital to its creation. If someone reads our work, we are lucky. A researcher must fulfill two requirements to reach an audience.

First, an audience must be convinced of the work's veracity. Why did I make these choices? How did my theoretical sampling lead to my results? Where does the evidence presented match the claims made? Where does it fall short? Research must deal with contestability, the degree to which readers are able to judge the work's trustworthiness because the researcher has provided them with the information and tools to make that judgment.

Second, even if they find the work good, if they think that it is true, an audience will not respond if the work is not useful to them. This book must be about something more than "just" Boystown for it to matter. An audience finds a work useful by being able to relate it. The theories must be able to be used in other situations. The stories must help them think through a part of their own life. The author must provide them a new way to think about themselves and their problems or to formulate new questions. Research must deal with extendability, the degree to which readers are able to extend the information presented to other situations similar and dissimilar by way of an author being as specific as possible about the limits and extensions of the work.

I presented *Boystown* in the way that would allow it to be contestable and extendable. Traditional social science deals with its inferiority complex—vis-à-vis the natural sciences—through the tools of incontestability: universalism, inaccessibility, and authority. By writing in inscrutable ways, presenting work as though the author is indisputable, the work hides its mistakes and seems to apply to every situation. Instead, I practice "disagreeable science" (Orne and Bell 2015), allowing the reader to disagree with me by providing the tools to do so. I provide many different voices through the text (heteroglossia) and present evidence from different angles (triangulation). I also present mistakes or counterexamples that seem to disprove my thesis (disconfirmation). There are no outliers in qualitative research. I must deal with everything that happened, and I want the reader to be convinced I did not leave something out because it was inconvenient.

I used novelistic and creative nonfiction also to make the work extendable. Sociologists find extendability through positioning the work within an intellectual history, a niche of work to which the data speak. Every chapter refers to those histories to which I connect, often building bridges between them so that researchers in other areas can see connections, especially the intersections between race, class, and gender that sexuality bridges and entrenches and the importance of sexuality to space.

However, those are not the only aspects of *Boystown* and my work that I wanted readers to find useful. I also want readers to connect to the feeling of Boystown and erotic spaces. Can someone understand what it is like to be down in the Hole? What about dancing with friends at Chloe's? Watching music videos at Sidetrack? Resisting a sandwich in front of the pretty boys on Lake Michigan? These are experiences. They cannot be described only intellectually; they must be felt and imagined. They must be embodied. My method of presentation and the types of data I collected reach readers through these intuitive understandings.

A FINAL NOTE

I also wrote *Boystown* for myself. It is the book I wanted to read. It captures a spirit I worried was disappearing, but the process of researching and writing this book ultimately convinced me the erotic sensibility of queer cultures will live on. *Boystown* makes claims about the importance of sex that both sociology and straight society need to hear and that queers need to be reminded of. We don't have a language for describing why sex matters, why it is important. I found that language in Boystown.

NOTES

CHAPTER 1

1. As I shall explain, "gay" and "queer" refer to different identities. "Queer" is often used inclusively to signify all nonheterosexual identities. Here, I use "queer" to refer to a political-sexual identity that positions someone outside of the mainstream. BELIEVE and Frank are both pseudonyms, as I shall discuss later.

2. Not to be confused with "ex-gay," which refers to the movement of people who believe they have changed their sexual orientation to heterosexual through prayer, willpower, therapy, or other means. "Postgay" refers to the belief that we are in an era where society has transcended sexual orientation. That is, it doesn't matter whether one is gay or not.

3. Ghaziani 2014.

4. "LGBT" stands for lesbian, gay, bisexual, and transgender.

5. The notion that gay identity is a stage to be surmounted is reminiscent of Venicinne Cass's (1979) "identity synthesis" stage of gay identity, a disproven theory (Kahn 1991) that nevertheless haunts gay studies with its unfounded assumptions and homophobic stance (Orne 2011).

6. In her essay, "Thinking Sex," Rubin ([1983] 2011) proposed the charmed circle as a way to describe the connections between stigmatized forms of sexuality. I propose it as a tool to understand assimilation.

7. D'Emilio 1983.

8. *Bowers v. Hardwick* 478 U.S. 186 (1986).

9. *Lawrence v. Texas* 539 U.S. 558 (2003). See Carpenter (2012) for discussion of the racial and sexual background behind the *Lawrence v. Texas* decision.

10. Warner 2000.

11. Duggan 2004.

12. Ward 2008.

13. Discussing this chapter with someone later, this description alone caused them to exclaim: "Oh, Josh!" Apparently, he is popular.

14. Or at least it wasn't. As I discuss later in chapter 11, "Girlstown," even the Shoe eventually was full of bachelorette parties once Cocktail shut down.

15. See Moore (2004) for discussion of the cultural impact of HIV in the 1980s on queer sexual life. What I cover here is how these impacts play out twenty years later in a new context of assimilation.

16. See Sullivan (1996) for an articulation of these views by a proponent and see Duggan (2004) for a critic's point of view.

17. Today, 3.6 percent of men identify as gay or bisexual (Gates 2010), although self-identified gay or bi men would have been lower in the 1990s. In 1992, according to the U.S. Census, the U.S. population was 256.51 million. Sixty percent of gay men in the nineties lived in the largest cities, where HIV cases were most prevalent. Therefore, there were 1.44 million urban gay and bi men in 1992. Fifty-two percent of new HIV cases in 1992 were from men who have sex with men, in health lingo—57 percent, if we include men who reported having sex with men and injection drug use. Before 1992, these numbers were higher, but I'll use the lower estimate. The Centers for Disease Control and Prevention (1995) recorded 249,199 adults diagnosed with AIDS from the start of the epidemic to 1992. Approximately 68 percent of them died from AIDS. Thus, 12 percent of the urban gay and bi male population died from AIDS by 1992. Repeating these steps for 1995, 21 percent had died. See Black et al. (2000) for more on estimates of the gay population during the 1990s.

18. "Neighborhood effects" are as discussed by Sampson (2012), which I will discuss in greater detail in later chapters.

19. Here, I refer of course to habitus, which I discuss in later chapters of this book, but do not use as a term now because of the term's theoretical and confusing nature.

20. "Carnal sociology" is discussed by Loïc Wacquant (2004, 2005, 2015) in a series of articles and books over the last decade.

21. See Eliasoph (2005) for discussion of how carnal sociology as currently articulated is more like "corporeal sociology."

22. Doty 2002, 9.

23. "Enactive ethnography," as I discuss in the appendix.

24. As Collins (2015) suggests in his reply to Wacquant's discussion of enactive ethnography, as I discuss further in the appendix.

25. A bear is a hairy gay man, usually larger, bulkier guys. Their scenes have a body culture that is opposite of the classic gay-clone stereotype: fat over thin, hairy over smooth (Hennen 2005; Monaghan 2005).

26. I write about men who are cisgendered, biological, trans, genderqueer, or otherwise. I am claiming not that I employ an essentialized gender perspective, but that these spaces are undeniably masculine, rooted in the history of men—who, as I shall discuss, had the economic freedom to create them in the first place.

27. Many excellent books have been written about queer women's lives, both in the United States and globally, among them, Moore (2011) and Wekker (2013).

CHAPTER 2

1. The banning of straight women from this particular bar is a subject that attracted national attention, including a reference on *The Chelsea Handler Show*.

2. Tom of Finland was the pseudonym of Touko Laaksonen, a Finnish artist known for his drawings of hypermasculine men and fetish art.

3. What did she find embarrassing? Not their ignorance of Manhole, but the acknowledgment of their sense of novelty. I'll return to her later in the chapter.

4. Stafford 2013.

5. Ian Betteridge is a British technology journalist who coined this journalistic law, which helps readers identify lazy titles. If the title asks you a question, the answer is no, otherwise they would have titled it affirmatively. "Is this the cure for cancer?" Probably not.

6. Gates 2010.

7. Although, interestingly, Manhole became a regular occurrence. Manhole became a club, then shut down, then opened again, as of publication—yo-yoing in and out of business, as one might expect, given the business realities of heritage commodification discussed in this book.

8. The sexual field is a Bourdieuian approach to the study of sexuality (Green 2008, 2011, 2013). While I find the field concept less useful analytically, I discuss habitus taught in these spaces in the second half of the book.

9. Goffman 1959.

10. Jason Orne, Gina Spitz, and Michael M. Bell, "Goffman and a Deck of Cards: The Trick of Power" (manuscript in progress).

11. Urry 2002.

12. As discussed later in "Becoming Gay" (chap. 8).

13. From *In Our Words*, a Chicago-based online essay salon (Crowley 2012).

14. After identifying Jackhammer as a potential important site, I accepted brief employment opportunities to get a better look at the other side. I acquired this access because my husband, Austin, worked briefly as a bartender there.

15. Lest you think I'm including this for my ego, I'm "fit" only in the context of the largely older and more bearish men that frequent Jackhammer. See the supplementary material in "Producing Ethnography" in the preceding section of this book for discussion about my sexuality within this study or my work in progress, "The Sexual Ethnographer," for more on attraction and sexuality in the ethnographic context, especially the issues within enactive ethnography.

16. Moon (2013). For a historical account of the development of cruising, see Chauncey (1994).

17. For a revealing discussion of cockblocking as itself a sexual act, see Kahan (2013).

18. An interesting connection between perceived masculinity, which could be interpreted as an internalized heterosexism since it implies gay men are not "real men," and perceived erotic power at being able to "turn" a man otherwise uninterested in men. These stereotypes also interact with race, as I shall discuss in chapter 5, "Sexual Racism," giving further evidence of the intersectional knot.

19. Chicago's liquor laws are complicated. There are a limited number of each license type, often depending on the local alderman's whims, as when Alderman Tom Tunney declared he would not issue more licenses for the area surrounding Belmont, where Berlin is located (Ambrosius 2013).

20. A "40" is a forty-ounce beer.

21. The Recon Party is so named because it is cohosted by the fetish dating and hookup website Recon.com.

22. Leather harnesses are expensive! Typically, they run between $100 and $250. I didn't get one until later that year when Austin bought me one for my birthday.

23. Saint Andrew's cross is an *X*-shaped cross on which someone can be strapped for BDSM play. It is so named for the cross on which Saint Andrew was crucified.

24. For more on augmented reality as social theory, see Jurgenson (2011).

25. The line between people who were friends and those who were ethnographic participants and had blurred to such an extent that I'm not sure any group could tell any other group were participants. No one mentioned anything to me to indicate they had guessed as much. Although one might think this compromises ethnographic "objectivity," as Michael Bell and I discuss in *An Invitation to Qualitative Methods* (Orne and Bell 2015), friendship is one of the great promises and rewards of fieldwork.

26. Curran 2013.

27. "Pegging" refers to a woman using a strap-on dildo to fuck a man in the ass.

28. Of course, two opposite-sex people having sex doesn't mean that they weren't queer. Both could have been bi, or one could have. If they were queer, then it was their space, though unusually claimed. If they weren't, then my argument here remains. Regardless, I argue these spaces are queer in ways other than sexual orientation, though typically only queer men use them.

CHAPTER 3

1. "Uncrowning" is a term from Bakhtin that I discuss in detail later.

2. Bourdieu 2002.

3. Simmel 1957, 296.

4. Goffman 1959.

5. Although their paper is about collective action in terms of social movements and politics, I'm informed here by Emirbayer and Goldberg's (2005) work on pragmatism and emotion. The emotions that I am discussing here are a collective state of consciousness connected not to an essentialized psychological entity but to a relationship among people and to a space. I am concerned not with what arises "exclusively from people's heads or hearts, rather . . . [what is] between actors and their situations (which contain other actors)" (486). The account of Durkheim's collective effervescence that follows should be read in the spirit of modern sociology of emotions. See Turner and Stets (2006) for a review of that literature.

6. Durkheim 1995.

7. Indeed, doing the same thing together at the same time makes you feel good (Wiltermuth and Heath 2009).

8. Durkheim 2003, 123.

9. Ibid.

10. Schachter and Singer 1962.

11. Durkheim 1995, 221.

12. Bell 1994, 69.

13. Dean 2009.

14. Sexually permissive people tend to have more friends than non–sexually permissive people—see Vrangalova and Bukberg (2015). There are major causality issues with the correlation in the Vrangalova and Bukberg study, but it jives with the work that we see here.

CHAPTER 4

1. When I asked him if I could call him Deveaux in the book, he responded: "But I already chose a damn name! Although that one's good too, honey."

2. Because Deveaux is a drag queen, I use both female and male pronouns for her, since that reflects how people talked about her at Jackhammer.

3. The numbers don't quite add up, even considering his family history and age, but that's not Deveaux's point, of course.

4. For a review of communities and neighborhoods and how they influence our lives on the grand scale, see Sampson (2012).

5. Green 2008, 2013.

6. Winterson 2011, 59.

7. Dunne, Prendergast, and Telford 2002.

8. Dave (2014) provided the text of the speech to me.

9. The definition of community as "face-to-face intimate, affective relations" comes from Sampson (2012), 56.

10. Gay Standard Time.

11. Moore 2004.

12. Ibid., 13.

13. See D'Emilio (1983) for more on this historical development of gay identity from displacement due to war and changing economic circumstances. I discuss these factors in more depth in chapter 7, "Gay Disneyland."

14. A street in downtown Chicago.

CHAPTER 5

1. How groups connect, compete, and cohere is referred to as intergroup contact or relations. See Hogg (2003) for a review of the social psychological literature in this area. "Social psychologists," though, is a misnomer since many are actually sociologists; so, perhaps they should more rightly called microsociologists or psychosociologists.

2. For example, Park 1914, 1937.

3. As summarized by Lyman (1968); remnants remain, such as the use of interracial relationships as social barometers (Song 2010) and contact and conflict hypotheses (Kilson 2009).

4. Twine and Steinbugler 2006.

5. Fryer 2007; Song 2010.

6. See Henry (2006) and Kilson (2009) for two modern discussions of the contact hypothesis and its legacy in social science.

7. Changing the definition of a group to not include a romantic partner is the topic of Okitikpi (2002).

8. On entrenchment, see Yeakley (2000).

9. Henry and Hardin 2006.

10. I was holding a similar assumption as I am about to critique, that moments of diversity must reflect processes that reduce racist attitudes, rather than reflecting them.

11. Using the same phenotypic observation of a Midwestern white guy that I've used throughout the book. That is, I used racial categories as I saw them. For this discussion, I'm not interested in the reification or troubling of racial classification boundaries. Instead, I want to focus on only whether interracial contact occurred.

12. See Ward (2008) for more on this concept of racial diversity within queer spaces.

13. I will address this theory of sexual racism in greater detail in a work currently in progress.

14. Triangulation is a qualitative methodology technique of using multiple sources of data about an event or process. If the sources agree, leading to the same conclusion, researchers can put more faith in the reliability and accuracy of their conclusions.

15. David here is referring to images of women in American Indian garb, often to sexualize them.

16. Logan and Shah 2013.

17. Thus, sexual racism is itself an example of the intersectional knot. You cannot untangle one aspect of power without considering the others.

18. Negging involves subtly insulting a person. People typically respond in one of two ways. In a situation of equal social power, they would be insulted. However, if the person who has been targeted has less social power, they will attempt to make you like them. I admit that I've used this tactic with certain members of the plastic social group after noticing its common use by other members with financial rather than bodily capital. By acting as though I had social power, using the upper hand to make them like me rather than the reverse, I noticed that I was more accepted in the group as a member worthy of talking with and confiding in.

19. "SGL" stands for "same-gender loving," a term often used in Black communities

20. CD4 is a medical term for a group of glycoproteins associated with regulatory T-cells that the HIV virus uses to gain entry into the T-cell.

21. Warner 2000, 35–36.

22. Warner 2000, 36.

23. Schilt 2012.

CHAPTER 6

1. I use this conceit to explain four "properties," à la grounded theory and dimensional analysis (Glaser and Strauss 1967; Charmaz 2006). Properties are a theoretical tool used by qualitative researchers to map concepts, areas they explore to fully understand a concept before they feel they understand it well enough to be "saturated."

2. Indeed, I suspect that many of the assumptions about queer men and women occupying separate spaces are based on white queer people. The spaces for queer people of color in Boystown were always more integrated, pushed against the white assimilationist assumptions of the rest of Boystown.

3. Both the University of Texas at Austin and the University of Wisconsin–Madison are known as party schools with heavy drinking.

4. On the white, muscular, masculine flavor of male physical attractiveness, see Childs (2005); Shiao and Tuan (2008); Levine and Marano (2009); and McClintock (2014).

5. TPAN is the Test Positive Aware Network, an HIV nonprofit in Chicago.

6. If such a detail as drink choice doesn't strike you as mattering much, remember these consumption habits in chapter 8, "Becoming Gay."

7. Bourdieu (1998). The conspicuous consumption by the rich of time more so than money is something I discuss in considering the concept of habitus later in chapter 8, "Becoming Gay."

8. Nott 2012.

9. Ignore the misattribution of homonormativity to frequent random sex, which as I've been arguing is exactly the opposite—though it does fit with my later discussion about the sex-negative atmosphere of queer leftist spaces. See chapter 13, "Queer Is Community."

10. See Han (2008) and Robinson (2015).

11. Robinson 2015.

12. On people's willingness to be explicit about preferences, see Robinson (2015).

13. Unlike Jackhammer's the Hole, for instance, which is a bar used for sexual purposes, not a sex club.

14. I'd like to point out that these kinds of thoughts indicate that I'm not some more enlightened person. I have some of the same kinds of struggles with sexual shame that other people have. My work has led me to certain views about the inherent morality about the charmed circle, but that doesn't mean that I don't struggle with those in my own life.

15. I take that back. I'm sure Michel Foucault was using his own form of biopower in fairly raunchy sex games: the bathhouse as sexual panopticon.

16. In the main, they tend to block known sex workers that have gotten in trouble with them, and drug users that seem to be tweaking (i.e., engaging in frantic and compulsive behavior often associated with methamphetamine abuse). Steamworks has a strong no-drugs policy and enforces it.

17. See *Tearoom Trade* by Humphreys (1970), which, while having major ethical problems, is still enlightening.

CHAPTER 7

1. As my friend Jennifer said on hearing me refer to it as the New Modern Grill: "Sure it is." I have never heard anyone actually call it by that name. Or any name, frankly.

2. Brown-Saracino 2010.

3. Sampson (2012). It's worth noting that these gentrified neighborhoods are often really "mixed" neighborhoods demographically when they begin gentrification. In Sampson's analysis, there was never a single all-Black neighborhood in Chicago that became all white.

4. Remember the phrase "tastes changed" for later.

5. Airbnb is a website that connects travelers with people that have spare space.

6. Pilsen and Logan Square are neighborhoods in Chicago.

7. Bronzeville, Chinatown, and Humboldt Park each correspond to a major ethnic group in Chicago, a point I return to later in chapter 12, "Take Back Boystown."

8. A bit of a chicken and egg problem, eh? Are they here because it is the gay destination or is it the gay destination because services are unavailable elsewhere?

9. Ghaziani 2014.

10. D'Emilio 1984.

11. Rich 1980.

12. Gamson 1995.

13. Ghaziani 2014.

CHAPTER 8

1. Halperin 2012, 13.

2. I threw a huge party to celebrate the ten-year anniversary of my first coming out that June. It was an excuse to have people over and eat a giant rainbow cake.

3. Simmel 1903.

4. Oldenburg (1989), although Grazian (2009) argues that these spaces are also seen only as drivers of social cohesion, which Anderson (2009) rightly points out as homogenizing these spaces. My work here is in this vein. Sexy community is a kind of third space and transforms intergroup relations, though all kinds of space teach us something. It's just that all of its lessons might not be good.

5. Wacquant 2004, 2011.

CHAPTER 9

1. Style can be viewed here as a reflection of one's habitus.

2. Although people come out repeatedly during the course of a lifetime (Orne 2011), people count gay age from when people first come out and start to attend gay events and visit gay spaces. That is, how much time have they had to "become gay"?

3. Alexander's explanation for his lack of gay cultural knowledge because of low dating opportunities is consistent with other research on the role of body size in mainstream gay spaces (see Whitesel 2014). Although, as I shall argue, there were other factors at play.

4. I do not repeat our exact conversation here for confidentiality reasons. The texts are simply too revealing.

5. Hicklin 2012.

6. Portes and Zhou 1993.

7. Zolberg and Woon 1999.

8. See, for example, Conrad (2011).

9. See Sullivan 1996.

10. Nair 2013.

11. At least, psychically. American families take many forms today, as sociologists amply demonstrate, though researchers continue to assume the nuclear family as the model, and so do everyday people themselves, even when they don't see the model around them (Edin and Kefalas 2005).

12. Although this characterization of gay men's sexy communities reeks of Vivienne Cass's (1979) "identity synthesis "stage, which has haunted scholarship about gay identity (see Orne 2011).

13. Moore 2004, 48–49.

14. I find it synchronicity that Moore then turns, in his next chapter, to the life of Fred Halsted, famed pornographer, who "created the world of gay sexual art and experimentation ... [and] then watched it, and himself, be destroyed by AIDS, a sanitizing of gay sexual tastes" (58), although Boystown's Halsted Street is no relation, named instead for Philadelphia bankers who ceded the property to the city (Hayner and McNamee 1988).

15. Warner 2000, 60, 61.

16. Warner 2000, 60.

17. The It Gets Better Project is documented in Savage and Miller 2011.

CHAPTER 10

1. Vague to the point of uselessness? I am striking a fine line between details that help you as the reader place him, without identifying him in the small group of business elites of Boystown.

2. Prideaux 2003.

3. See McKercher, du Cros, and McKercher (2002) on the "heritage management" side of those producing heritage commodification, while see Prideaux (2003) for a noncritical review of causes and consequences of heritage commodification within tourism.

4. As indicative of these trends, Manhole reopened after the final draft of this book was written.

5. Ambrosius 2015.

6. Nisbet 1969.

7. Boyd 2008.

CHAPTER 11

1. Christian Farr, "Wrigleyville Bar Identified in Weekend Sexual Assault," 5NBCChicago, June 3, 2014.

2. Grazian 2008.

3. Bourdieu 1984, 175, 573.

4. Nussbaum 2013.

5. Collins 2000; McCall 2005.

CHAPTER 12

1. Comments quoted from the Take Back Boystown Facebook page.

2. "Third Boystown Stabbing in as Many Weeks Caught on Video," *Huffington Post*, July 5, 2011, http://www.huffingtonpost.com/2011/07/05/third-boystown -stabbing-i_n_890411.html.

3. Sosin 2011.

4. Greene 2014.

5. Demarest 2012, 5–6.

6. Quillian and Pager 2001.

7. Women probably perceive a greater incidence of crime because they actually do feel more at risk in public spaces than men, as I discussed in chapter 11, "Girlstown."

8. Waters 1990.

9. This assertion comes from my conversations with several older bartenders in the area.

10. hooks 2000; Collins 2008.

11. On queer-of-color critique, see Ferguson (2004).

12. As Michael Bell, Loka Ashwood, and I discuss in a paper in progress. We call this feeling "heritas."

CHAPTER 13

1. At the time, Chelsea Manning had not yet announced her transition. Though many knew she identified as female, the literature still gave her name as Bradley Manning. She announced shortly after that she was named Chelsea.

2. Ward 2008.

3. A GIF is an animation made from still pictures, often image captures from popular TV shows and movies. A meme is a picture with text, often repeated pictures that come to represent a type or character.

4. As discussed in chapter 12, "Take Back Boystown."

5. Orne 2012.

6. Again, I am protecting their jobs here. The Center on Halsted is very concerned with their image and who provides information to outsiders. This is understandable, given their large budget and precarious position in the community, as I discussed in the previous chapter.

7. Ward 2008.

8. An oppression Olympics creates the "circular firing squad" of everyone insisting that their issue is the "real issue" of oppression in society as discussed in my essay, "The Circular Firing Squad: A Facebook Flamewar Wins Gold in the Oppression Olympics."

9. "Beginner's mind" references the concept within Buddhist philosophy that someone new to an activity does not come in with expectations, and thus enjoys

the activity more, and that someone should attempt to take on the beginner's mind when practicing an activity they are expert at.

10. "No platforming" refers to the practice of shutting down a speaker or event to prevent them from having a platform for their speech.

11. On homonormativity, see Duggan (2004).

12. Orne 2013.

13. Hochschild 2012.

14. Orne 2013.

15. Goff, Steele, and Davies 2008.

16. This is a kind of stereotype threat, in this case, the stereotype that whites are racist, which is then activated by reading the racially charged article.

17. Green 2007.

18. Sacks 2002

19. Ibid.

20. Not to be confused with universalism as in Christian Unitarian Universalists.

21. Green 2007, 29.

22. Bell 2011; Orne and Bell 2015.

CHAPTER 14

1. Winterson 2011, 130.

2. Stein and Plummer 1994.

REFERENCES

Ambrosius, Andy. 2013. "Liquor Licenses Banned in Crime Hot Spots around Belmont CTA Station." *Patch* (blog). January 15. http://patch.com/illinois/lake view/liquor-licenses-now-banned-in-crime-hot-spots.

———. 2014. "Hydrate Aims for 'Totally Different Feel' after Major Renovation." ChicagoPride.com, January 15. http://chicago.gopride.com/news/article.cfm /articleid/52002025.

Anderson, Tammy L. 2009. "Better to Complicate, Rather Than Homogenize, Urban Nightlife: a Response to Grazian." *Sociological Forum* 24 (4): 918–25.

Bell, Michael. 2011. *The Strange Music of Social Life*. Philadelphia: Temple University Press.

———. 1994. "Deep Fecology: Mikhail Bakhtin and the Call of Nature*." *Capitalism Nature Socialism* 5 (4): 65–84.

Black, Dan, Gary Gates, Seth Sanders, and Lowell Taylor. 2000. "Demographics of the Gay and Lesbian Population in the United States: Evidence from Available Systematic Data Sources." *Demography* 37 (2): 139–54.

Bourdieu, Pierre. 1984. *Distinction*. Cambridge, MA: Harvard University Press.

Boyd, Michelle R. 2008. *Jim Crow Nostalgia*. Minneapolis: University of Minnesota Press.

Brown-Saracino, Japonica. 2010. *A Neighborhood That Never Changes*. Chicago: University of Chicago Press.

Carpenter, D. 2012. *Flagrant Conduct: the Story of Lawrence v. Texas*. New York: W. W. Norton.

Cass, Vivienne. 1979. "Homosexuality Identity Formation." *Journal of Homosexuality* 4 (3): 219–35.

Charmaz, Kathy. 2006. *Constructing Grounded Theory*. Thousand Oaks, CA: SAGE.

Chauncey, George. 1994. *Gay New York*. New York: Basic Books.

Childs, E. C. 2005. "Can We Ignore the Perspective of Black Women on Their Own Experience?" *Du Bois Review: Social Science Research on Race* 3 (2): 471–79.

Collins, Patricia Hill. 2000. *Black Feminist Thought*. New York: Routledge.

Collins, R. 2015. "Visual Micro-Sociology and the Sociology of Flesh and Blood: Comment on Wacquant." *Qualitative Sociology* 38 (1):13–17.

Conrad, Ryan, ed. 2011. *Against Equality*. Lewiston, ME: Against Equality Press.

Corbin, J., and J. Morse. 2003. "The Unstructured Interactive Interview: Issues of Reciprocity and Risks When Dealing with Sensitive Topics." *Qualitative Inquiry* 9 (3): 335–54.

Crowley, Bobby. 2012. "Why I Sometimes Feel Uncomfortable around Straight People." *In Our Words* (blog), July 3. https://inourwordsblog.wordpress.com /2012/07/03/why-i-sometimes-feel-uncomfortable-around-straight-people/.

Dave, Naisargi N. 2014. "Vibrant Morphologies" Keynote address at the Queertopia conference, Northwestern University, Evanston, IL, May 3.

D'Emilio, John. 1983. *Sexual Politics, Sexual Communities*. Chicago: University of Chicago Press.

Dean, Tim. 2009. *Unlimited Intimacy*. Chicago: University of Chicago Press.

Demarest, Erica. 2012. "Citywide Crime Down in 2011, Slight Decline in Lakeview." *Windy City Times*. April 4.

Devault, M. 1990. "Talking and Listening from Women's Standpoint: Feminist Strategies for Interviewing and Analysis." *Social Problems* 37 (1):96–116.

Doty, Mark. 2002. *Still Life with Oysters and Lemon*. Boston: Beacon Press.

Duggan, Lisa. 2004. *The Twilight of Equality?* Boston: Beacon Press.

Dunne, Gillian A., Shirley Prendergast, and David Telford. 2002. "Young, Gay, Homeless and Invisible: A Growing Population?" *Culture, Health and Sexuality* 4 (1): 103–15.

Durkheim, Émile. 1995. The Elementary Forms of Religious Life. New York: Free Press.

———. 2003. "'A Discussion on Sex Education'." In *Émile Durkheim: Sociologist of Modernity*, edited by Mustafa Emirbayer, 122–24. Malden, MA: Blackwell Publishing.

Edin, K., and M. Kefalas. 2005. *Promises I Can Keep*. Berkeley: University of California Press.

Eliasoph, N. 2005. "Theorizing from the Neck Down: Why Social Research Must Understand Bodies Acting in Real Space and Time (and Why It's So Hard to Spell Out What We Learn from This." *Qualitative Sociology* 28 (2):159–69.

Ellis, C. 1999. "Heartful Autoethnography." *Qualitative Health Research* 9 (5): 669–83.

———. 2009. "Autoethnography as Method (Review)." *Biography* 32 (2): 360–63.

Emerson, R. M., R. I. Fretz, and L. L. Shaw. 2011. *Writing Ethnographic Fieldnotes*. Chicago: University of Chicago Press.

Emirbayer, Mustafa, and Chad Alan Goldberg. 2005. "Pragmatism, Bourdieu, and Collective Emotions in Contentious Politics." *Theory and Society* 34 (5–6): 469–518.

Ferguson, Roderick A. 2004. *Aberrations in Black*. Minneapolis: University of Minnesota Press.

Fryer, R. 2007. "Guess Who's Been Coming to Dinner? Trends in Interracial Marriage over the 20th Century." *Journal of Economic Perspectives* 21 (2): 71–90.

Gamson, Joshua. 1995. "Must Identity Movements Self-Destruct? A Queer Dilemma." *Social Problems* 42 (3): 390–407.

Gates, Gary. 2010. *Sexual Minorities in the 2008 General Social Survey: Coming Out and Demographic Characteristics*. Los Angeles: Williams Institute. http://bibpurl.oclc.org/web/41145.

Ghaziani, Amin. 2014. *There Goes the Gayborhood?* Princeton, NJ: Princeton University Press.

Glaser, Barney, and Anselm Strauss. 1967. *The Discovery of Grounded Theory: Strategies for Qualitative Research.* New York: Aldine Publishing.

Goff, Phillip Atiba, Claude M. Steele, and Paul G. Davies. 2008. "The Space between Us: Stereotype Threat and Distance in Interracial Contexts." *Journal of Personality and Social Psychology* 94 (1): 91–107.

Goffman, E. 1959. *The Presentation of Self in Everyday Life.* Garden City, NY: Doubleday.

Grazian, D. 2008. *On the Make: The Hustle of Urban Nightlife.* Chicago: University of Chicago Press.

———. 2009. "Urban Nightlife, Social Capital, and the Public Life of Cities." *Sociological Forum* 24 (4): 908–17.

Green, Adam. 2007. "Queer Theory and Sociology: Locating the Subject and the Self in Sexuality Studies." *Sociological Theory* 25 (1): 26–45.

———. 2008. "The Social Organization of Desire: The Sexual Fields Approach." *Sociological Theory* 26 (1): 25–50.

———. 2011. "Playing the (Sexual) Field: The Interactional Basis of Systems of Sexual Stratification." *Social Psychology Quarterly* 74 (3): 244–66.

———. 2013. *Sexual Fields.* Chicago: University of Chicago Press.

Greene, Theodore. 2014. "Gay Neighborhoods and the Rights of the Vicarious Citizen." *City and Community* 13 (2): 99–118.

Halperin, David M. 2012. *How to Be Gay.* Cambridge, MA: Harvard University Press.

Han, Chong-Suk. 2008. "A Qualitative Exploration of the Relationship between Racism and Unsafe Sex among Asian Pacific Islander Gay Men." *Archives of Sexual Behavior* 37 (5): 827–37.

Hayner, D., and T. McNamee. 1988. *Streetwise Chicago: A History of Chicago Street Names.* Chicago: Loyola University Press.

Hennen, P. 2005. "Bear Bodies, Bear Masculinity: Recuperation, Resistance, or Retreat?" *Gender and Society* 19 (1): 25–43.

Henry, P., and C. Hardin. 2006. "The Contact Hypothesis Revisited." *Psychological Science* 17 (10): 862–68.

Hicklin, Aaron. 2012. "Nate Silver: Person of the Year." *OUT Magazine.* December 18.

Hochschild, Arlie Russell. 2012. *The Managed Heart.* Berkeley: University of California Press.

Hogg, Michael. 2003. "Intergroup Relations." In *Handbook of Social Psychology*, edited by John DeLamater, 479–501. New York : Kluwer Academic/Plenum Publishers.

hooks, bell. 2000. *Feminist Theory: From Margin to Center.* Cambridge, MA: South End Press.

Humphreys, L. 1970. *Tearoom Trade: Impersonal Sex in Public Spaces.* Chicago: Aldine.

Jurgenson, Nathan. 2011. "Digital Dualism versus Augmented Reality." *The Society Pages* (blog). February 24. https://thesocietypages.org/cyborgology/2011/02/24/digital-dualism-versus-augmented-reality/.

Kahan, Benjamin. 2013. *Celibacies*. Durham, NC: Duke University Press.

Kahn, M. 1991. "Factors Affecting the Coming Out Process for Lesbians." *Journal of Homosexuality* 21 (3): 47–70.

Kilson, Martin. 2009. "Thinking about Robert Putnam's Analysis of Diversity." *Du Bois Review: Social Science Research on Race* 6 (2): 293–308.

Laumann, Edward O. 2004. *Sexual Organization of the City*. Chicago: University of Chicago Press.

Levine, M., and H. E. Marano. 2009. "Why I Hate Beauty." In *Readings in Social Psychology: General, Classic, and Contemporary Selections*, edited by Wayne Lesko, 156–62. London: Pearson.

Logan, Trevon D., and Manisha Shah. 2013. "Face Value: Information and Signaling in an Illegal Market." *Southern Economic Journal* 79 (3): 529–64.

Lyman, S. M. 1968. "The Race Relations Cycle of Robert E. Park." *Pacific Sociological Review* 11 (1): 16–22.

McCall, L. 2005. "The Complexity of Intersectionality." *Signs: Journal of Women in Culture and Society* 30 (3): 1771–1800.

McClintock, E. A. 2014. "Beauty and Status: The Illusion of Exchange in Partner Selection?" *American Sociological Review* 79 (4): 575–604.

McKercher, B., H. du Cros, and R. B. McKercher. 2002. *Cultural Tourism: the Partnership between Tourism and Cultural Heritage Management*. Philadelphia: Haworth Hospitality Press.

Monaghan, L. F. 2005. "Big Handsome Men, Bears and Others: Virtual Constructions of 'Fat Male Embodiment.'" *Body and Society* 11 (2): 81–111.

Moon, Jennifer. 2013. "Cruising and Queer Counterpublics." PhD diss., University of Michigan.

Moore, Mignon. 2011. *Invisible Families*. Berkeley: University of California Press.

Moore, Patrick. 2004. *Beyond Shame*. Boston: Beacon Press.

Nair, Yasmin. 2013. "No More City on a Hill" *In These Times*. October 23.

Nott, Mark. 2012. "It Doesn't Have to Be All about Sex: Exploring the Rituals of Grindr." *In Our Words* (blog). August 8. https://inourwordsblog.wordpress.com/2012/08/08/it-doesnt-have-to-be-all-about-sex-exploring-the-rituals-of-grindr/.

Nisbet, Robert. 1969. *The Quest for Community*. New York: Oxford University Press.

Nussbaum, Emily. 2013. "How 'Sex and the City' Lost Its Good Name." *New Yorker*. July 29.

Okitikpi, O. 2002. "Managing Intimate Interracial Relationships." PhD diss., Brunel University London.

Oldenburg, Ray. 1989. *The Great Good Place*. Boston: Da Capo Press.

Orne, Jason. 2011. "'You Will Always Have to "Out" Yourself': Reconsidering Coming Out through Strategic Outness." *Sexualities* 14:681–703.

————. 2012. "When Bahktin Is in Boystown." *Queer Metropolis* (blog). April 20. https://queermetropolis.wordpress.com/2012/04/30/when-bakhtin-is-in -boystown/.

————. 2013. "Queers in the Line of Fire: Goffman's Stigma Revisited." *Sociological Quarterly* 54 (2): 229–53.

————. 2013. "The Circular Firing Squad: A Facebook Flamewar Wins Gold in the Oppression Olympics." *In Our Words* (blog). January 24. http://inourwords blog.com/2013/01/24/the-circular-firing-squad-a-facebook-flamewar-wins -gold-in-the-oppression-olympics/.

Orne, Jason, and Michael M. Bell. 2015. *Invitation to Qualitative Fieldwork*. New York: Routledge.

Park, Robert E. 1914. "Racial Assimilation in Secondary Groups with Particular Reference to the Negro." *American Journal of Sociology* 19 (5): 606–23.

————. 1950. "The Race Relations Cycle in Hawaii." *Race and Culture* 1:188–95.

Portes, Alejandro, and Min Zhou. 1993. "The New Second Generation: Segmented Assimilation and Its Variants." *Annals of the American Academy of Political and Social Science* 530:74–96.

Prideaux, Bruce. 2003. "Commodifying Heritage." *International Journal of Tourism Sciences* 3 (1): 1–15.

Quillian, Lincoln, and Devah Pager. 2001. "Black Neighbors, Higher Crime? The Role of Racial Stereotypes in Evaluations of Neighborhood Crime." *American Journal of Sociology* 107 (3): 717–67.

Robinson, B. A. 2015. "'Personal Preference' as the New Racism Gay Desire and Racial Cleansing in Cyberspace." *Sociology of Race and Ethnicity* 1 (2): 317–30.

Rich, Adrienne. 1980. "Compulsory Heterosexuality and Lesbian Existence." *Signs: Journal of Women in Culture and Society* 5 (4): 631–60.

Rubin, Gayle. (1983) 2011. *Deviations*. Durham, NC: Duke University Press.

Sacks, Jonathan. 2002. *The Dignity of Difference*. London: Bloomsbury Publishing.

Sampson, Robert J. 2012. *Great American City*. Chicago: University of Chicago Press.

Savage, D., and T. Miller. 2011. *It Gets Better: Coming Out, Overcoming Bullying, and Creating a Life Worth Living*. New York: Dutton.

Schachter, Stanley, and Jerome Singer. 1962. "Cognitive, Social and Physiological Determinants of Emotional State." *Psychological Review* 69:370–99.

Schilt, Kristen. 2012. "Gender as Pleasure." Paper presented at the panel "Is Undoing Gender Possible?" American Sociological Association annual meeting, Denver, CO. August 15.

Shiao, Jiannbin Lee, and Mia H.Tuan. 2008. "'Some Asian Men Are Attractive to Me, but for a Husband....'" *Du Bois Review: Social Science Research on Race* 5 (2): 259–85.

Simmel, G. 1903. "The Metropolis and Mental Life."

Simmel, Georg. 1957. "Fashion." *American Journal of Sociology* 62 (6). The University of Chicago Press: 541–58.

Sosin, Kate. 2011. "Hundreds Pack into Boystown Violence Forum." *Windy*

City Times, July 7. http://www.windycitymediagroup.com/gay/lesbian/news/ARTICLE.php?AID=32676.

Song, M. 2009. "Is Intermarriage a Good Indicator of Integration?" *Journal of Ethnic and Migration Studies* 35 (2): 331–48.

Stafford, Zach. 2013. "Time to Bust Out of Boystown?" *Redeye Chicago*. April 10.

Stein, Arlene, and Ken Plummer. 1994. "'I Can't Even Think Straight': "Queer" Theory and the Missing Sexual Revolution in Sociology." *Sociological Theory* 12 (2): 178–87.

Sullivan, Andrew. 1996. *Virtually Normal*. New York: Vintage Books.

Tavory, I., and S. Timmermans. 2009. "Two Cases of Ethnography: Grounded Theory and the Extended Case Method." *Ethnography* 10 (3): 243–63.

Turner, J. H., and Jan E. Stets. 2006. "Sociological Theories of Human Emotions." *Annual Review of Sociology* 32:25–52

Twine, F. W., and A. C. Steinbugler. 2006. "The Gap between *Whites* and *Whiteness*: Interracial Intimacy and Racial Literacy." *Du Bois Review: Social Science Research on Race* 3 (2): 341–63.

Urry, John. 2002. *The Tourist Gaze*. London: SAGE.

Vrangalova, Z., and R. E. Bukberg. 2015. "Are Sexually Permissive Individuals More Victimized and Socially Isolated?" *Personal Relationships* 22 (2): 230–42.

Wacquant, Loïc. 2011. "Habitus as Topic and Tool: Reflections on Becoming a Prize-fighter." *Qualitative Research in Psychology* 8 (1): 81–92.

———. 2004. *Body and Soul*. Oxford: Oxford University Press.

———. 2005. "Carnal Connections: on Embodiment, Apprenticeship, and Membership." *Qualitative Sociology* 28 (4): 445–74.

———. 2015. "For a Sociology of Flesh and Blood." *Qualitative Sociology* 38 (1): 1–11.

Ward, Elizabeth Jane. 2008. *Respectably Queer*. Nashville: Vanderbilt University Press.

Warner, M. 2000. *The Trouble with Normal: Sex, Politics, and the Ethics of Queer Life*. Cambridge: Harvard University Press.

Waters, Mary. 1990. *Ethnic Options: Choosing Identities in America*. Berkeley: University of California Press.

Wekker, Gloria. 2013. *The Politics of Passion*. New York: Columbia University Press.

Whitesel, Jason. 2014. *Fat Gay Men*. New York: New York University Press.

Wiltermuth, Scott S., and Chip Heath. 2009. "Synchrony and Cooperation." *Psychological Science* 20 (1): 1–5.

Winterson, Jeanette. 2011. *Why Be Happy When You Could Be Normal?* New York: Random House.

Yeakley, A. 2000. "The Nature of Prejudice Change: Positive and Negative Change Processes Arising from Intergroup Contact Experiences." PhD diss., University of Michigan.

Zolberg, A. R., and L. L. Woon. 1999. "Why Islam Is Like Spanish: Cultural Incorporation in Europe and the United States." *Politics and Society* 27 (1): 5–38.

INDEX